Smile More, Pray More

Moving from Rural Texas to See the World

Smile More, Pray More

Martha E. Couch, PhD

Edited by:
Teresa Criswell Smith, MS
Sharon Robinson, PhD
Jori Kennedy, BS

ARCHWAY
PUBLISHING

Archway Publishing books may be ordered through booksellers or by contacting:

Archway Publishing
1663 Liberty Drive
Bloomington, IN 47403
www.archwaypublishing.com
1 (888) 242-5904

Because of the dynamic nature of the Internet, any web addresses or links contained in this book may have changed since publication and may no longer be valid. The views expressed in this work are solely those of the author and do not necessarily reflect the views of the publisher, and the publisher hereby disclaims any responsibility for them.

Any people depicted in stock imagery provided by Getty Images are models, and such images are being used for illustrative purposes only. Certain stock imagery © Getty Images.

ISBN: 978-1-4808-8415-1 (sc)
ISBN: 978-1-4808-8414-4 (hc)
ISBN: 978-1-4808-8413-7 (e)

Library of Congress Control Number: 2019920687

Print information available on the last page.

Archway Publishing rev. date: 1/20/2020

Contents

Preface

Since I have encouraged others to write a book, tell their life story, etc., I am owning my words and writing my life story. Through my work with the 4-H program, helping members and families with their stories, I have completed hundreds of trainings about creating 4-H record books, so I am owning my advice.

Here I am in 2019, and I am doing it: writing my life story! I am calling it *Smile More—Pray More*, in which you will read about the incident that led to this title.

In my sixty-ninth year, I find joy in this project.

Thanks to those of you who have said, "Martha, you should write a book!" You may be sorry, but I am following up on your advice.

Additionally, I want to encourage you (yes, you!) to write your story (or stories) for you and your family. With the digital age, stories may be lost. In the past, many historians have counted on letters or even postcards to reconstruct their family story. Generations to follow will be glad for an insight to the nineteenth and twentieth centuries of our families.

I know that I cannot believe it is already 2019!

I have traveled a great amount during my life, and this travel has lent itself to many stories to share. Sometimes learning about the view of America and Americans while visiting other countries gives us an increased perspective.

It has been a blessing to meet and visit with people from 110 countries. Generally, people are excited to visit with people from the United States, and it is great fun for me to meet them and learn about their countries. It has nearly always been true that we and our media give us a certain view of others—and our media may give the rest of the world a certain view of us. I count it as a great travel benefit to really learn about them, their families, their homes, their plans, and their goals.

In the 1980s, everyone we encountered in Germany wanted to know "who shot J. R." This was the first time I realized the global impact of the United States media.

In 2019, when others learned we were from the United States of America, the questions related to gun control … why don't we have it?

I find listening more powerful than telling.

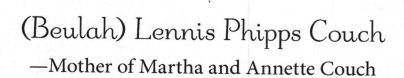

(Beulah) Lennis Phipps Couch
—Mother of Martha and Annette Couch

Mother (Lennis Phipps Couch) would be so proud that I did not use her first name. She (until her last breath) did not like her first name, which was Beulah. (I do not know what she was thinking; her mother lived with the name "Fleta" her entire life.) She had trouble with "Lennis" because she received a draft notice and other mailings aimed at males her entire life. I do not know where her parents found the name.

The advantage of being named Lennis is searching for information in genealogy sites. *She* is the only one! This works even better when you search for Fleta.

I do not have a great amount of information about her youth. She mainly spoke about it as "hard times" and "doing without."

Moving to Howard County—They lived in a rural area near Winters, Texas, on a farm. I have many questions now because I do not know if they owned the farm or were sharecroppers. I do know that they bought the land that I own today in northern

Howard County in 1927. Mother's sister, Helen, and her husband had moved to this area before this time.

Mom graduated from high school (there were only grades through eleven), but the Depression hit, so Mom and her parents could not afford to move. The expression "hunkered down" was what Mother said they did—and waited for better times.

Almost ten years later, they moved to Howard County in 1937. Mother was in her eighteenth year.

I know that it was very, very difficult. They first dug a cellar to store canned food and vegetables and a lean-to, in which they lived. Enoch Noah Phipps (born 1894) and Fleta (no middle name) Dietz (1889) were her parents. They, of course, brought a mule and a trailer load of farm equipment and personal belongings. They were *not* planning to return to their previous home.

Getting the Cotton Crop Going—I have photos of Enoch with the horse and the one-blade plow breaking the ground. Breaking the ground means the horse pulls the plow through the earth to break the surface of the dirt. Following the row that is created, seeds are placed into the soil and then covered by the boot of the farmer. Next, pray for rain!

Besides getting this grassland turned into cropland, Enoch would have been getting a cow or two to have milk. Fleta and Mother would have been getting a garden ready to grow vegetables the next season.

Not only did they have to get the land and farm up and running, but they also had to have electric lines run from the highway to the house, which was about a quarter mile from the highway. This was daylight-to-dark work, and it was every day but likely not on Sunday. They took a day for church and a bit of rest.

Mother was very involved with the farming. Her journal details that she "pulled hay," cleaned out the chicken houses, milked the cows, gathered vegetables, and handled all other farm chores. She and her father worked cattle, which means that cows were wormed or calves were birthed. She never shied away from work that was required.

Women's Work—I know that even though she was a young woman, Mother had to help some with farming. But she and Fleta would have been churning butter, starting small chicks on their way to becoming hens and roosters, and canning vegetables for the rest of the year. I have Mother's personal journal that she began in 1937 (the year they moved), and they did take time to make ice cream. Now, I have a vision of this process. They would make ice cream and need to eat it immediately since there were no freezers available. What a problem or a blessing!

Because of the heat, Mother would write in her journal during the "heat of the day." They also took naps during this time and probably did mending and other household chores while inside.

Romance—Check later in the book where I have included a transcription of Mother's journal, which will lend many more day-to-day details of romance.

Soon after they arrived in Howard County, Mother's diary mentions dating Charles and their communications via the mail. When the mail arrived at the farm/ranch, Mother would watch for it and immediately check for letters addressed to her. If there was a letter from Charles (likely Tuesday or Wednesday), she would read it while she walked the quarter mile from the highway to the house. She would immediately sit down and write a response to Charles. "Yes, you can pick me up Friday night for a date!" She would put the letter in an envelope and *walk* 1½ miles from the ranch to the Luther Post Office, where the postman would be returning from the mail route to the north and stopping on his way back to Big Spring.

Mother had to be very organized and aggressive about following this timeline so she could go out with Charles. In her journal, there are weeks and weeks of reporting this behavior. She did not marry Charles, and she began a job in the kitchen at the Big Spring Medical Center, so she had less free time.

My Father, John Thomas Couch (1919)—She does not record in her diary nor did I get exact details about this time. The first entry in her diary about Dad was August 31, 1940, when she says she received a "letter today from dear John." This short note thrills my soul. He was (forever) the one because she never referred to Charles as "dear" with such fondness. What insight into them and their relationship!

Dad Goes to War—Dad joined the US Army Corps before they were married; she stayed in Howard County and worked at the hospital the entire time he was deployed to the Pacific theater. He was a right gunner (he shot at Japanese airplanes from the "bubble" on the right side of the bomber plane). They would fly each day from Tinian (an island in the South Pacific) over "the hump" to provide support to those airmen who were bombing Japan.

Mother and Dad both told a story about her not hearing from him for months. Mother wrote his commanding officer, and she received a letter in a short time from Dad. As you have read in history books, several of the letters were redacted, which means that words, locations, etc. were blacked out so the reader could not see them.

Married Couple—Dad returned safely from the war, and Mother and Dad were married on December 30, 1945. They went to the Methodist minister's home and were married there. The report, which was verified by Mother, Dad, and Dad's brother (Archie) and sister-in-law (Alice), was that they drove to Abilene, Texas (about ninety miles) to spend their honeymoon night with Archie and Alice. Their entire lives Mother and Dad were very close to Archie and Alice. Archie was just one year older than him. Today, my closest Couch cousins are their children, so it carries across generations.

First Home—Their first home was in Big Spring (yes, only one spring!) on North Twelfth Street. It was a small two-bedroom house. They had great neighbors who gathered at each other's houses to play dominoes and cards. I remember sitting on the sidelines and watching these games, or maybe it was when Mom and Dad visited them after we had moved to Luther.

Enoch Dies Unexpectedly—Grandfather Phipps died unexpectedly, and Grandmother was left alone to manage the farm/ranch. Mother and Dad drove back and forth to help when they could. But plans were developed for us to move to Luther. Much of the delay was because there were no funds to build a house, and Grandmother had lived in the 1938 house that was built from a lean-to. So mostly we went back and forth frequently.

Struck Oil—In the fall of 1953, oil was found in the Luther community. A few years later, two wells were drilled on our property. This was life changing. Grandmother had a new home built and moved in there. We moved into her old house and gradually added on to accommodate our sister, Annette. A second bathroom, a garage, a den, etc. were added.

We were settled in time for me to start Gay Hill School in 1956.

Funds for College—After the war was over, there was a nationwide move for savings bonds and savings accounts for college funds. The family started these for our college education, and we were encouraged to add our allowance and small job earnings to those funds.

Mother and Dad really emphasized this part of Annette's and my life and supported all efforts needed. We would be the first generation in which college was a real possibility. Mother and Dad were very supportive of the idea that both of us go to college.

After I finished four years of college, Mother was startled that I was taking a graduate class in the first fall after graduation. She could not understand this. She knew no one, except our medical doctor (Dr. Thomas), who went to more than four years of college. She, of course, had her life plan for me that included marriage and grandchildren. For much of my adult life, we had numerous discussions about this life path that I was seeking.

Mother Travels—Mother started traveling with Dad to his Air Force reunions. I have the phone call memorized from the time she and Dad called to tell me that they were going to his Army Air Corps reunion in Ohio. It was good for them and especially great for Dad. Mother knew that Dad was relishing this, and she wanted to support him.

Annette traveled with them some, but I only went with Dad to China and with Mom after Dad died.

I organized for her to go on her first cruise. She was in her element. This type of special treatment, where you could travel the ocean blue and stretch out on the bed in your cabin while being waited on by others, was very special to her.

We had a ship captain incident. Mother was so tired when we arrived at the ship that sailed out of Florida that she did *not* attend the emergency drill for evacuating the ship. They, of course, took roll and sent Mother a reprimand! I still have the letter. It was serious but also a fun thing.

Either Annette or I took Mother to eleven different Air Force reunions. They had an organized women's group that provided support to former Air Corps members. Mother was involved in this group. I still receive Christmas cards from several of these women. They were and are a blessing to our family.

Mother's Reaction to my Trip to the White House—This was 2008, and it was the one-hundredth anniversary of the Texas 4-H program. Our supporters were able to arrange an event at the White House with President George W. Bush. A photo of this event appeared in most Texas newspapers. Mother was excited and became a celebrity at the assisted-living facility where she now lived. I called her from the White House to report exactly where I was at the moment. She was thrilled. I am sure that she told everyone who would listen at her residence.

Mother's Last Days—She was taken from the assisted-living facility to the hospital and was in intensive care. The hospital called me, and I immediately traveled to Big Spring. When I arrived, the doctor told me that "it would not be long." She had pneumonia and other infections.

I sent Annette home because her liver condition made her immune system weak, and I did not want her to catch something from Mother. I sat with Mother, and she was in and out of consciousness. She was in her eighty-ninth year of life. One of the times she was lucid, she asked me if I had ever heard of someone just up and dying. I told her no, but I had such a moment of thought about Mother.

She had lived through the Depression. She had moved a great distance from her childhood home. She had survived Dad's death. She had managed her life for nearly twenty years by herself. She thought that her life was endless. She was such a strong warrior! I wish this for all of us.

John Thomas Couch
—Father of Martha and Annette Couch

John Thomas Couch (June 5, 1919) was the eighth child and the sixth son of General Jackson and Armanda Josephine Caledonia Ross Couch.

First Memories—I do not have real memories of this, but I saw pictures of Dad, Mom, and me on a car trip to Colorado. Dad was driving, and Mom was operating the movie camera. I was leaning over the seat and watching all the scenery. Mother was wearing a black dress with large white polka dots, which were reflected in the windshield on *all* of the film. Studying these old movies today, I realize that this was the summer of 1953, and Annette (as an embryo) was traveling with us—so I have the first pictures of her on record!

But, for my story, it was Daddy until I was a teenager. Then, I thought it would be grown up to call him Dad. He is forever tied to my earliest memories, since (as I said in my story about my sister Annette) he carried me to the nursery to meet her the first day of her birth. I had mixed emotions and caused trouble by playing under Mother's hospital bed! I did not know that Mother could discipline me from her hospital bed!

A Man of Patience and Empathy—It was true every day that Dad was a patient man. When he was at work and we misbehaved, Mother would threaten us with "the belt" when he returned home. The belt was an unfinished leather belt with no buckle that was stored on the top of the icebox (or refrigerator, as it's known as today). It symbolized the threat of punishment, but neither Annette nor I were ever whipped with it. I knew then (and know now) that this was not Dad's life plan. He was a caring man, who wanted to be sure that we were strong and safe and knew how to behave.

Early each morning, Dad would wake, milk the cows, change his clothes for work, have breakfast, and travel the sixteen miles to town (Big Spring) to his job as an electrician. After returning from World War II, he went to electrician school in Kansas City, and this was his lifelong vocation.

Some nights, after supper, he would do small electrical repairs for elderly neighbors. He was a good man, milking cows, working all day, and then returning to milk the cows again and do electrical repairs for neighbors. Additionally, one year, he went with Annette to school at night to learn "new math." I do not think that you could find a better dad.

Family Income Tax Forms—He really exhibited patience when I handed out the draft copies of the family income tax to friends. We were playing office. Dad had thrown the draft copies of our income tax forms into the trash. I found them, and they were quite interesting looking. I made notes on them, and when friends came over, I handed them out. You can imagine the "discussion" that occurred at the kitchen table. I had no trouble with this again.

Religion—A serious area of contention or misunderstanding was with church. Every Sunday, Dad stayed home while Grandmother Phipps, Mother, Annette, and I went to the First Methodist Church in Big Spring. Mother and her family had been Methodists their entire life. Mother was a steward in the church. I remember being confused and sad every Sunday. Dad's family was Baptist, and their historic church was only three miles from our home.

After Grandmother's death (October 28, 1966), we had a family meeting, and Mother, Annette, and I joined the Luther Bethel Baptist Church and began to go to church as a family. I am certain that this decision was important to my Christian life. Seeing my entire family (including Dad) embrace our Christianity together was an important base for my life.

In another chapter, I detail the great story of Dad and my trip to China. He loved to travel, but most of it was by car, except for his trips to Army Air Corps reunions in several US locations.

Preparing Martha for Life—Dad worked hard to prepare me for life. It began with my first (well, second if you count my birth) visit to the hospital. I had to have my tonsils out and found myself in the local Hall and Bennett Hospital. The nurse said it was time to go. Dad put me on his shoulder and carried me to the operating room. With that one gesture, he made me feel safe, but he also made it clear to me that this had to happen. "You will be okay, and we will be right here!"

I healed quite well but got carried away with on my tricycle going round and round in the garage, and I found myself with an emergency visit back to the hospital. Dad helped me to understand about following the rules of "resting and healing."

Once I was out of college and in the workforce, he spent a Saturday teaching me how to change (and/or rotate) the tires on my car. I think of him now as I drive my car to the dealership to have this done for me. His instructions on tire changing likely caused me to always organize my money to have funds for someone to rotate my tires! When we were in the driveway and I was changing tires, I could envision this long-term plan. Dad was always arming me for the future.

This was radically different from Mom's approach, which was to question me all the time about what I was doing to get married. Dad could see my future from a much more accurate viewpoint than my mother! Thank you, Dad.

Photo History of Our Family—Like me, Dad loved photography. He was an early adopter of 8mm film. He had a camera and a light bar. He could light up the entire living room for Christmas and birthday filming. He had battery packs and carried his equipment everywhere.

I remember him sitting at the kitchen snack bar working on his photos and films. He had a splicer and could cut and splice all of Annette's birthdays together or all of our Christmases together on one reel. He loved it and spent hours working on this project. I developed my interest in photos, creating photo stories, and collecting equipment from him. Thank you, Dad. All these memories are precious!

Before Dad began to work on this hobby, we mainly had school photos and studio family photos. Now our family photo history is more complete.

Fortieth Anniversary—I do not know why, but I had a sense that we should celebrate Mom and Dad's fortieth wedding anniversary and not wait until their fiftieth. Because of World War II, they did not marry until 1946 between Christmas and New Year's Day. They married in the preacher's home in Big Spring. They spent their first night (honeymoon) in Abilene at Dad's brother and sister-in-law's house. Remember, this soon after the war funds were scarce.

We had the fortieth wedding anniversary reception at the Howard County Junior College facility. We were successful at keeping it a surprise. The four of us went to lunch and diverted to the college campus, where we surprised Mom and Dad with a crowd gathered for the reception. Great day! One slight problem was that I borrowed Mother's address book. She did not keep it thoroughly updated, so I invited *dead* people. None of them appeared at the reception!

Communication with a Busy Daughter—When I was working as the District 1 (Amarillo area) and District 2 (Lubbock area) 4-H specialist, I was on the road nearly every day. There was not yet wide use of cell phones, so I would make a weekly cassette tape while I was on the road. I would try to do this on Tuesday so I could get it in the mail for my parents to receive before the weekend.

I just pretended that I was talking to them and giving them an update of what I was up to and where I would be that week. It was the best way for me to help them to understand my job and the travel required. They, of course, knew no one who had a job like mine!

From the Garden to Heaven—The day Dad died in 1990, I was working at the office preparing for big volunteer training on aerospace, and Annette was a volunteer at the office, helping me with this project. (Remember, this was the time before wide use of cell phones.) Mother and Dad were in the garden, which was about a quarter mile from the house, and they were picking squash. Mother was joking about finding squash bugs and moving them to other squash plants. She was *done* with the crop of squash.

She heard a noise as Dad collapsed between the garden rows. She could not help him, so she went to the car and drove for help to the nearest house, which was three-fourths of a mile away. That neighbor performed CPR on Dad, but he was gone. The ambulance arrived, and he was taken sixteen miles into Big Spring where they tried to revive him, but he was already in heaven.

Mother began the struggle to find us and let us know. We had finished my work project but stopped at a restaurant on the way home. Mother called two friends—one who drove to the office to look for us and the other one who drove to our house to wait for us to get home.

We knew that something was *very* wrong when we got home and saw Catherine and Delaine Crawford parked in our driveway.

Within the hour, we were on our way to Luther to support Mother. The last part of that day is sealed in my memory forever—an ordinary Saturday that left my life as it had never been before. I thought, *He was only seventy-two. Why didn't I ask him more about his time in World War II, and why didn't I organize my life to spend more time with him?*

He was such an honorable man, who approached every day with a plan to help people and with love for others. He was truly an example of the Greatest Generation!

Blessed Sister Annette

The birth!—When my only sister was born on November 3, 1953, I was confused! In the middle of the night, Dad took me to stay with Grandmother, who lived right next door, and left me. I did not know what was going on and did not know to worry.

On the next day or two, Dad took me to the hospital. (I do not know exactly how long it was before they took me to meet her—one of the thousands of questions I should have asked Dad, Mother, or Annette, who have all gone to heaven.) Mother was in a different bed than I had seen before, and it was tall enough for me to crawl under and play.

After a few minutes, Dad picked me up and put me on his shoulders. We walked upstairs in the hospital to the nursery. He pointed to Annette and told me that she was my sister, and she was going home with us! I was very upset and *not* happy. I learned later that I like time to plan and survey a situation.

I asked Mother several times, and she always said, "In 1953, people did *not* tell their children about new family members arriving." I certainly would be more comfortable with modern times, in which sisters and brothers are told they are getting a new family member.

Annette was a great sister for sixty-one years. And, she was my best friend. It is not possible to express my love for her, but some of the fun stories presented here will give thought to her great personality and her approach to life.

Prayers—It was a family tradition to have prayer before meals, and sometimes it was Annette's or my turn. At about four years of age, Annette prayed for Elvis Presley. Likely all of us, including Elvis, needed prayer, but it did not sit well with Grandmother!

Two or three years later, Annette prayed for a dog, and one showed up in a day or two. Now, this is a small miracle because we lived in the country one mile from other houses. Annette named the dog, and it became hers. Next, she prayed for a horse. And, yes, a horse showed up at the house a few days later. This was problematic because the "lost" horse had to be returned.

Annette Tried to Kill Me—There were many dangers around the farm/ranch property as we were growing up. Annette was about four years old and I was seven years old when this event occurred. We were playing in the backyard. Do not think of your backyard. This was at the back side of the house but between the house and the barn.

In this area, there were old worktables where Mother and Grandmother killed and cleaned chickens, shucked corn, and did other messy projects that were best completed outside of the house.

After they had gone into the house, Annette and I stayed there to play. I began to use a crowbar, pretending I was removing some of the boards. Annette panicked and thought that I was going to get in trouble, which was likely.

She picked up a small pipe and whacked me on the head to stop me. Of course, it did stop me. You know what they say about a head wound—that it bleeds a lot. And it did.

Mother threw me into the car and raced me to the hospital. Annette stayed with Grandmother. She told my sister that she had probably killed me! Of course, I survived, but we all learned a lesson.

Annette and Grandmother Phipps—Probably because she was the baby grandchild, and also probably because she was very rambunctious, Grandmother Phipps was always correcting her and giving her directions. Apparently, this gave Annette permission to be bold with Grandmother. One day after dinner, time was a-wasting, and Annette began to worry that if Grandmother did not go home very soon, we could *not* watch *Highway Patrol* (a popular 1950s television show starring Broderick Crawford). So Annette said that to Grandmother.

Much trouble ensued, and Annette had to go to our bedroom. But, the truth was that all of us wanted to watch *Highway Patrol*. After the skirmish, Grandmother headed home, and *we all* were able to watch Highway Patrol. All's well that ends well.

Annette Goes to College—Annette went to Howard County Junior College in Big Spring for two years and lived at home. I had gone to work, so I do not know as much about her day-to-day college time as I wish I did.

She worked on the annual staff and had a part time job to help with expenses.

I do know that she graduated with an associate degree and

headed to West Texas University in Canyon, Texas, in the fall of 1974.

It worked very well for me during the two years she worked on her bachelor's degree at West Texas. I was working a great amount in and out of the Amarillo area, so I stayed with her. She did not have a roommate, so it was very convenient. She was so tickled that I had to sign in and out of her dorm when I came to stay. I was tickled that they thought I was her younger sister!

Her degree from West Texas University was in communication specialization.

Annette at Work—When Annette graduated from West Texas in 1976, she already had a job at the radio station in Spearman, a town north east of Amarillo. She did everything from music to sports to news at the radio station.

Annette and I decided that she would move to Lubbock, and she did. She started a part-time job during the Christmas rush with Texas Instruments in Lubbock. Later, she also worked with Texas Instruments in Temple and Dallas. She had a thirty-plus-year career with the company and retired after this time.

Because the family home in Luther was empty, Annette moved back there and volunteered with the Big Spring Symphony. She loved this and used her communication education and people skills working there.

It is accurate to say that Annette was very adaptable and joined workforces in different places with great skill. She met people easily and enjoyed all of the groups and individuals with which she worked. Until the end, she kept in touch with all of them.

Besides work, she volunteered with the Red Cross. She loved

assisting families whose homes had a fire, and she helped them relocate and find new resources.

She also held a position with the Blue Cross Center in Midland. Midland was about fifty miles from Luther, where Annette lived. She was able to return to her customer-service roots that she enjoyed so much at Texas Instruments. It was a full-circle opportunity.

Dallas Cowboy Games—We loved (and I still do) the Dallas Cowboys and Cowboy games. We went to our first game in 1971, which was the opening day for the season and for Texas Stadium. We lived in Lubbock then and took quick flights to most of the games. We probably went to two or three games per year. In the eighties, we bought season tickets, and our seats were located in the end zone. We loved it and made friends with other fans in our section.

In January 1992, we were on our way to the second NFL playoff game we had attended. And it was the first since we had become season ticket holders for the Dallas Cowboy games. The Cowboys were playing the San Francisco 49ers.

The day was beautiful. We parked across Highway 183 (of course, this was in the old days at Texas Stadium) because it was cheaper, and we thought the Joneses, who owned the team, had enough money of their own. Parking at this location meant that we had to walk down the overpass embankment under Highway 183 to get to the stadium.

I was walking ahead of Annette, when she called me back. She had fallen and said her leg was broken. Of course, I was thinking, it is the *playoff* game ... so I told her I would help her up so we could continue on to the stadium. She insisted that her leg was broken and wanted me to look under her sock to see if the bone was sticking out!

When I finally stopped and looked, her lower leg was at an odd angle. A blessed nurse, walking to the game with her family, stopped to help. It was a laughable sight because she was wearing blue-foam moose antlers in support of Darrell "Moose" Johnson, a Cowboy player.

As others stopped, they flagged down cars on Loop 12 to use their car phone (the walk-around cell phones were not available yet). Someone called 911, and very quickly EMTs arrived with a fire truck, a police car, and an ambulance. And, to add to the scene, the traffic helicopter was hovering over us and reporting on the incident to let fans know that they might encounter additional or slowing traffic.

They secured Annette's leg, loaded her into the ambulance, and off they went to Parkland Hospital in Dallas. Being very optimistic about getting this fixed and coming back to the game, I returned to the car (negotiating with the parking attendant to save my parking spot) and raced off to Parkland.

After clearing three sets of X-ray and security machines, I found Annette on a gurney in the hall of the emergency room. She found no humor in my speculation that she might be in the same area as President Kennedy was in 1963!

We saw the emergency room doctor (who was a graduate of Texas Tech University like me), and he said that it was a bad break and surgery was in her future. I told him about the play-off tickets, and he said that he was off duty at three o'clock and could go to the game with some help from that fact that doctors could park near the stadium. I bartered these precious tickets for a transfer out of emergency into an individual room (with a television), and we saw most of the game.

The Cowboys won! They beat the San Francisco 49ers!

I finally "forgave" Annette the next year when the Cowboys were in the NFC Championship (we were in attendance) and beat the Green Bay Packers to go to the Super Bowl again. My sister and I went to Cowboy games for twenty-three years. What great memories!

These great memories of our Cowboy game adventures help me to keep my sister's memory alive. I still attend all the home Cowboy games in the new AT&T Stadium.

Annette and Martha Travel—After we were out of college and began to work, my sister and I loved to travel together. She won a trip to New York City at a Red Cross fund-raiser. We had a wonderful trip, which included dinner at the top of the World Trade Center. I would not take for that time. It was special to us as country girls in the big city.

The food and service were great, and, of course, the views were unbelievable! It was very expensive but worth it to have this great joint memory in light of the later history of the World Trade Center.

We had a crazy time getting back to the hotel with a taxi driver who kept banging his head on the steering wheel!

It was so surreal when, years later, the towers fell during the attack on America. Annette and I connected via phone that day and relived our experience.

I was in New York City again in December 2017, and the decorations were great. The city was so beautiful. I loved it again. This time I went to the *Today* show and was interviewed by Al Roker.

Golden Globe Awards—Another outstanding trip that she and I took was to the Golden Globe Awards in Beverly Hills, California. Annette investigated how to get Golden Globe tickets, and plans were made. (These are expensive tickets, so you may not want to try this at home!)

We love movies and had gone to as many as five in one day. Historically, many movies would open in our towns during the Christmas holidays. We were both off work, so we would plan a movie marathon.

At the Golden Globes, we were in the grandstands at the red carpet and saw the celebrities arriving, stopping for interviews, and modeling their gowns and tuxedos. That day alone we saw fifty-seven famous people—if you do not count us.

Next, we watched the broadcast and award announcements on closed-circuit television in our hotel suite. We loved it and gathered many stories to tell.

Rose Bowl Parade—Another California trip was to the Rose Bowl Parade. Just like for the Golden Globes, there were tickets available. These tickets are very affordable. But, considering the time change from central time in Texas, the parade is *very* early in the morning. This event is very family friendly.

International Travel—Annette and I also enjoyed international traveling. Our biggest trip was to Australia and New Zealand, but we also took several cruises in the Caribbean. Annette embraced the joy of traveling. This trip was her favorite. She seemed to have an affinity for Australia and constantly followed the events occurring there after we visited in the 1980s. We rode in a Shotover jet boat on the river and saw the fairy penguins as they left their nest at night. Also, we took a cruise into Sydney harbor and traveled under the Harbor Bridge.

Annette was a serious Russell Crowe fan, and she met him several times. She followed his movies and music with great interest and passion. I was fortunate enough to meet him several times as well.

In 2018, when I went back to Australia on a cruise, I carried Annette's ashes to return her, symbolically. She loved Australia very much, and I found joy in thinking of her while I was traveling there again. I sensed that she was with me, and I talked her through the changes that I saw.

After we discovered cruising, we also enjoyed Caribbean cruises and other international trips.

Things I Learned (or Tried to) from Annette
Caring for others—Even though her name was Annette, she was the biblical Mary to my biblical Martha. She was caring, almost to a fault. Of course, that is just "the Martha view." She immediately embraced new friends. She listened. She got involved in helping them.

Taking care with being proud—She was not overly proud. I was always worried (and still am) about appearances. She preferred having the time with people, even if she did not have the right dress or the right gift. She embraced them and what they could add to her life.

Listening—When she broke her leg on the way to the NFC Championship game, where the Dallas Cowboys played San Francisco, I told her, "It cannot be broken. Come on. Get up and

I will help you get to the game, and later we will have it checked."
She taught me to listen!

Keeping your sense of humor—She had a great sense of humor,
but thankfully, not in the sarcastic, "say anything to get a laugh"
sense that I have. She did not think it was that funny when she
was at Parkland Hospital with her broken leg, and I observed,
"I wonder if President Kennedy was right about here where you
are on the gurney."

*Not letting the circumstances of life stop you from moving for-
ward*—Even when our grandmother told her, "I do not believe in
people dying their hair, but if mine was your color, I would dye
it," that did not stop her from holding her red head high.

Blessing those who come into your life—In her last days at St.
Joseph's, nurses, therapists, and doctors who had treated her
came by her room to tell me what a great patient she was. In her
worst of times, she had blessed others, had patience with others,
and remembered their names.

Taking care of yourself, so you can care for others—She believed in
following through with her goals, such as getting four jobs after
retiring from Texas Instruments, and saying "I love you." We
agreed that we would never separate without hugging.

Do not just be an observer of life—In the mid-1980s, I was at
work and listening to the radio. (Yes!) The station was having
a contest to win George Michael concert tickets. He was going
to appear the next weekend at Texas Stadium (the home in the

eighties of the Dallas Cowboys). You had to give a reason why you deserved tickets to his concert. I called and said, "The only thing I have seen in Texas Stadium is the Dallas Cowboys, and I deserve better!" I won!

So the next weekend we were off to Dallas (actually, Irving, Texas) to see his concert. It was a sold-out stadium. I was so in shock that I was there with fifty thousand others that I just stood still and observed. Annette turned to me and said, "At least clap; you look like a nark!" As an aside, when I revealed this at Annette's funeral, my minister reported to all that he was also at this concert, which was before we knew each other.

"You can do it"—This mainly relates to technology. Annette was great with technology. As I said earlier, she worked for Texas Instruments. Almost daily I would call her with some tech trouble. She would always laugh but try to help me. I am thinking of her especially as I am writing this book. I could *really* use her help. When you read this, I hope that you can hear laughter from heaven as I do.

Bravery!—In case you did not know her, she was brave—brave about trying new things, brave about tackling new careers, brave as a friend, and brave when she knew she was leaving this earth.

I wish I was eloquent enough for you to know her better with what I have written.

Love you, Sis!

Grandmother Phipps Stories

Grandmother Phipps—we called her Grandmother, as she decided—was alone the entire time we knew her. Grandfather Phipps had died in July 1951. I was not even two years old, so I have no memory of him. I treasure the photo that I have of me on his lap; it seems like a happy moment. I was their oldest living grandchild. (My Aunt Helen and Uncle Virgil had a son who died as a very small child before I was born.)

She lived next door, which will give an inaccurate picture in the reader's mind. We lived in the country, and ours were the only two houses, but they were built close enough as if we were in town on a city block. We spent a great amount of time going back and forth between the two houses.

A Nighttime Walk in the Winter—I stayed with her many, many hours and sometimes days. Annette was younger and more rambunctious, so she was unable to be quiet and still. I could sit quietly and read … staying out of her way.

One of my most dramatic experiences, especially as a young child, was when I stayed with Grandmother while Mother and

Dad were out of town. Annette stayed with neighbors, who had young children her age.

It was in the winter. About 7:00 p.m., the electricity went off. Grandmother panicked. We had no phone, so she had me put on my winter coat, and we were to *walk* in the dark for 1½ miles to the Littles' (Aunt Helen, Uncle Virgil, and cousin Betty). It was very cold, and little girls did not wear slacks in 1954.

Our houses were a quarter mile off the highway on a gravel road. This part of the walk was scary, but I was more scared at the thought of the traffic on Highway 667 that ran in front of the houses.

We walked on the highway and watched (maybe hoped) for cars. None came by, and we continued to walk. We turned off the main highway onto the smaller (although still paved) road. It seemed like hours had passed.

Finally, we arrived at the Littles' house. There were no lights showing from inside the house. We knocked on the door, and no one was home! I was even more cold and frightened.

All there was to do, according to Grandmother, was to walk home. Her logic was that we did not know when they were coming home, and we could not wait on the porch. Remember, phones were rare! We had a party line at our house, but I guess we did not have a key to the Little's house.

We walked about one-third of the way back to our house and saw a car light. Small miracle, it was Aunt Helen, Uncle Virgil, and Betty.

"What are you doing?" was the question that greeted us, but they quickly got us into the car, and we were on our way back to Grandmother's house. It was an electric breaker, and the electricity was back on immediately.

An interesting fact is that Grandmother's house had a butane heater, so it was *warm* the entire time we were out in the freezing weather. It was just dark, which was not really a problem in my very young view. Safety was such a blessing, but I had trouble sleeping from being so traumatized.

I was not privy to the conversation with my parents and grandmother when they returned.

Nancy Drew and Hardy Boys Books—From the time I learned to read, I loved it. We lived sixteen miles from town, and we only went into town once a week. The library had a rule that only four books per visit could be checked out. This was so upsetting to me. I really had to pace myself since we only made the trip into town once a week on Wednesday.

This was also the day that we delivered fresh eggs to several regular customers. I always helped get the eggs into the customer's house. These were "rich" (compared to us) customers. The women were like women on television, who walked around their homes in high heels and shirtwaist dresses!

I loved reading all the Nancy Drew and Hardy Boys books. Grandmother insisted that Mother give her several of my books. Two or three days later, Grandmother came back to the house for dinner and promptly announced that these books were *not* fit for me to read!

I continued to read them but in secret. This was the first time I noticed that Mother organized us to keep secrets from Grandmother.

Television Shows—This was another area in which Grandmother tried to protect us from sin. We could not watch any television shows, except *Lassie*, when she was at the house.

Religious Radio Broadcast from Mexico—Radio was the main entertainment during these times and for Grandmother. Late in the night, she would listen to a religious broadcast from Mexico. The preachers would set up large broadcast towers and send nightly radio broadcasts across the United States, but certainly in Texas, since we were relatively close.

Even before the internet, there was great merchandising of products by these religious broadcasts. Grandmother ordered books, stationery, and (my favorite) bean pods from Israel. I should not have made fun of her because it might run in the family. When I visited Israel, I bought carved wooden crosses, camels, etc. So the apple does not fall far from the tree. I just traveled far from the tree to find similar objects.

The Long View for the Enoch Phipps Family—I really loved Grandmother, and I know that in the long view, she was sad because Grandfather had died relatively early in their planned time together. They had lived through the Depression; moved their family from near Winters, Texas, to Luther, Texas (hundreds of miles); started over; lived meagerly; and worked so hard breaking grassland into farmland using a horse and a one-blade plow.

There was a very large garden and a herd of cattle and, then, a cotton farm to tend. Work was from daylight to dark. Resting and relaxing were infrequent. It is impossible for us to really understand this commitment to life, freedom, and a future for their family.

Less than one year after Grandfather died, oil was discovered in the area, including on their property. Grandfather's honorable life of hard work and sacrifice gives me a family legacy to honor by giving to my church, starting scholarships, and sponsoring youth leadership programs.

Life in Luther, America

Rural Upbringing—I was born in Big Spring, Texas, and lived the first three years of my life in a two-bedroom house on Twelfth Street. We had a big backyard and great neighbors. Many nights, neighbors were at our house with the adults playing dominoes.

Mother was a stay-at-home parent, and Dad was an electrician, working at a small electrical shop in town. Dad's parents lived in Big Spring, too, so there was considerable time spent at their house, especially on the weekends.

In 1951, when Grandfather Phipps died, plans began to develop for us to move to Luther (sixteen miles north of where we lived) to support Grandmother with the farm and cattle operation.

Life changed forever with the discovery of oil in Luther in the mid-1950s.

Oil Country—After my first memory of Annette joining our family, my next memory was oil gushers, which are oil wells drilled into the layer of oil below ground with the oil spewing out in a massive gusher. The oil would blast in the air maybe hundreds of feet high.

Our elementary school mascot became the Gay Hill Gusher. This shows the influence of the oil industry in our community. This influence continues today and will remain long into the future.

The pumps that were on the wellheads to bring the oil to the surface made a banging noise about every ten to fifteen seconds. Friends who visited would ask Mother how we could sleep with all this noise. Mother proclaimed, "We wake up when the noise stops."

Big Spring, Texas, is in Howard County and clearly in West Texas. It was cotton country when I was born in 1950, but very soon it began to be known as oil country. It is even more so at the writing of this book in 2019.

I just made a visit to the property, and oil production is all about fracking. If "old" people thought that oil rigs changed the skyline of Luther in the 1950s, fracking rigs have really changed the skyline today, but more dramatically than ever.

There is hardly any room on the land for farming. It is now all oil rigs, storage tanks, barracks for workers, and other oil field dwellings.

Turbines—The horizon today also includes wind turbines. They have changed the sunset, which previously was a beautiful view to the west. I loved the view from the back porch and the calmness at the end of the day. No more!

Now the massive turbines twirl, and a strange whistling noise interrupts the quiet. It may be reminiscent of the pump jacks, which were affixed atop the hole where the oil wells were drilled.

These pump jacks brought oil to the surface and into the pipeline that moved the oil to refineries.

Pecan Trees—During our time in Luther, our three-bedroom house was built. Mother had a rule that we needed a guest room, so Annette and I shared a room until I was twelve or thirteen years of age. I loved finally having my own bedroom! I even did a 4-H bedroom improvement project. This project was featured in a home tour for a 4-H scholarship interview. I received a small, but important, scholarship for college.

Mother started to landscape the property, which included four pecan trees. She had always wanted these for shade but really for the pecans.

There also were fig trees (we called them trees, but they were really bushes). Mother was famous for making strawberry preserves with figs and strawberry Jell-O. Those Depression-era mothers loved a cost-savings plan for feeding their families.

Back to the pecan trees. Mother announced to me that she had planted these pecan trees so there would be pecans for my wedding. Sixty years later, there are *no* pecans and *no* wedding!

Rattlesnakes on the Farm—It is West Texas, so there are too many rattlesnake stories! We learned early about snakes and which ones were poisonous. It was an extremely important survival skill for all of us. I am just going to recount two significant rattlesnake stories.

To those of you who are not familiar with West Texas, you might be thinking, *Why did you not move away from this place?* Well, simply, it was our home. Many days were a struggle, but the challenge was always met, and until today, survival is possible.

The first big snake event was on a beautiful spring day when

I went to visit Mother for the weekend. This was after Dad died, and I think the number of rattlesnakes is related to the decrease in activity out and around the farm with Mother living there alone.

It was a Saturday morning when I was visiting. We were making the rounds to check the yard and flower beds for additional plantings. As we approached the south flower bed, there were rattlesnakes everywhere. There were five to seven adults, some that were mating, and there were thirty to forty baby rattlers.

The old wives' tale states that baby rattlers have stronger, more consecrated venom than full-grown rattlesnakes. A neighbor joined us with his shotgun, and he began to shoot snakes right and left. Snakes were escaping by slithering in every direction. Probably twenty-five or thirty snakes were killed, but many escaped into the cellar.

The next day, Mother called the cement company, ordered a truck of cement, and filled the cellar. I have a vision that hundreds of years from now, a team will be excavating, and they will find this slab of snakes encased in cement, along with hundreds of jars of preserved food and her wedding dress, which had always been stored in a gallon Mason jar!

The second snake story occurred in 2017 when I made one of my trips to the Luther ranch house. Vandals had burned down the Bethel Baptist Church (the original Couch family church, where most of the General Jackson (G. J.) Couch family went for several years). It had stood for more than one hundred years and was the center of the community, but it was gone in the middle of one Saturday night.

This news made me realize that the vacant family home 1½ miles from the church site was not safe.

I began the process of moving out of the house. It was not

my main home but the family home. This was a difficult decision. My ancestors had kept this through the Depression, and I
struggled with having to give it up but for the safety of the house.

I moved out some of the remaining special items, mainly
Christmas decorations from the garage. One notable item was a
1950s aluminum Christmas tree that Dad had cared for so carefully that each limb was still stored in the brown paper tubes.

I moved the box with the Christmas tree into my car and took
it to my home in College Station. The next day, Craig Peterson—
the manager of our farm/ranch as well as many other family
farms, including his own—called me to tell me that they had
found a six-foot rattlesnake in the garage—the biggest one I have
ever seen on this property.

I considered this snake a sign that I had done all that I could
do to leave our Luther home in the safe hands of others who were
better prepared to handle the day-to-day environment.

We survived with stories to tell, but as is true in rural
America, survival is more likely when neighbors are there to
help! Thank you to all; they know who they are!

Hiding in Plain Sight in the Early Days—The Luther home was a
quarter mile from the highway, and we had a family drill where
we could clean the house and be prepared for company before
they could drive from the highway to the house. This was a drill
for which we had a lot of practice. We could clean the house in
forty-five seconds.

We also practiced the "hide from the Watkins, encyclopedia,
Avon, etc. salesman/woman" drill. Of course, it was weak since
all the doors (remember screen doors?) and windows were open
to cool the house.

If we wanted to see or visit with those driving down the road from the highway to the house, we had another drill in which we could change our clothes, straighten the living room, check the guest bathroom, and be ready for company. We each had certain duties to make this plan work. It was an organized and successful plan. Friends and neighbors reading this may be surprised.

Or maybe every family does this!

Grandmother Bought a Race Car from the Local Television Station—Continuing with the earlier story about Grandmother Phipps trying to kill me on the late-night walk to the Littles' home, she once bought a soap box derby car from the nightly television news show. The "car" had no engine, so it had to be pulled behind the pickup truck because there were no hills to coast down in Luther.

When I was eleven years old and Annette was eight years old, Mom would sit in the back of the pickup and hold the rope that was attached to the derby race car. Dad would drive us down the highway. Between Annette and I, the one of us not in the car would watch for traffic on the highway. There was some fun involved with the wind blowing on your face as we raced along, but I never thought it was worth the risk.

The race car is still in the chicken house at the ranch. I am sure it is broken down but safely stored there so as not to hurt anyone.

Even though some of these stories are about danger, I appreciated my days on the farm/ranch. There was time for family relaxing and time together.

Gay Hill School Closing and the Supreme Court Case—The news was not to be believed, but it said that the Big Spring School Board had met and annexed Center Point (the school district between us and Big Spring) and the Gay Hill School District (our school) into the Big Spring School District. Our school was *16 miles* from Big Spring.

The conversation centered on "How could this happen?" We did not know there was a meeting and that this was on the agenda. Our school was *our* school.

Meetings began to occur several times a week. Our whole family went as did all the other families. We felt we were in the fight of our life. They were taking our school!

We worked on saving our school three ways: (1) legally, with attorneys and petitions; (2) with public opinion, using the media and talking to friends and neighbors; and (3) economically, by boycotting all the businesses of the school board members.

For four years (for me this was from the third grade to the seventh grade), we fought! The legal case went all the way to the U.S. Supreme Court. I have a file cabinet drawer with all the legal documents and newspaper articles.

When it was all over, my family and many others transferred us to an adjoining school district. This was traumatic and involved a thirty-minute drive each way to school. (Previously, we were two miles from our school.) We had lost our school, and change was upon us.

Mom and Dad bought a car, and I drove Annette and me to meet the Borden County School bus each school day. Borden County built a parking lot at the county line where we could leave our cars while we were at school in Gail.

This was life changing! Annette was only in the third grade, but she went to Borden County ISD, also.

One result of our fight was that *all* of the businesses owned by the school board members were closed. We boycotted them all. And we informed our friends to boycott, too.

In the long run, this may have been a good thing for Annette and me. The Borden County Schools were small, attentive, and a great place to be educated. Many times, the blessings are not known until later.

A Hard Day's Night

—Movie Arrived at the Ritz Theater in Big Spring

A Hard Day's Night was released in the summer of 1964. I had a summer job (more about that in another chapter), and Annette and Mother went to stand in line at the Ritz Theater in Big Spring to get tickets. They said there was a big crowd trying to secure tickets! I do not remember what the tickets cost, but I also do not remember Mother complaining about the cost, so it must have not been too expensive. She was an enthusiastic team member in helping us get tickets. I think that she liked being one of the girls.

I took a day and night off work for the three of us to go to the movie. It was the *midnight* show, so we left our house sixteen miles from town at 11:00 p.m. Remember, we lived next to Grandmother, and she was *not* to know that or where we were going. We went in Dad's pickup because Grandmother owned the car we used. Now, the pickup operated on both gasoline and butane, a factor that may be hard to understand today. There was a switch under the steering wheel to change from one fuel to the other.

Apparently, when Mother got in the pickup in the dark, she

bumped the switch and turned off *all* fuel to the pickup! About halfway from the house to the highway, the pickup sputtered and stopped.

Being the oldest (the answer to many choices or decisions made for me), I walked back to the house (in the dark) to get help from Dad. He was watching to see that we were getting off safely and started toward us when the pickup died. He, of course, knew exactly what the problem was.

As we were walking toward the pickup, I could see Grandmother looking out her bedroom window. I do not know, but I will bet there was a conversation the next day with my parents (or Mother) to which I was not privy!

So, it restarted, and we were again on our way. When we completed the sixteen miles to the theater, we found a line of like-minded fans around the block, and we took our place near the end of the line.

At midnight, the theater doors opened, and we quickly moved inside and raced for seats. We had to walk carefully because the police officers and sheriff deputies were standing in the center aisle to keep us safe in the process.

I remember that there were no previews, although I do not even know if there were always previews for upcoming movies back then. The movie and the screaming began at the same time. I could not believe it! I was also excited and ready to see the movie, but I also wanted to hear it.

As younger people have seen old black-and-white footage of these 1960 events, you can begin to picture what we were seeing. As you know, I was only thirteen, but I remember being fascinated with the look of people in England and London. Clothes were different, and, of course, the accents were so interesting. I think this was the first time I knew I wanted to travel there. At this writing, I have traveled to England twelve times.

But, back to the story. The movie was enjoyable. And, as it all turned out, we were safe. We returned home by 3:00 a.m. and slept well, but we had stories to tell, except to Grandmother … in her case, we were mum!

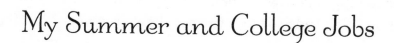

My Summer and College Jobs

Working at the Andersons—I was thirteen, and we were all focused in my family on going to college. I imagine this conversation happened in many US households in the 1960s. There
was constant promotion of college funds that banks were offering. The family started funds for us with a "matching funds"
emphasis.

Along with savings accounts, Mother introduced to me to
the idea of a summer job, where I would stay at the Andersons
(who lived ten miles to the east and in the country were considered "close" neighbors) and help with housework and cooking
for Opal and Walter Anderson. Opal's husband was "bedfast"
(a term that was used during this time for individuals who were
not ambulatory).

I do not remember my decision-making plan, but money for
college was the key factor.

My first summer at this job was 1963. I packed my belongings
and moved away from home for the summer. Probably, my stays
with Grandmother Phipps gave me the experience to think that

I could do this. I had my four library books per week, and I was ready.

I stayed in the guest room, so I had my own space. I could not decorate it, but the bedroom was very nice. I shared a room with Annette at home.

I was responsible for light housework (dusting, sweeping, vacuuming) and light cooking, which also required washing dishes. Mrs. Anderson took a nap in the afternoon, so I had time to read.

Mrs. Anderson worked on her journal every day. She had lovely leather-bound journals. Watching this prompted me to begin journaling, which I do to this day. It is always a blessing, but especially during times of crisis, while traveling, and for keeping memories.

During my first year, I went into town with Mrs. Anderson to shop and do errands. She was a lovely "fixer-up" lady or a ranchwoman. These are Texas terms. We were farm people, and ranch people dressed differently from farm people. There are entire Family Studies theories about the size of families and the apparel for Texas farm and ranch citizens.

Because ranchmen work much of each day on horseback, the sperm count (from the heat of the horse) is lowered, which decreases the likelihood of pregnancy. So, farm families historically were larger families, and ranch families were smaller.

Back to my story. The first year went well, and I was adding to my college savings account, so I agreed (more accurately, was persuaded) to work again the summer of 1964. This was more fun, probably because I was better prepared but more likely because my bedroom was in a separate area of the house—across the breezeway (a open, roof-covered passageway between one part of the house and another). When I had free time, I felt like I was returning to my apartment!

I had my driver's license by that time. Yes, in Texas in 1964, you could get your license at fourteen years of age. I even had driver's education at Borden County High School. We had a class period dedicated to it, and the women's coach taught it. Our school was in such a rural area that it was easy and safe to drive on the highway as we were training.

Mrs. Anderson had a Buick, which was a luxury automobile. I could drive it as the chauffeur when we made our weekly trips into Big Spring. We bought groceries and other supplies. Usually, we would have lunch in town, too.

Other days, I would cook meals and do light housework. There were some inside and outside flowers to tend as well. Mrs. Anderson had a very organized schedule for each day, but the work was not any more difficult than my chores at home.

I did this job for four years and saved money for both Howard County Junior College and Texas Tech University. Besides that, this was a great exercise in independent living, practice for college and my career when I lived in the Gaines County city of Seminole.

In looking back, it probably was not a normal teenage growing-up process, but it was invaluable to my family and me. I was financially and emotionally prepared for leaving home and going to college.

College Jobs—As a student at Howard County Junior College (a two-year college in my hometown), I was able to get a part-time job. I was the total caregiver for drop-in kids at the Jack and Jill Day Care Center on Saturdays. I never knew from Saturday to Saturday how many kids would be dropped off.

I began to panic one Saturday and knew I needed help. I convinced the day care center that I needed help, so it hired Annette for one dollar per Saturday to assist. We were certainly safer, and so were the kids. Some Saturdays we had twenty-five kids, so prayers of safety were answered weekly.

At Texas Tech University, I had student-worker jobs where I worked for two different professors in the Department of Food and Nutrition. The first one was Opal Wood, who taught a first-year food and nutrition class that counted as basic science. Many football, basketball, track, and other athletes who needed a science credit had to visit Miss Wood's office to prepare for class. It was fun to work in her office!

The other professor was Moselle Holberg. I was glad to have the job, but she did not have anything for me to do. It was exhausting to try to look busy. I was always afraid that they would discover I was not needed, and I would be dismissed!

Ultimately, all of these jobs prepared me for many different challenges I would face when I was employed. Thanks to all.

Living a Christian Life

I was raised in a Christian home, but there was discord. Mother was a Methodist, and Dad was a Baptist. Unfortunately, they did not work this out before we—the children—joined them.

Sad memories abound, as every Sunday morning, Mother, Annette, and I would go with Grandmother to the Methodist church in Big Spring. I did not ask, but I felt sad that we did not go together as a family.

Mother had Annette and I go through confirmation class at the First Methodist Church. This happened for me when I was nine years old. I was fascinated with the historic stories and the leader's explanations of their significance. I was confirmed in 1959, and Annette was confirmed when she was in the same age range.

When I was a teenager, my cousin Betty Lou Little gave her personal witness to me. I rededicated my life to Christ at an evening service the next Sunday after that night.

Since I have now read Mother's journals, I understand that she was a steward in the Methodist Church soon after she and her family moved to Howard County. This is an interesting fact to know since I have served on the board of stewards at the Christ United Methodist Church for the past ten years.

Back to our personal family religious conflict: I was not invited to my parents' meeting, but at dinner one night, it was announced that we were all joining the Bethel Baptist Church (three miles from our house), which was Dad's original family church. An intervening factor was that Grandmother Phipps had died, and Mother and Dad made a family decision.

We met with the pastor for arrangements. This is when we learned that Mother, Annette, and I would need to be baptized. Mother was fifty, Annette was sixteen, and I was nineteen years of age.

For those of you who do not know about traditional Baptist baptism, it is a full-body dunking, not just a sprinkling, as in the Methodist church. It was a very emotional and religious event. I was blessed by this life-changing total family event. It was significant to me for the fact that the family was united.

Sadly the Bethel Baptist Church, in 2001, was burned to the ground by vandals, who were illegally living in the church. They were cold, and they set a fire for warmth. So, at the end of that winter day, the church that was historic to the General Jackson (G. J.) and Josie Couch family was ashes. This signaled the painful end of this over one-hundred-year-old church.

Currently, I find great joy in being an active member of the Christ United Methodist Church in College Station. I serve on the board of stewards and the church council, serve as volunteer director of the Care Ministries, lead a group of volunteers who serve dinner for members and guests most Wednesday nights, and volunteer as the church receptionist.

I find great joy in my life serving and worshipping God through serving his people with hours of volunteer time. My personal walk with Jesus Christ blesses me each and every day.

College Life

—Martha

From early memory, we were going to college. Those parents who survived World War II came home, went to work, got married, had children, and began to want a better life for their children.

Part of that life was to go to college. We and all of our friends started bank savings accounts for college. Annette and I were encouraged to put any babysitting, birthday, and Christmas money into our college accounts.

Banks had little savings books where we could watch our accounts grow. My account book is currently in the cedar chest showing all the deposits and withdrawals.

High School—I was pretty dedicated to school and worked to keep my grades at a high level. Dad was the family member who helped Annette and me. After dinner, he would help with homework, type reports or papers for us, and quiz us on assignments.

I graduated salutatorian of my 1968 class. Making one of the graduation speeches was not too traumatic since I had significant practice in the 4-H and youth program. Kenny Hensley was the valedictorian.

Howard County Junior College—I do not remember when or how it was decided that I would go to Howard County Junior College, which was located in the town closest to us. Reasons included "it is local," "it is less expensive," and "you can ride to town with Dad." So, off I went.

The first day was registration. Dad dropped me off on his way to work at about 7:30 a.m. I got in line to register for classes. When entering the hall, I was handed a card on which to complete my schedule.

I went from table to table to register. I was going to be on campus from 8:00 a.m. until 5:30 p.m., so I signed up for as many classes as I could fit in that time frame. When I arrived at the final check, a blessed advisor helped me. I had signed up for twenty-one hours, and he told me to drop my class hours back to eighteen, which he said was a full load. Bless him!

While at Howard County Junior College, I worked every Saturday at the Jack and Jill Day Care. Because it was a drop-in care center, each Saturday I had *no* idea how many would arrive for care, and this became a problem mid-fall! I convinced the day care owner that I needed help.

I was hired as a work-study student for two dollars per hour. They let me hire Annette for one dollar per hour, but it made the children we cared for safer. Ironically, in retirement, I worked on a team to develop training modules for childcare providers. During that project, I celebrated how much progress had been made in the safe care of children.

Texas Tech University—In 1969, I started my sophomore year at Texas Tech University. Ironically, Texas Tech changed its name from "college" to "university" that same year. I always wanted to go to Texas Tech, but financially it was a family decision for me to attend Howard County Junior College for my freshmen year.

I moved into Doak Hall with my roommate from Fort Worth, Carolyn Hutton. We had written letters back and forth to decide on dorm room decoration plans. It was a good sophomore year. The campus, of course, was much larger than Howard County Junior College, but distances were manageable.

I began to make friends, several of whom I am still friends with today. There were the usual dorm antics. Once all of my clothes were stolen from the laundry room. I creatively managed and would admit to no one that my clothes were missing. I learned early: do not let them have the satisfaction!

For my junior year, Carolyn moved off campus, and I shared a dorm room with Anita Lindsey from Azle, Texas. She was from the Fort Worth area, and we had a great two years sharing our room and are friends to this day.

To say that we set our dorm room on fire would be accurate. The incident involved small votive candles and falling asleep while studying. We both woke up suddenly and put out the fire with water (luckily we had a sink in our room). We quickly opened the windows to let the smoke out.

I do not know how we could be so lucky, but when we went to make a report to Ann Beard, the dorm mother (yes, they called them that), the next day, she told us that they were going to turn our room into a "demonstration" room for an entire dorm redo. Whew!

My graduation in 1972 was the same year Annette graduated

from Borden County High School, but there was no schedule conflict, so the entire family attended both ceremonies.

As you can read in another chapter, I went to work at Texas Extension Service in May, right after graduation. My mentor and supervisor encouraged me to immediately start on my master's degree in the fall of 1972, so I barely stopped going to college. My master's degree was completed in May 1976. At the same time, Annette graduated from West Texas, so we had a big day of graduations.

Then it was on to my doctorate degree, and I graduated in 1980. Annette was my technical assistant on this degree. My research was tallied on computer punch cards, and she would work with me at night and on Saturdays at the computer center on campus. This research was on volunteers who attended the South Region Leader Forum.

Dr. Martha Elaine Couch—I was the first in my family to receive a doctorate. This focus and challenge that Dr. Catherine Crawford gave me made a great difference in the remainder of my life. Her words of encouragement and challenge made me eligible to serve as the Texas 4-H and youth development leader. The Texas 4-H program was the largest in the nation with one million members, and all the hours and sleepless nights in college were worth every minute, hour, and day to be eligible for this important position!

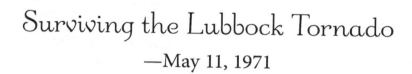

Surviving the Lubbock Tornado
—May 11, 1971

I had just finished my last final exam and planned a nap before going to a movie with my friends, Shirley Poston and Carolyn Hutton. We went to a theater near the Texas Tech University campus to see *Cactus Flower*, which starred Goldie Hawn, Walter Matthau, and Ingrid Bergman.

When we exited the movie, it was lightning, and storms were approaching. We started toward the campus with Shirley driving. I was in the front seat, and Carolyn was in the back seat. It began to rain hard, and we could barely see out the front window.

Next, the hail began to hit the car. Carolyn covered herself with a blanket that was in the back seat. We saw several people parking their cars and running away. Shirley and I agreed that the car was safer and kept us from being hit by debris.

I had a feeling of high pressure in the air a few seconds before the car windows blew out. We were covered with shards of glass. Shirley stopped the car. I ordered her to drive on. We crossed University Avenue and tried to drive onto the Texas Tech campus. We had to drive up over the sidewalk and onto the lawn to work our way around the fallen trees.

And Carolyn was still under her blanket!

The rain had slowed. We could see the sky in front of us to the west. We exited the car after getting Carolyn out of the back seat and ran to the Administration Building about a block away. On the way to the building, we could hear the constant piercing sound of the sirens.

Upon entering the building, we heard voices and headed for the basement. There we found hundreds of students and professors huddled together. Many people were injured, but we just had small cuts from flying glass.

After a safe amount of time, we were dismissed. All three of us walked to my room in Doak Hall. After we cleaned up, we waited. There was no sleeping. There were few students remaining in the dorm with the end of the semester, but the police had evacuated people who lost their homes or apartments into our dorm.

On the morning of May 12, we went to breakfast, and there was another sight that I will never forget. Hundreds of people wrapped in bandages and blankets were eating breakfast with us. It reminded me of scenes on the television news about the Vietnam War evacuations.

The next morning, the three of us walked out to inspect the damage to Shirley's car. Of course, it was sitting in the middle of the Texas Tech lawn right where we left it. We'd even left one of the doors open in our hurry to get to safety.

This was before the time of cell phones, but it would not have mattered because all the electric and phone lines were down.

My parents learned of the tornado when Dad's brother, Asa Couch (who lived in Birmingham, Alabama, which was in the

Eastern Time Zone), saw the report on the early news and called Mother and Dad.

Mother immediately got in the car and headed to Lubbock. She said that she panicked more and more as she drove north. The panic was because the farther she went, the more emergency vehicles with emergency lights blazing passed her on the highway. She began to travel at ninety miles an hour with them.

Seeing her face at my dorm door was a relief for me and for her, too. We told her the whole story. Pretty quickly, she packed me up to go home to Luther.

Later in the month, Dad, Mother, and Annette made a trip to Lubbock to see the damage. Dad made several trips in his lifetime to view storm damage, so I was not surprised. But I was definitely *not* returning to Lubbock to see tornado damage! I had already seen it and experienced it firsthand!

The Beginning of Forty-Nine Years in the 4-H Program

The first time I heard about the 4-H program was at a presentation by the Howard County Extension agent at our elementary school. He had a filmstrip telling us about the program. This low-tech presentation was not the best way to recruit youth to 4-H, but it worked.

At home that night, I told Mother and Dad that I wanted to join 4-H. We talked about the annual family garden as a 4-H project, and now I realize that it was a good plan for them to get me interested in working in the garden.

I am not a person who likes being outside. I am not a person who likes digging in the dirt. Later, as I worked for years with the 4-H program in several leadership roles, I pointed out that it was *easy* to recruit youth to the 4-H program if you can recruit me to the garden!

I joined the Gay Hill 4-H Club (named after our local school), which met monthly in the school. After our school was taken over by the Big Spring Independent School District, we met at the Bethel Baptist Church two miles away.

We were very modern because we had both girls and boys in our foods and nutrition group. At our meeting, we would have a lesson on nutrition, prepare a food item, and then enjoy eating the prepared item. Since we met after school, this was very popular. Several of us entered the local food show, which was held at Howard County Junior College.

Francis Zant, a local seamstress, volunteered to lead a group of us in a clothing project. We learned to use the sewing machine and make our own clothes. Francis sewed for others in her home; this was her career. I am pleased to have been able to meet and work with Francis.

She was the first divorced woman I had met, and she kept her son and her safe through her career. Yet, she took valuable time from her work to help us learn to sew. She was another mentor from which to learn.

My interest in sewing was so high that Grandmother bought me a Singer Sewing Machine, which I still own today. In the first fifty years of my life, sewing was the primary source of my professional clothes.

In adulthood, knowing how to sew led to having sewing weekends. Several of us would have a "sew fest" and support each other with projects and deadlines for getting garments ready. I do miss the camaraderie of those times, but currently I am working on other hobbies.

Conceptually, the 4-H program is based on learning by doing, so I started a bedroom improvement project. With support, both financial and labor, from my parents, this project led me to redo my bedroom. Prior to the redo, the wallpaper had *large* floral blooms of bright pink on a light blue background!

Afterward the room had light beige walls with natural-colored wood doors and baseboards. Then I added my favorite colors in the curtains and bedspread. It was a very different bedroom, and I felt calm and loved it!

Later, my bedroom was involved in a tour when I was interviewed for a Howard County 4-H scholarship. Other 4-H projects included citizenship and leadership. These prepared me for my work life and my extensive travel.

4-H Record Books—Another life skills part of 4-H was the record book program. Most 4-H members were encouraged to keep records of their project and leadership work. There were about thirty to forty subject categories that paralleled the projects, i.e., beef, clothing, leadership, etc. Record books were both a way to teach youth about recordkeeping and a recognition event.

Any former 4-H member in my age group will remember the yellow national report form, which had columns and squares to enter numbers of events you attended and hours you spent. If I did not know better, I would think that the National 4-H or Texas 4-H offices were in cahoots with the IRS since that best describes these forms.

Dad was a great help. I would complete the forms in pencil, and he would type them—over and over again as we made changes.

My level of involvement with the 4-H Record Book Competition was all the way from competing myself and helping Annette to training volunteers in helping youth and parents to complete their record books. I guess I loved it since I spent hours training and promoting this life skill.

Today, I think this significant background supports my effort to write my life story.

Texas 4-H Roundup—This is another significant event that involves thousands of Texas youth and families annually. The main event occurs on the Texas A&M campus as part of the partnership with the Texas A&M System and Texas AgriLife Extension Service.

Texas 4-H Roundup was a significant part of my 4-H experience and has been for forty-five of the forty-nine years that I have been involved in 4-H. The only reason it was not forty-nine years is because you could not attend until you were fourteen years of age.

In each club and county, youth prepare, practice, and demonstrate knowledge, judging skills, speaking skills, creative and critical thinking, and recordkeeping skills through many projects and competitive events.

My first trip to the roundup was when I became eligible in 1964 and I attended with a method demonstration. This is quite shocking since I have trouble with public speaking! I traveled with the assistant county extension agent and three other 4-H members, who were older than me. They had attended the year before. When we arrived in Gatesville (about halfway between Big Spring and College Station), one of the other 4-H members had come prepared with fake vomit! As we arrived at the first traffic light, she pretended to throw up.

We almost had an accident as our agent tried to get off the street and into a "filling station" (yes, that is what we called them, not service stations like today). The culprit dashed into the bathroom, which back then was outside the station.

I was as startled as the agent and waited in the car. One of the other 4-H members went to "check on the sick one." Of course, all was well, but what a start to my forty-plus years of traveling to Texas 4-H Roundups. After I went to work for the extension, another trip involved carrying a lamb in the back seat of the car. We were not lamb people, so I was not prepared for the noise they can make. This noise did help to keep us awake, however, in our nine-hour drive very early in the morning.

It was always a blessing to work with these key volunteers, who, as partners in youth development, assure that young people from Texas receive a college education. It's a partnership that has existed for more than one hundred years.

My blessing was that mentors came along at the right time and the right place. My parents had no idea about the opportunities awaiting me.

Annette and I always entered the speaking division—method demonstrations or public speaking. This was such great training for college and my career because there were many opportunities to practice life skills and job skills.

I made it from the district contest to the state contest for all five years I was eligible. I did not know it at the time, but it was exactly what I needed. I could not remember my speech the first time I participated when I was nine years of age. I even called out "Mother" at a local presentation. But by the time I was finished with 4-H, I had excellent speaking skills.

Roundup as the Associate Director of the Texas 4-H and Youth Development Program—There are not enough words to express the feeling of walking on the stage during the Texas 4-H Roundup in 1997 as the director of the Texas 4-H program. It was an unbelievable honor and a great but long journey to this point.

Who could ever think that a girl from Luther, who joined the 4-H program in 1959, could serve in this position? God has given me more blessings than I could know and pray for to occur!

Extension 4-H and Youth Development Specialist

My Area Was Forty Counties in Texas

This was a great job because I could use my communication and presentation skills to do training for extension agents, volunteers, and members. I traveled across the entire Texas Panhandle working with forty counties. I had great partners, who were 4-H specialists and district administrators. We worked together to design curriculum and presentations. These were great times, and I enjoyed helping agents, volunteers, and youth leaders.

I had offices at both the Lubbock Research and Extension Center (South Plains, District 2) and the Amarillo Research and Extension Center (Panhandle, District 1).

I so enjoyed finding creative ways to provide training. I once ordered thirty helium-filled balloons to use at a training session in Levelland. They fit perfectly in the back of the Dodge station wagon I had reserved from the motor pool, which was a group of cars assigned to our office by the state organization. Off I went.

I suddenly noticed that there was a great amount of traffic on the rural highway into Levelland. The highway was four-lane, so I worked my way past all the traffic. As usual, I was on a tight time schedule.

After passing more than twenty cars, I saw the lead car from a funeral home. I was passing a funeral procession! What was there to do but keep driving? If I slowed down, all the cars would pass me again and have more time to write down the name—Texas

Agricultural Extension Service—to call and complain! I told the agency director that "name recognition is everything!"

Electric Camp—One of the very popular activities in my area of Texas, which I helped organize,, was the 4-H Electric Camp. It was in New Mexico and a four-hour bus drive from either district—Amarillo or Lubbock. At this educational camp, youth learned about how electricity works, as well as safety and conservation practices.

An advantage was that the event was usually in July in the New Mexico mountains, so it was cooler than staying at home. Part of the experience was the bus ride and getting acquainted.

The youth as well as the chaperones loved it. Getting away. No phones. No television. Challenging youth to learn about safety and electricity. But, mainly, there were no distractions from media or home duties.

The evenings provided great opportunities for social gatherings with games, dancing, and fireside motivational moments.

4-H members from all over the Lubbock and Amarillo area reported great fondness for this leadership and educational event. For us in the Lubbock and Amarillo area, which is a very flat part of Texas, going to the mountains was quite an experience, especially in July when it is hot as hell in Texas. In the New Mexico mountains, it was cool, relaxing, and fun.

We had challenges in the form of downpours, hail, bears, snakes, and fatigue, but if you ask any of those who attended, they would get in line to board the bus again tomorrow!

For electric camp, there was a wonderful forty-plus-years' partnership with the Amarillo and Lubbock Electric Companies. They paid for the camp attendance for all youth, volunteers, and employees. They conducted educational safety workshops and led all recreational activities. Donors are a special find, but donors who will not only give money but also teach youth at a camp in the mountains out of state are *real* partners!

Citizenship Washington Focus and Heritage Tour—Twice I chaperoned this great trip, where one to four buses of youth and adults traveled from Texas to Washington, DC. This was a two-week trip with travel and a one-week workshop at the National 4-H Conference Center.

Besides learning about our national government, attendees met with their senators and representatives at their offices. This is a great life experience for all of us, but especially for our high-school-age youth.

One of the trips overlapped with the American Bicentennial in 1976, and our group was seated at the Washington Monument for the fireworks on the Fourth of July. It was not only a very important memory for the youth, but for me also.

Seventy-fifth Anniversary of 4-H in Texas and County Leadership Training—Because of the size of Texas and my overzealous behavior, I sometimes got myself overscheduled! Friends are saying, "Ha-ha!"

I was one of the chaperones for the statewide 4-H Tour of Texas, in which a team of youth representing the state flew around for a media tour. It was a great event and much positive interpretation for the 4-H and Youth Development Program. I loved it and was blessed to be asked to help.

When the tour ended, I flew back to my main office in Lubbock. I was picking up an extension vehicle to drive to the Moore County Youth at Risk camp at Palo Duro Canyon, near Canyon, Texas. When I went to pick up the car, the gas tank was empty. I had to go back into Lubbock to buy gas and was finally on my way after 11:00 p.m. It was about a ninety-minute drive to the youth camp.

Ten minutes from the highway turnoff to the camp, I fell asleep! I woke up when the car and I went into the median of the divided highway. I successfully got the car stopped in the median. I was now fully *awake*! I took several breaths and began to continue my journey.

As soon as I got the car back on the highway, the right-side front tire blew out. It was the middle of the night, so I decided not to try to change the tire but to drive very slowly—on the flat tire.

After a mile or so, another tire blew out! For some reason, I was not very worried because the tires that were flat were on the same side of the car. So, slowly on I went. By this time, it was 3:30 a.m.—time flies when you are going four miles an hour! I knew that I could not go all the way to the camp because it was in a canyon, and there was a steep downward incline approaching the canyon.

I parked the car at the top of the hill and freshened up, changed clothes, etc. I was preparing for the day, and my presentation was at 8:30 a.m. At about 6:00 a.m., a camp employee came by on his way to work. Extension agents, who were conducting the camp, organized a plan to help me. The camp loaned them a tire, and into town they went. Within a few hours, they brought the car back fully functional.

They also changed the time for my presentation so I could get some rest. Blessings! It is true that the entire time I worked in districts one and two, the county staff was extremely supportive. I felt like we were always on the same team to make 4-H a great organization that helped many youth and families.

Partnerships, Friendships, and Sharing Expertise with Other 4-H and Youth Development Specialists—After serving as an assistant county agent for Gaines County in Seminole, Texas from 1972 to 1975, I was promoted to 4-H and youth development specialist in districts one and two. This was a forty-county area of Texas, surrounding Amarillo and Lubbock.

For years, I was in over my head, but I had great mentors in Catherine Crawford, Bill Gunter, Paul Gross, and Sue Farris. They were district extension directors, who supervised the employees with whom I worked. Agents have expertise in agriculture and home economics. As a 4-H specialist, I brought expertise in youth development, public speaking, competition, and volunteer training. We were in a partnership for the 4-H program in this area of Texas.

All four of them were great mentors because I needed great support to accomplish these important tasks. They encouraged and supported me every day (and two are still living and continue to support me).

Other great partners who supported me in developing skills for these important tasks were 4-H specialist coworkers. We were located across the state and had similar assignments and challenges to support the 4-H program and its employees and volunteers. Professor Dan James and I developed an aerospace project for the 4-H emphasis in science and technology. We knew an average amount about aerospace, but we developed a partnership with NASA and launched this project statewide. For those of you not familiar with the current 4-H program, it is not just cows and cooking but also has a high level of science and technology. Dan brought me along as we led the first high-tech effort in the Texas 4-H program.

Professor James and I went through the struggle together

regarding professorial rank. I served on the agency committee that set the requirements for the professional ranking system for extension specialist. Once the system was in place, Dan and I talked long and hard about this.

Current long-term specialist employees could choose to request a professional rank with accompanying vitae supporting the request. Or, they could wait the three or four years for the establishment of the system and apply for rank. Back and forth we went, but we decided to begin with a requested rank. Thank you, Professor Dan from Professor Martha.

Other Great Specialist Teammates—Dr. Shiretta Ownbey and Iris Kalich Hegemier were 4-H specialists in Fort Stockton and San Angelo. We had a wonderful working relationship and inspired each other to be more creative. We met many times in a central location and worked on lesson plans for volunteer and youth training.

Each one of us had creative skills but in different areas, so this was a great working group not only for us but also for the Texas 4-H program. As with our other coworkers, we shared our resources across Texas. We had working retreats to develop programs, and then each of us used them in our districts.

When I was meeting with them, I lived in Lubbock (population 100,000), and one night, when Iris was complaining about the availability of resources in San Angelo, I said to her, "Iris, if you lived in a real town, there would not be a problem!"

Now, she lives in San Antonio and I live in College Station, and she frequently repeats back to me, "Martha, if you lived in a real town!" I love these friends and the great times! The great times led to innovative curriculum and projects for Texas 4-H and youth development.

Serving as a District Extension Administrator

I never had in my life plan to serve in an administrative position. I loved serving as a 4-H and youth development specialist with all the teaching possibilities and opportunities.

But an unexpected opportunity came alone with the sudden death of Dr. Judy Flynn, who was the district administrator in Amarillo. I had worked extensively with Judy developing the self-esteem project titled "It Is Up to *Me!*" The team, with Judy's leadership, launched this statewide project to help young people be in charge of themselves and their decision-making. It was a great success.

Judy died suddenly during a district extension director's retreat in the valley area of Texas.

Some months after her death, it was announced that her position was to be filled, and I applied. Two fears that I had were (1) I had never served in a position with supervisory responsibilities, and (2) I would need to move to Amarillo. I had lived in Lubbock for nineteen years, and I loved it there. It was a big enough city to have great restaurants, movies, and other forms of entertainment.

Lubbock was also closer to Mother, and I was her primary caregiver. Telling her that I was applying for this job in Amarillo was stressful, but she tried to focus on my success.

I was chosen for the position and put my Lubbock house on the market. It sold pretty quickly and packing began. I have a clear memory of Mother sitting in a lawn chair in my driveway while the moving company loaded my stuff. She appeared sad, but I think deep down she was proud. I promised to travel often to see her. She could not know, nor could I, that in less than four years, I would be moving even farther away.

I had to wait to move to Amarillo until my house sold, so I lived in an apartment with all of my furniture and other belongings. I moved everything I had into the apartment so I would know where it was. During the move, my car was broken into one night while I was staying in a hotel waiting for my belongings to arrive from Lubbock.

There was much work to do to get acquainted with official paperwork, supervisory responsibilities, etc. I knew all the employees who worked in district one, but now I would have a different role with each of them. My coworker, Paul Gross, had been my extension agent when I was a 4-H member in Howard County, so I knew him. He was great to work with and supported me as I learned the ropes.

I worked one year with Paul before he retired. He singlehandedly helped me prepare to do this job well. I was familiar with the twenty counties since I had served as their 4-H specialist, and I felt like they embraced me as their supervisor. A new challenge was working with the twenty county commissioners' courts and county judges. They provide part of the funding for our county extension agents positions, so they are an important partner in extension education.

Paul was a serious early riser, and we would meet at the office at about 6:30 a.m. and be at the county office we were visiting or working with by 8:00 a.m. on any day. I reset my personal clock (which still exists today) when I worked in district one.

Paul retired at the end of our first year working together. I had (and have) known him since 1969, and he has been a great coworker, a great supporter of me and my career, and a great friend. The agricultural agents planned a wonderful retirement party for him, which included presenting him with a new pickup (that is what we called them, even though most people now call them a truck).

After Paul's retirement, my coworker was Dr. Bob Robinson. We first met in 1975 when he was an assistant county extension agent in Potter County. Since then, he has been the county extension agent in Randall County and the extension director in district two, Lubbock, Texas.

Very early in our team time, we communicated to all county extension agents how much they were appreciated and exactly what our expectations were of each of them. This environment of clear expectations led us to successful times, serving the employees and citizens of this twenty-county Panhandle area.

As we traveled together almost daily around the twenty-county area, we had several fun episodes—three of them related to gas stations.

The first one was in Hemphill County (Canadian), where it was so cold that the gasoline pump dispensed fuel about a tablespoon a minute. We had to have gasoline, so we waited and waited and laughed and laughed!

Another time, we needed gas for our return trip from Ochiltree County (Perryton) to Amarillo after a planning conference with the Ochiltree County Extension staff. After a day-long meeting, we left for home. The gas pump worked fine, but the gasoline station did *not* accept our Texas State credit card.

I waited in the car while Bob went in to pay. Minutes went by, and Bob did not return and did not return. When he finally did return to the extension's vehicle, I asked him what happened. He said that the station did not accept our credit card. Bob had attempted to use his negation skills to try to get our card approved, and on and on the time went with no results. He finally had to pay for the gas from his personal funds.

After listening, I said, "Bob, you will have to learn that it is a waste of time to negotiate with a part-time employee who is making less than five dollars per hour (the going wage in the early 1990s). In the future, pay and let us keep moving!"

Our supervisors were coming from College Station for our annual performance appraisal, and I asked Bob if Cleo's weekly cleaning lady could clean out the trash from the extension's Suburban. We needed to travel around Amarillo with our bosses, and Bob was notorious for keeping the Suburban less than tidy. We laugh about these three incidents even today.

In 1997, I applied for and was chosen as the Texas 4-H and youth development leader. Bob celebrated with me, but we knew that we were going to miss our great working team. I am pleased to report that Donna Brauchi followed me with great programs and successes in the Panhandle area after I moved to College Station.

I started my new job on May 1, 1997. District one held a fun going-away party on April 30th, so I did not fly to College Station to start my job until early in the morning on May 1. Bob insisted on taking me to the Amarillo airport. Bob could walk me to the gate since at this time there was limited security.

We had a tearful goodbye, although I was only moving from Amarillo and not leaving the earth (I told him).

God placed a nun in the seat next to me on my flight. She comforted me as I left one of my favorite jobs and favorite places, not only in Texas or the United States but in the world as well. I was greatly cared for that day.

Professor, Associate Director
—Texas 4-H and Youth Development

Leading the World's Largest State 4-H and Youth Development Program

Throughout the time that I worked as a 4-H specialist, I had great Texas 4-H and youth development leaders. Dr. Don Stormer hired me, and he was a leader in innovation. He worked to have 4-H specialists out in Texas (and not all in College Station). He challenged us to complete further education. He led the development of many new and innovative curriculum approaches.

I did not know him well until he became by boss, but he challenged me to a complete professional and personal development plan.

He led the administration's effort to have a 4-H specialist in every district in Texas. There were parallel positions in agriculture, and he gave vision to that plan for 4-H. This really brought professionalism to the 4-H program. I know that I was not his choice for the Amarillo and Lubbock 4-H specialist, but he supported me and my future. Thank you, Dr. Stormer.

The next Texas 4-H and youth development leader was Dr. John Pelham. He continued the great professional approach for 4-H. He supported me as I completed my PhD, when my mother said, "I do not think Martha is ever going to stop going to school!"

My blessing was that mentors came along at the right time

and the right place. My parents had no idea about the opportunities that were awaiting me, so it was key to have additional
mentors.

When John was leaving for a position in Missouri, he said to
me, "I hope that you will consider the position of Texas 4-H and
youth development leader sometime. You are state leader material." Few others had ever expressed this to me. Thank you, John.

On May 1, 2008, I was appointed assistant director and Texas
4-H youth development leader. No honor has been greater, nor
had one been more challenging.

Youth leaders, adult volunteer leaders, and county extension agents, specialists, and donors lead the largest 4-H and
youth program in the nation. And the Texas 4-H and Youth
Development Program should well be the largest because our
millions of youth deserve access to out-of-school education and
leadership opportunities.

Most every day (and certainly at the end of every day), this
position of leadership was a blessing. There are great stories to
tell, which will *not* be told. From a storytelling point of view,
they are great stories, and lives were changed, but these youth
and volunteers deserve to tell their own stories, and I hope that
they will. The joint history of the 4-H program is worth sharing.

Promoting the value of the 4-H program in communities,
counties, and states, as well as nationwide, and worldwide is all
of our responsibilities. Please continue to share our story.

*100 Anniversary of Texas 4-H and Being Honored at the
White House*—The Texas 4-H program was approaching its
one-hundredth anniversary, and because we have a style that
says, "We do not do anything in a small way," we planned to
celebrate the anniversary and promote 4-H in a Texas way!

Many, many people had a hand in this great plan to visit the White House and celebrate our anniversary with President George W. Bush. I want to give much credit to Ed Smith, extension director and friend since January 1975. It is a compliment for Ed to say that he is a great political animal, and I thank him for being my partner in this endeavor.

Arrangements were made, people were called, letters were written, money was raised, and God blessed us with this happening. The Texas 4-H and Youth Development Program was being honored at the White House for one hundred years of youth development.

Fifty of us from all over Texas went to represent our 4-H and Youth Development Program. It took two airplanes to secure enough seats. We required a floor in a DC hotel near the White House because we needed to walk to the White House with our large group.

We had a practice lineup the night before in the hotel. We knew that we were going to be on risers, and we knew that we would be arranged in order of height, so we did that in the hotel lobby and assigned everyone a number to deploy us to the risers.

One little unplanned event was that one of our 4-H members became sick from lunch in the DC subway (not the restaurant!). Blessed Justin Benavidez and I talked, and we called his mother and told her that he would not be able to go to the White House; we had to leave him at the hotel. While on the phone with his mom, Justin spoke up and said he *was* going and to count on him making it. We could not keep him from going because in 4-H we teach following through and letting nothing stop you from your goals.

So a new plan was developed. Justin and I would get in a taxi while the others walked, and we would go slowly. We made it! I did forget and left Justin too long on the risers during the ceremony, but he stayed upright. Today, he tells me he would not "ever forget this trip," and the memory is important.

A funny moment occurred after we arrived in the East Wing of the White House. I had our entire group line up in the entry hall in the order they would stand on the risers. When the photographer arrived, we methodically got on the risers and stood. The photographer ascended the ladder, looked at us, and said "Hmmm." They had planned extra time to get our large group arranged on the risers, and we were ready at first attempt.

The disadvantage of getting organized too early was that we had to stand for ten or twelve minutes on the risers waiting for President George W. Bush, but every second was worth it!

The president entered from the East Wing and headed toward us in a crisp walk. It was a sight I never thought I would see. Following close behind him was an assigned soldier (Marine) carrying the "football"—nickname for the case with the defense system launch codes. When I called my sister, Annette said, "I cannot believe that they let *you* in the room with the launch codes!" Love her!

As soon as the media and the White House photographer took several photos, they were dismissed. President Bush left the risers and stood in front of our group and spoke to us for twelve to fifteen minutes. Imagine! The president of the United States took time from his busy and extremely important day to talk to all of us about service, making a difference, and standing up for what you believe. Words to live by even today.

What a proud day for the Texas 4-H program, each of us, and our families.

My advice to all is do not back off of big, seemingly impossible goals!" They are achievable, and a difference will be made.

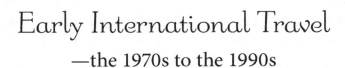

Early International Travel
—the 1970s to the 1990s

Travel to Mexico—My Texas Tech University roommate, Anita Lindsey Hatchett, and I wanted to take a trip to Mexico, which would be my first international trip if you do not count quick trips across the border to Mexico with my birth family.

For the first time, we worked with a travel agent. The flight from Dallas to Mexico City stopped in Monterey, which was required for immigration purposes. What a shock to be in Mexico City, which was very exciting but different from home.

A significant visit was to the Basilica of Our Lady of Guadalupe. I was raised in relatively small West Texas churches, and this was a sight to see. Visitors from other countries were making a pilgrimage and were very prayerful. I loved this, and it was one of my early epiphanies in foreign travel—the experience of watching others worship, whichever faith is involved. Religion around the world became a target for me in future travels.

Next, it was on to the mysterious Teotihuacán Pyramids (the first pyramids I ever saw), which were built around 100 BC as the centerpiece of an enormous ancient city often compared to ancient Rome. They were inexplicably abandoned for centuries before the arrival of the Aztecs, who called the ancient architectural marvel the "birthplace of the gods." This site was tough for me physically. I have had this challenge with foreign sites that have many steps and no handrails because of my fear of falling!

As with later sites, I did not make it to the top but loved the visit. I have learned since that time to (1) get others to take my camera to take photos and/or (2) buy postcards for the view from the top and celebrate! Of course, Anita made it to the top.

The next portion of the trip was via charter bus from Mexico City to Taxco. For a flatlander from West Texas, this was quite a drive with curves, big drop-offs from the side of the mountain, and much traffic. Other buses with local citizens and their belongings hanging out the windows were passing us on curves! We made it, but it probably is one of the factors that has added to my age.

Taxco was a beautiful small town, and I loved visiting there. There were many local craftspeople, and I probably developed my shopping habit there—and, I'd have to say, my jewelry habit as well. I, of course, still have a ring I bought as a souvenir. I recommend jewelry as a souvenir. You can wear it everywhere and share about your trip when people ask about your new piece of jewelry. And, it easily fits in your luggage.

The bus trip continued as we traveled to Acapulco, which is a beautiful Pacific Coast resort. We were in a great high-rise hotel with wonderful views of the coast. You will have to ask Anita about the quality of sunburns that can be accomplished at this location!

As do all tourists, we visited the cliff divers and saw them perform. This is an amazing team of athletes. I love looking back at these photos, even though they are 110-type Kodak photos that I have scanned into my computer. I still enjoy renewing these memories.

There were other delights, including the joy of staying and dining in a modern resort, which I did not have near me in rural Howard County, Seminole, or Lubbock.

Anita found too much joy in sunning on the beach and received quite a burn. There were challenges in traveling home via bus and plane with this discomfort. I am sure that Anita remembers this today.

Travel to the Orient—I was working in Lubbock, Texas, at the time, and I really was getting into the idea of international travel. I was a Texas girl, and only Dad had traveled internationally. My former coworker in Seminole, Elinor Harvey, agreed to go with me to the Orient. We worked with a travel agent (remember those?). Gill, our agent, was a travel expert, and with all that occurred, he was a godsend.

This is still the only trip for which I borrowed money to travel. Forty years later, Elinor and I were reminiscing, and I learned that both of us had to borrow money! And, each of us did not tell the other one before the trip.

Our trip included Japan, Hong Kong, Singapore, Taiwan, and Thailand. This was quite a trip to plan for two single women in 1978! There were new challenges in getting passports, visas, and travel documents.

The day before our flight was to depart, the airline went on strike. Gill rescheduled our flights and met us at 6:30 a.m. at the Lubbock airport with new tickets. Instead of flying from Lubbock to Seattle to Tokyo (two flights), our new plan was to fly from Lubbock to Albuquerque to Denver to Seattle to Anchorage to Tokyo (tripling our number of flights and quadrupling our travel time). But we made it!

My luggage did *not* make it, or to be more precise, half of my luggage made it, but half did not. As a relatively novice traveler, I thought that putting all my shoes, makeup, and underwear in one checked suitcase and all my outerwear in the second checked suitcase was a good idea. I know what you are thinking, but you have 2019 knowledge and experience. Also, you are thinking, *What? You got to have two checked bags?*

The suitcase with all the underwear and shoes arrived! I had the challenge of washing out my one dress (yes, dress; remember 1975 attire) each night. We were at a great hotel that supported my difficulty with laundry detergent and other aids. I had a floral pin that I wore every other day to change the look!

I view this as great early travel experience that prepared me for numerous other travels. I never, ever had this difficulty again. Always put some of each garment type in each suitcase!

We had five days in Tokyo and traveled to Mount Fuji for a great overnight stay. At Mount Fuji, a hostess came to our room to "fit" us in our kimonos. Remember how petite Japanese women are, and no kimono available would fit. Instead we wore our sleeping garments, which were not nightgowns but hand-made polyester robes we brought because they traveled easily and did not wrinkle. You would call them muumuus. I have photos to prove this, but don't worry, you will *not* see them!

The ceremonial dinner was wonderful and started a long history of similar experiences around the world. I treasure these examples of people showing their best selves to visitors.

It was on to Kyoto. One of the features there was a forest (yes, a forest) where, legend has it, a shogun built a new shrine, and neighboring shoguns sent gifts to honor him and his shrine.

Other shoguns sent statues, jewels, and urns, which were the usual gifts. A young shogun sent ten thousand sapling trees, which his servants planted around the shrine. Today there is a forest in this area of Japan.

One point to remember is that gifts may be short term, so think about legacy giving. I try to practice this. It was a significant learning experience for me so early in life. Travel can be life affirming.

We left Japan for Taiwan, which is a tiny island country in the Pacific. Remember the history: In 1945, following the end of World War II, the nationalist government of the Republic of China, led by the Kuomintang, took control of Taiwan. In 1949, after losing control of mainland China in the Chinese Civil War, the government withdrew to Taiwan. That is the Taiwan we visited and know today.

It was bad, but I was not clear on this history when I traveled there. I trusted my travel agent and the travel company when I planned this trip. It was a good lesson for me: I needed to do my own research when I plan to travel.

Obviously, we were safe, but it is *not* a good idea to be this surprised when you visit a country. All our luggage was scrutinized at a high level, which was decades prior to our current travel security. We could not take certain reading materials into the country.

I had to purchase a lovely ring to secure my memory of this visit and to promote relaxation!

Next, it was on to Hong Kong, one of my favorite places to visit, ever. I have visited there six times. Hong Kong is an island with the city of Kowloon adjunct to the mainland. During this 1975 trip, it still belonged to the British. The people used British money because they were citizens of Britain.

Before I went, I heard about Americans going there to have clothes (very nice clothes) tailored. This was true! It was a real shopping mecca. We enjoyed a dinner cruise and tours of historic and religious sites.

We were on our way to the most different place to visit thus far: Bangkok, Thailand. This was (and is, as I have visited several additional times) among the most beautiful places in the world.

It was so different from the ornamentation and structures I had seen. I loved it! I felt safe, and the Thai people were very friendly. They also have great and unique shopping opportunities.

The people were (and are) lovely, caring, and communicative about their country. It may be shocking to you, but it is known for its tropical beaches, opulent royal palaces, ancient ruins, and ornate temples, displaying figures of Buddha.

Bangkok, the capital, has canal-side communities and the iconic temples of Wat Arun and Wat Pho and the Emerald Buddha Temple.

We flew home from Bangkok exhausted but changed forever. We had been overzealous in planning this time, and sometimes it nearly did us in!, But neither of us will ever forget this early travel experience.

Spain, Portugal, and Morocco—Wynon Mayes, Hale County Extension agent, found and chose this trip because we could attend the World Expo in Seville, Spain. The theme for the Expo was "The Age of Discovery." My interest in travel was revving up, so I planned to go with her. It was basically a bus trip. We landed in Madrid and traveled to Milan (hottest place I had visited at the time of this trip). Milan was the first city I visited where there were metal window covers for privacy and protection from the heat. I really thought that they added to the heat. At the time, I pronounced this the hottest place on earth, but I would revise this after traveling to many more locations.

We crossed the Mediterranean Sea in a large ferry with many trucks, buses, and cars that were *all* on board with us. I had never done this before, but we left the bus in the bowels of the ferry and found window seats in the observation/dining area. I found it enjoyable. We had a view of the African coast. It was going to be my first time on the African continent, and I was hoping for this to be exotic travel. There was even a bit of shopping on the ferry, so it had everything!

Morocco was an entirely new place. There were sights like I had never seen before. We went to Fez, Marrakesh, and Casablanca. This was as foreign as a moonscape to me. I could not believe it. As was our usual procedure, we threw our luggage into our hotel room and tried to head out into the town. The doorman told us that women could *not* travel alone or leave the hotel. There are no words to describe how we felt. We could not take it in, and we had no plan. We sat in the lobby and wrote postcards.

We had some cultural fun with a stage show that evening in Morocco. I could not believe that I was sitting quietly at a dining table with a snake charmer charming a *giant* snake on the stage. I had spent my entire life avoiding or killing snakes, and here I was having dinner and being entertained by them! I kept hoping that this was some sort of mechanical fake snake! This, of course, was wishful thinking.

This was also our first experience with aggressive local citizens trying to sell their wares. They would follow us on motor scooters from stop to stop. Of course, in later travel, we viewed this frequently.

We did not plan it this way (or we did not know to plan it

this way), but we traveled back across the Mediterranean Sea to Portugal, and this was great. Portugal was beautiful, and we loved it. It was cooler and very scenic. This is one of only three countries that I returned to in future travel.

There was joy in all of this early travel, but it helped to set my preferences for future excursions. I loved these trips, and as you will read, I have combined events with travel many other times.

More about Wynon Mayes, Who Challenged Me to Travel

I have traveled a great amount during my life, and this travel has produced many stories to share. Sometimes learning about the view of America while visiting another country gives us a great perspective.

It has been a blessing to meet and visit with people from 110 countries. Generally, people are excited to visit with people from the United States, and it is great fun to meet them and learn about their country and their lives. It has nearly always been true that our media give us a certain view of others—and, our media may give the rest of the world a certain view of us. I count it as a great travel benefit to really learn about them and their families.

In the 1980s, everyone we encountered in Germany wanted to know "who shot J. R." This was the first time I realized the global impact of our media.

In 2019, our most ask questions, when others learned we were from the United States of America, related to gun control.

I find listening more powerful and telling.

And Then, There Was Wynon—Wynon went to work for the Texas Extension Service at the same time I did, and we traveled from western Texas to College Station for new employee training. Before I met her, people told me that she was "a card." I did not know what that meant, but I do now. She was the Eveready bunny. When we arrived in a country, she would make us throw our belongings into the room, cabin, etc. and get out into the country, street, or camp to explore. We had to explore immediately. "Time is a-wasting!" to quote Wynon.

Our first trip was a class project at Texas Tech University, for which we traveled to Europe. I even had to enroll in college and do a class paper to travel with Wynon, but "no" was not an answer. I learned her fast pace of travel and how to shop—jewelry stores, markets, vendors, etc. If the merchandise was purchase worthy, we were there.

Know that this was the time of travel when luggage was not limited, and there were *no* extra charges for luggage. Wynon had six grandchildren, and she loved thinking about them and shopping for them when we traveled. She also found great joy in shopping for her "once-in-a-lifetime special finds!"

Australia and New Zealand—Our second trip was the trip of a lifetime (or so we thought) to Australia and New Zealand. We traveled with my sister, Annette; Elinor Harvey; and a co-educator from Idaho. We were to meet in Los Angeles. Annette, Wynon, and I started from Lubbock, Texas. Elinor started from Houston, Texas, and, of course, our other friend started from Idaho.

Our first flight was Lubbock to Dallas. Then Dallas to Los Angeles, where we were to meet the others. Near the New Mexico state line, we had an engine blowout and had to make an emergency landing in Albuquerque, New Mexico. Wynon and I planned to get a flight out of New Mexico. And Annette cried.

Wynon, who was on the aisle, positioned herself to exit the plane as soon as the door opened. I told her to not stop for anyone until she got us booked on another flight. I put all my money in my bra and got organized to follow Wynon. Annette cried. I told her to get her things together to get off the plane.

We were warned about the landing, and it was rough. As we landed, we went into a skid, but we were able to stop safely, and the good news was that Albuquerque had a very long runway. As predicted, Wynon got off the plane and got us booked on another flight. I calmed Annette down, but we had no cell phones back then to let our other passengers in Los Angeles know our plight.

Everything worked, and they held the LA to Brisbane flight for us—and all my money was still in my bra!

First Trip to Russia—In 1997, I went on my first trip to Russia. It was a wonderful, informative, and educational trip. For my entire life, Russia had been the enemy of the United States. It was unbelievable to be walking freely around Red Square. It was a great blessing to meet Russian citizens.

I made it a goal (which I hope I accomplished) to represent the United States well, no matter where I have traveled. As with Russia, I went prepared to learn about the citizens of this country. Landing in Moscow was a stark event. Paperwork for visas, etc. was troubling and not well organized. I really was surprised that we got in and out. I had thoughts of being held in a country that considered the US its enemy,

We saw Red Square and walked by the door to Russian president Putin's office! He was president then and now.

The trip included a river cruise up the Volga River, and we

lived on the boat in Moscow for five days. This was my first river cruise, and I was not prepared for the boats parking side by side. You might have to walk through four or five boats to get to the dock.

Once we left Moscow and were traveling up the Volga to St. Petersburg, it was very beautiful. The boat docked in small rural communities, and the locals would bring out card tables to sell their crafts. Meeting the citizens and having informal exchanges with them along the river was a highlight.

An unexpected event occurred. We traveled to Russia in early May on the first cruise of the season, and the Volga River froze over when we were half a day from St. Petersburg. Our boat was frozen in the river. We were trapped in Russia, which should have been a worry but was more of an adventure. An ice cutter was sent to rescue us. The ice cutter carved a path for our river cruiser to navigate close to it, and we made the trip into St. Petersburg,

An extra benefit of this trip was meeting a frequent traveler and the first person I ever met who knew about the Century Travel Club, of which I have been a member for seven years. The Century Travel Club allows membership when an individual has traveled to eighty countries, but many members that I have met at meetings have traveled to more than three hundred countries!

Wynon Mayes, who got me to go on this trip, was my traveling mentor. She was fearless and challenged me to go to new places. Her approach was to throw the luggage on the bed and get out to see the new place we were visiting. We both loved shopping at local grocery stores. There you could learn many things about local citizens and their families.

We had a running gag. She was *very* sensitive about her age. She truly believed that if people knew her age, they would discriminate against her. Many times I kept her age a secret when we were traveling. Once, she rented a Chinese bridal sedan chair have four Chinese men carry me around the town square. I refused and told her that if she made me, I would write an article about our trip for the *Amarillo Globe News* (her local newspaper) and reveal her age. Needless to say, she rode in the wedding lair herself!

Her rule of seeing everything was one I learned to practice. In New Zealand, we were the only ones in our group to ride the Shotover jet, a speedboat on a local river that was only inches deep! I gripped the boat so tightly that I broke off my fingernail tips! Since that was 1987 and I am writing this now, we lived through that adventure.

Olympics in Atlanta 1996—Wynon and I began planning for the journey eighteen months before the trip. The only way to secure tickets (for civilians) was to go to the Lowe's Home Improvement store (an Olympic sponsor) and pick up a form to order tickets. We could only buy tickets using a Visa credit card (another Olympic sponsor), and neither of us had that card.

The challenges were (1) to find a friend or coworker with a Visa card; (2) ask them about their credit limit on the card; (3) ask them if they had enough credit space on their card, which meant we had to reveal the cost of the tickets (many family members and friends thought that we were crazy with our extravagant travel hobby anyway!); and (4) borrow the card.

We accomplished this with Wynon's coworker! The order was in, and the waiting had begun.

We ordered tickets for the opening ceremony and one sporting event each day—women's basketball, men's baseball, fencing (which we knew very little about), and Greco-Roman wrestling (which we knew nothing about).

For lodging, Wynon had found an ad in her Rotarian magazine (reading while she was sitting on the toilet), and a great family from the Atlanta area hosted us in their home.

We were ready, and the tickets arrived! We were going to achieve another one of our lifelong goals. Wynon instilled in me the "lifelong goal" approach, which I carry forth today.

Of course, another challenge was finding tickets to fly into Atlanta by the time the Olympic tickets arrived. Not to be deterred, we flew into Birmingham, Alabama, and rented a car. Off we went.

The host couple from the Rotary was so wonderful. They drove us to the MARTA (rapid rail system), and we headed to downtown Atlanta. Walking the streets, we found a crowd (dumb luck) that was waiting for the Olympic torch to be carried by a series of former US Olympians. In a few minutes, Bruce Jenner ran right by us carrying the torch. Sometimes you just have to count on luck because you cannot plan all of this.

The opening assembly was the first event we attended, and it was a challenge because of the heat that day! We waited for some hours under the stands in our assigned sitting area for the sun to set. We had the cheap seats where we faced the afternoon sun.

A welcome backpack awaited us at our seats. I still have these souvenirs today. Just writing this account brings the memories directly back to me: the heat ... the crowd noise ... and the athletes from all the countries of the world entering the stadium.

We were so hungry that I finally had to go for concession-stand food. I waited in line for food as the athletes entered from all the countries, Botswana to Zaire (which I have just recently visited).

But I made it back to our seats before the American team entered. The US team entered last as the host.

Seeing the torch entering the stadium and Muhammad Ali lighting the Olympic flame is still ingrained in my memory.

Alaska—Wynon booked us on my very first combo cruise-and-land tour to Alaska. We were way ahead of our time as there are now millions of cruises to Alaska.

We met the group in Seattle for orientation and a tour of the city. Seattle is still one of the great cities in America, and I loved my first visit there. On to the cruise ship, which was just a boat compared to today's vessels, but we loved it anyway! The scenery was beautiful, majestic, and breathtaking.

For a shore excursion, we took an eight-passenger airplane—really a biplane that took off and landed on the water right there in the Juneau harbor. If you have not done this, know that the water comes over the plane when you take off!

Remarkable views of the Juneau harbor and city abounded. The flight over the mountain and the glacier was like nothing I had ever seen! More miraculous was landing the plane on a glacier lake near a mountain cabin. But we made it! The family whose cabin we were visiting prepared dinner. Of course, we saw dogsled races and great fishing. But all during this time, I had to think and pray about the flight back to Juneau—taking off in the lake.

The time arrived for our return flight. Prayers were answered, and we landed safely in Juneau! Upon exiting the plane, I told Wynon that we had to find a church immediately because "I have to make a sizable donation!" And, I meant it!

After a seven-day cruise, we joined a shore excursion that went up the river to Fairbanks. We took the train to a lodge at the base of Mount McKinley, which we saw while approaching on the train, but the next day on our tour, the fog completely covered McKinley.

An additional adventure was riding in a river raft in Denali National Park. There was more bailing water than rafting!

The last day of the trip was spent in Anchorage, Alaska, at a wonderful hotel. My suggestion for all of you is to "rough it" during travel if you must, but on the last night, stay in a great hotel to recuperate and celebrate what a great trip you have experienced.

While enjoying our hotel, Wynon was preparing for our return to Texas when she admitted she was so tired. She begged to use my new wrinkle cream for her face. I told her, "Wynon, I am not prepared. You will need industrial-strength wrinkle cream!"

In this book, you will find other stories of traveling with Wynon, and different locations are featured.

I quote her many times, even today. "I have made a mistake and worn my stand-up dress with my sit-down shoes!"

Bless her! I know that she is saving a place for many of us in heaven!

1988 Trip to China with Dad's 58th Army Air Corps Group

Traveling with Retired Army Air Corps Members—After my first trip to the Orient, I shared this trip with Dad with fondness because I learned that I got the travel bug from him. The stories around the family were how stressful World War II had been, and as with many American families, the men returned home and did not talk about it. This was Dad's story about the revisit.

In the early 1980s, the 444th Bomb Group planned a reunion, and Dad's B-21 group was hoping for an individual gathering, as well. I was shocked when Mom and Dad called to tell me of the plan. Later, I learned to be so proud. This was a real turning point for Dad and his ability to talk about his World War II experiences.

Mom and Dad attended several reunions and came back with this story about a group trip to China. I, of course, jumped at the chance to go with him and told Dad that I would go with him. Mom was not interested or maybe not able.

This was organized by Dad's commander and was excellent. There was a national reunion in Los Angeles that Mom and Dad attended. At the conclusion, I joined him for the group trip to China. There were fifty-six of us, and besides the trip, it was great to meet some of those who had been in the Pacific theater with Dad.

Dad was a side gunner on an airplane, which meant that he manned a gun turret from a bubble that extended out of the side of the fighter plane. From that gun, he fired at Japanese fighter planes that were attacking American planes or ships sailing in the Pacific Ocean. Having seen the fighter planes, I cannot imagine that any of them came home. What warriors!

They traveled with the B-29s to provide air cover. It was so amazing to meet other soldiers in his unit and hear their stories. Dad seemed so relaxed around them. He was a person who did not draw attention to himself, so it was a blessing to hear stories from other soldiers.

China Air—We met in Los Angeles to gather and have orientation for the trip. The next day, we boarded a plane to Hong Kong, which would be my second trip to that location. Our destination the following day would be Beijing. There was no Jetway. All movement from the ground to the plane and back to the ground was via the stairs. We had fallen back in time.

Our seats were at the back of the plane, so it was interesting to look over the travelers and see where the American or European travelers were seated. There was a dramatic variance in hair color between our group and the Asian travelers. Later, I learned from the tour guide that they all dye their hair!

Airplane service was simple and not what we were accustomed to even thirty years ago. As I have traveled recently from the United States to Europe and Africa, we may be returning to this type of service. We had boiled eggs and juice boxes but were glad to have them. We had pre-information, so we carried many nutrition bars as supplements.

Hotel in the Country—Our hotel was "in the country," which was ten to twelve miles from Beijing. Breakfast was an attempt at American food with fried eggs and toast. We had to wrap our eggs in the paper napkin to remove the grease so the eggs were edible. Before the trip, all the information encouraged us to take plasticware, so we had plastic "silverware" for sanitation. We were told that the chopsticks would likely be reused. But we survived, and I embarrassed Dad by taking the plasticware to him at his table. After all, he and these men survived horrible things, and I was worried about the chopstick sanitation. As I write this, it does seem ridiculous!

Restrooms—Daily restroom usage was a challenge for me. They were not yet ready for tourists, and there were *no* Western toilets. They were all ground level, and many were just holes in the ground. I mainly did without liquids and waited to go the restroom back at our hotel. I have visited China twice since this trip, and it is modern and a wonderful place to see. Do not be deterred by my stories.

The second greatest advantage to this trip was timing. We arrived there before the great influx of world travelers. I feel like this first trip (I have been back twice) was very revealing, and I am very pleased with the timing of this journey.

The Great Wall—They call it one of the Seven Wonders of the World for a reason. It is. You can see it for miles as you approach (and the astronauts reported that they could see it from the moon).

We walked a mile or two on the wall. I was prepared for the unevenness, but I was not prepared for the height of the steps. It is the truth that I have relatively short legs, but some of these steps were impossible! Watching Dad enjoy it was a blessing.

I saved a bit of time for shopping, which was simple, but it was wonderful to see the local citizens' handiwork. I treasure these remembrances.

Tiananmen Square—We saw Tiananmen Square and Mao's Burial Tomb. I found it quite touching to walk freely around the square of the largest Communist country in the world. I had completely different feelings when, less than one year later, I watched on television the uprising that occurred there. The Chinese tank was about to roll over the young man right where I had stood months before.

Hong Kong—We left China and spent a night in Hong Kong before going home. To surprise Dad, I ordered hamburgers from hotel room service. When the hamburgers arrived, I had rarely seen Dad so happy! I can still smell those wonderful hamburgers! He was childlike. For seven days we had had enough Chinese food for a lifetime, and even as I write this, I believe that I can still smell our great hamburgers! Visiting other countries reminds us of memories of home that are priceless.

There was additional opportunity for shopping in Hong Kong on the way home. I discovered Diane Fries dresses, which were in my wardrobe for several years. I hid the price tags from Dad, so he would not be shocked by the cost. I found these professional and ready-to-travel dresses a great resource for my specialist and state leader positions at home. They were "warrior" dresses. Dad was a trooper as I tried on dress after dress and dragged him all over the shopping malls of Hong Kong looking for dresses and jewelry.

Thank you, Dad, for your service and the opportunity to enjoy this time with you.

Traveling and Cruising the World

Early Family Travel—The earliest family photos I have were taken with Dad's new camera when we were in Colorado. Dad is driving, Mom is in the front seat, and I am leaning over the seat watching as Dad drives up Pikes Peak.

We also took a family trip to San Antonio in the late sixties and visited HemisFair '68 World's Fair. We stayed in a motel, where each room had a drive-in garage attached to it. Three of us (excluding Mom) went up the Hemisphere Needle. The best part was family time together in a new environment.

With work and Dad becoming part owner in the electric shop, our family travel was limited. We only took short weekend trips and trips to family reunions and to visit relatives.

I Love Cruising the World—I discovered cruising forty years ago and love it. The ship moves, and you and all your belongings go along with it. I experienced many land trips before my first cruise, but now I am a cruise believer. It is quite relaxing because you are not continually packing and repacking.

I know that many reading this chapter will think that this is a bad idea, but I am on the "cruise team"! I have cruised more than forty times, both ocean cruises and river cruises. Both are great and easy.

Alaska—My first cruise was to Alaska in 1985. One feature that I used for this first cruise was a land tour option. Alaska is a beautiful state and offers many sights.

When I cruise, I love getting the luggage in the cabin. I even love the language of cruising and, of course, not having to pack and repack. This is just one of the best attractions.

See Alaska if you have not. I give more detail about this trip in another chapter.

Great Waves—The waves came over the twelfth deck! Yes, during a cruise around Cape Horn (the southern tip of South America), the waves came that high. I never felt like we were in danger, but waves landing on our balcony is not what you generally expect.

Circling the Globe—I was able to join a cruise trip that went around the world, or circumnavigated the globe. We flew to the west and joined the ship in Thailand. Then we cruised to Malaysia, Singapore, India, Oman, and Dubai. We flew home from Dubai.

This cruise was on the Cunard Queen Victoria, which is an ocean liner and not really a cruise ship. The difference is based on the shape of the ship and how far the ship sits in the water. The other Cunard ships (Queen Mary and Queen Elizabeth) are also ocean liners.

Another big difference in this cruise ship group is that it still has a two-class system for ranking passengers, which have to do with types of dining and other amenities. There is also early seating and late seating, while most other lines have open seating.

They are beautiful ships. I feel very classy when I cruise this line. It is great to talk to many longtime cruisers on these liners.

Quarantined on the Island Princess—We were on my second passage cruise through the Panama Canal, and I came down with one of my respiratory infections. The ship's doctor thought I might be contagious, so I was quarantined to my cabin.

The cabin was nice, and I was safe, but the funniest thing was that the ship's chef decided that because of my respiratory infection my diet could only include chicken soup and Jell-O. I survived, but the extra "care" was unnecessary.

Cruising with Former Coworkers—I finally convinced former coworkers, who are current friends, to travel with us. All four of them had worked with Elinor and me. Elinor was their coworker in Seminole, Texas. I had worked with all of them in Extension District 2. And Kyle, Ed, and I had worked together in extension administration in College Station.

Teresa Smith and I had worked together in Extension District 2 and in College Station. Elaine Smith and I had not worked together, but we both were in social groups doing community projects.

Anyway, they had requested that I take them with me on a cruise. I called this "cruise orientation," and we loved it. We have also done this with other friends. Probably, the cruise ship should let me travel for free for bringing these new customers!

We took a cruise out of Galveston to Mexico. The main tour was of the historic Chichen Itza Pyramid. This is the largest pyramid in our half of the world, and it had been on my list to

tour, which added an achievable goal to the trip. I love to simul-
taneously achieve multiple goals!

At breakfast, I had taken some bread rolls in my bag before
leaving the ship. I planned for these rolls to be lunch, since my
general rule is to not eat in Mexico.

As Mexican security approached us when we entered the
country, I was singled out by a drug-sniffing dog that jumped
on me and put his head in my tote bag. The drug dog was after
my bread!

The authorities detained me to search everything. Eventually
I was allowed to enter the country (without my bread). It was bad
that this happened, but it was especially bad that it was in front
of my longtime friends because everyone was going to know this
story at home.

Cruising Around Cape Good Hope —One of my favorite trips
was sailing around Cape Horn at the bottom of South America.
I had previously traveled to North Cape, which is the top of the
European continent and since then I have traveled to Cape of
Good Hope, South Africa, so I have been to three of the main
points on the globe.

On this trip, there was also a great amount of turbulence as
we were rounding Cape Horn. Wynon Mayes and I managed to
hold on to walls, rails, doors, etc. to maintain being upright, but
other passengers had broken bones!

Meeting Citizens of the World—It is impossible for me to tell you
what meeting citizens in their native land has meant to me. They
(still) love to talk to people from the United States. As our US
media sends communications to the rest of the world, they see

many of us and our events every day. It is great to talk to them directly.

As a US citizen who loves to travel the world, I try to be prepared to give the best answer I know. This dialogue gives me an opportunity to ask about their schools, the population of their town, what do they do for fun, what they do for a career, what they know about us, or if they have visited the United States.

I carry business cards to give to new people I meet so maybe we can exchange Christmas cards or notes. It is not completely accurate to say that "they are just like us," but the way they love their country and the way they love their families is universal.

I had many conversations with people from other countries who quizzed me about America. The questions depended on the decade and what was in the news from America: "Do you know who shot J. R.?" "Do you know President Trump?" "How much does an iPhone cost in America?" "Are you related to the Kardashians?"

Travel as a Benefit—As you can easily tell, I love travel, and I find in exhilarating and fulfilling. I have met wonderful people. For instance, on the Cunard I met one of the people you hear about who lives on a cruise ship. Her theory is that it is about the same cost as living in an assisted living facility, and she is well cared for on the ship. But she also is seeing the world. I love her theory and may practice it soon.

Travel over these decades has changed. More places are accessible to American travelers. More travel providers are available, offering you opportunities. More ships, airplanes, boats, helicopters, rafts, and other forms of transportation are available. And there are more organizations to help you find "like" individuals with whom to travel.

I find planning for travel thrilling, and the travel is also. I don't try to discourage people from traveling so it will be less crowded for me because I can find other ways to enjoy it.

Here's to great traveling!

Elvis

—The King of Rock and Roll and His Scarves

Elvis was coming to Lubbock, Texas, for a concert. My high school friend Shirley Poston, was a bigger Elvis fan than I was and wanted us to get tickets.

Shirley and I had gone to Borden High School together from 1963 to 1968. She lived in Gail, Texas, where Bordon School was located. I lived thirty miles south in Luther.

Now, we found ourselves in Lubbock, Texas, where we both worked.

The tickets went on sale on a Sunday morning at Lubbock Coliseum on the Texas Tech campus. I got in the line pretty early and was able to secure two tickets. It was festival seating, so we would have to get in line early on the day of the concert. The date was May 31, 1976, and the show began at 8:30 p.m.

The municipal coliseum was on the northwest side of the Texas Tech campus. Lines were long, but I waited. Success!

Three weeks later, off to the concert we went. We arrived early and got seats that were even with the stage on the right side, next to the piano.

As people did during this time, we dressed up for the concert. It was organized so entry to the venue was pretty quick. The coliseum seated about 7,600 people.

The final show setup, which we watched after we were seated, involved a "scarf wrangler" who tied a knot in each scarf and carefully placed them in a line on the top of the piano. Scarves were of all colors.

The show began, and it was a Las Vegas type show with the Imperials, a female singer, a male singer, and a comedian before Elvis took the stage.

Finally, Elvis appeared and began to perform (with the Imperials singing backup). Every minute or so, the scarf wrangler would put a scarf around Elvis's neck. He would wipe his brow and fling the scarf into the audience.

Suddenly, a miracle happened! Elvis flung a scarf in our direction, and Shirley grabbed one end of it. Unfortunately, the woman in front of Shirley grabbed the other end. A full-fledged tug of war began. Each of them hung on tight and pulled back and forth. This went on for a minute when, suddenly, the woman in the row in front of Shirley turned in her chair and began to bite Shirley's knee. Neither of them would let go.

A man, who was three seats to Shirley's left, stood up, took out his pocketknife, and split the scarf between their hands. Each of them fell back into their seats. And the show went on!

When she returned home, Shirley trimmed the ragged edge of her scarf and hemmed it so she could wear it. She gave me the ragged ½-inch-wide edge, which I have to this day.

Sixty Years of Being Starstruck

After A Hard Day's Night—As was well documented in an earlier chapter, I have loved being starstruck. This hobby has given me many interesting experiences and stories as detailed in this book.

My mother, who wanted to do fun things with the girls—such as seeing *A Hard Day's Night*—was on our team to go to concerts and other events. She would only buy two tickets and usually wait in the car. And she was all about writing us "medical excuses" to get us out of school. I feel that the statute of limitations has expired since this was the 1960s.

The first of these events was a concert with Paul Revere and the Raiders in Odessa, Texas. It must have been festival seating because we had front-row seats. This was great fun, and they put on an energetic show. Mother went to the box office to check on us, and the officials told her to "go on in." Suddenly, she appeared next to us.

We had a great trip home. Mother let us sleep, so we would be better prepared for school the next day.

The next year, we bought tickets to see Herman's Hermits and the Animals, who were appearing together in Lubbock. This was a bigger concert venue, but we had pretty good seats. Of course, right after the half-time intermission, mother appeared! She said she was "checking on her girls."

As of this writing, I have seen more than one hundred musical entertainers, including Garth Brooks, Reba McEntire, Mac Davis, the Oak Ridge Boys, MC Hammer (which was the first time I used a cell phone, borrowing one from the person next to me to report to Annette), Sonny and Cher, John Denver, Bon Jovi, Michael Bolton, Barry Manilow, Liberace, Dolly Parton, Donny and Marie and the Osmond Brothers, Glenn Campbell, Elton John, Paul McCartney, Tony Bennett, Lady Gaga, Elvis (as detailed in the previous chapter), LaDonna Gatlin Johnson, Willie Nelson, Lee Greenwood, Neil Diamond, and the list goes on.

Paul McCartney—I have seen Paul McCartney in concert nine times – Dallas (twice), Los Angeles (twice), Houston (twice), St. Louis, Kansas City, and Las Cruces.

The most effort that friend Colleen Chadwick and I made was for the Los Angeles concert. We were so naive and planned to meet Paul by carrying a large floral arrangement with some Buddy Holly souvenirs from Lubbock included in the bouquet. It was large, but we convinced Southwest Airlines to hand-carry the bouquet into the luggage compartment of the airplane. Happily and optimistically, we headed to Los Angeles.

It was Thanksgiving weekend. We arrived and picked up our rental car, which we needed to haul our *large* bouquet. We drove to the Staples Center and attempted to deliver our bouquet. Now, think back to the 1980s, when there was less security than we have now. The delivery was successful, meaning we left it at the Staples Center.

The concert was wonderful, and we were over the moon.

As we relived it and celebrated in our Motel 6-type lodging, we discussed seeing the concert the next night.

We were great planners, and we already had tickets to see the Christmas pageant at the Crystal Cathedral. We went to the hotel lobby and got a newspaper to look at the ads for tickets to the McCartney concert the next night. There were many ads, so we began to call—on the hotel pay phone.

We planned to meet a gentleman at a 7-Eleven convenience store and exchange money for tickets. Now, this was long ago before ATMs and the vast use of credit cards. My sister Annette wired us the money to the Western Union office, where we collected it. We were on our way to secure the tickets. One of us watched (in case one of us needed to go for help), and one of us met the stranger at the convenience store to secure the tickets. He was a nice man, and all turned out well.

The stage was set for us to go the second night concert. It was delightful, and we still thought it was worth it. Great effort was rewarded. We felt guilty about having Crystal Cathedral Christmas Pageant tickets and not using them, so we called the venue to tell them we would not be using our tickets. We did not want our money back.

107.1 Fever (Beginning of Smile More, Pray More)

The morning of July 1, 2007 began not like any other morning in my life because I was unconscious! The location was a San Antonio tourist hotel near the airport. How long I was unconscious or what I did while I was unconscious is unknown.

The hospital record reports that I arrived at the hospital *naked* with a temperature of 107.1 degrees. Probably, I should have put the fever before the naked part, but both were so shocking.

The days prior to that morning had me in San Antonio, Texas, which is about three hours from my home. Texas AgriLife Extension, my employer, was hosting a national conference for youth development specialists at a luxury hotel.

It was a great conference, and our team was very pleased. I was on a real high as I packed my things to move across San Antonio to a hotel near the airport for a Texas conference for youth whose families were serving in the military.

On Friday night, I did not feel great. I threw up, which was very unlike me. I called Annette in Dallas and told her my situation and that I was going to try to sleep it off. Early the next morning, I would be traveling to Big Spring to visit Mother.

I slept it off nearly into heaven! Annette, who was my backup, called me at 7:00 a.m. to make sure I was up and on my way to West Texas. I could hear the cell phone ringing, but my hand could not grip the phone. The phone fell to the floor. I don't remember, but phone records show that Annette tried to reach me more than twenty times. I had fallen onto the floor unconscious.

She understood that I was in crisis and began the struggle to save my life from two hundred miles away. She called the hotel many, many times. They dismissed her as a Saturday night prank, trying to disturb a honeymoon couple, etc. They would not do a health check for me in my room. She called both my work and personal cell phones, as well as my hotel room phone.

She knew that I had a close friend in San Antonio, who was retired and not involved with the conferences. She did not have her number. She worked that angle, trying to contact her, while still trying to get help from the hotel.

Thanks to her persistence, Annette called a friend in Oklahoma to get the phone number of the San Antonio friend and informed her that I (and she) needed her help. The friend headed to the hotel upon getting the call.

Annette also kept calling the hotel, and at 8:30 a.m., the day manager came on duty. He sensed her great concern and sent someone to my room. They could not get me to respond but knew that I was deadbolted (interesting choice of words) in the room. He called 911.

When the paramedics broke into my room, I was *naked* and lying on the floor. I was unconscious but have fragmented memories of tall, tall people calling to me in my room.

My friend Iris arrived about the same time and followed the ambulance to the hospital.

My next memory was of being awakened, packed in ice with at least four big fans blowing on me. My first communication was to beg for a blanket! There were a series of questions that the doctor fired at me. "What is your name?" "What is your address?" "What is your phone number?" I could remember some parts of each answer. He mercifully let me go back to sleep.

This process occurred several times throughout the day and into the evening. I continued to beg for blankets, which is part of the comedy, since I am generally hot natured and would find it great to be cooled off.

Eight or so hours into coming back to life, I was unpacked from the ice and taken to an intensive care area where I slept for several hours. I woke up suddenly, remembering my plight, and jumped out of the bed to sit in a chair and take it all in.

God sent an angel to my hospital room in the form of a roommate. Each time I raced by her bed (pushing my IV pole in front of me) to meet with the social worker, this blessed eighty-three-year-old woman would say to me, "Smile more. pray more!"

I continued to quietly review all that I could remember. I could not stop taking in the fact that I was alive and seemed well. I was still on an IV. A nurse and a social worker checked on me. I was able to retrieve my phones and talked to Annette, Mother, and my friends often.

Communicating with my office, we developed a plan for me to be "rescued" and returned to College Station. I befriended a great nurse, who ordered portable IVs to take with me for follow-up treatment. She trained me on their use and supported clearing me to be dismissed. Hallelujah! Praise the Lord.

My car was brought to the hospital from the hotel. Jeff Howard, a 4-H staff member, arrived from College Station, and I was dismissed. We traveled well, and I enjoyed my new life (I think of it as that to this day). Home health care professionals and my local team of doctors (including a doctor of infectious disease) kept a constant watch of my recovery.

No underestimate of the medical support that I reviewed in San Antonio can be concluded. But, this was an answer to others praying for me—and a miracle!

My local doctor of infectious disease developed a theory about how I contracted diphtheria, which is virtually eradicated from the United States. An employee of the hotel, who was likely an undocumented worker, brought the disease across the Mexico-US border. He or she was working (for example) in the laundry room, and the germs were on his hands and folded into the warm towels from the dryer. The folded towel was an incubator for the diphtheria germs.

The deadly towels were waiting for me in my luxury hotel room when I dried my face.

This event caused me to be even more goal oriented since I was given additional time for my life, and wasting any of the time given back to me was not an option!

Going Headfirst in Reno and Lake Tahoe

As many of my other stories begin, I was traveling to ... the Reno/Lake Tahoe area to present a speech to the International 4-H Travel Group. I am easily recruited to do these types of presentations if it meets two criteria: supports the 4-H program and involves travel for me

I had previously traveled through this area and always wanted to return—bucket list item!

It was a wonderful conference and great for my 4-H spirit as I visited with youth and adults involved with 4-H from all over the United States and many other places in the world.

On Thursday morning, after my presentation was complete, I had time off for touring. The conference was in Reno, so I took the beautiful drive from there to Lake Tahoe, celebrating the grandeur of our country all the way. It was a sunny day, and the temperature was delightfully cool and pleasant.

I parked the rental car in the small lot at an overlook, where both Emerald Bay and Lake Tahoe could be viewed. The view was worth the drive. I enjoyed this sight and took many pictures.

I had locked my purse in the car and went out with only my keys and the camera.

I continued to take in all the beautiful sights as I began to return to the car. This lack of focusing and my "lookie-lookie" behavior caused my life to be changed forever.

As I walked down the stairs from the overlook (and right by the stairs was a lovely ramp), I lost my footing, fell all the way down the stairs, and landed on my head. When I began to raise myself up to get off the ground, I saw blood dripping from my forehead!

By this time, several other tourists had raced to my rescue and were helping me. They said, "We are calling an ambulance!" I said, "No! No! Just get me to my car. I will be fine!"

Another tourist had brought a roll of paper towels from her car, and I was holding the entire roll to my head. It was becoming saturated with blood very quickly. While I was having these thoughts, I could hear the siren! I asked the people gathered, "You called an ambulance?" They said yes.

I was mad, of course, since I like to be independent and help myself. Thank goodness, however, that these people sent from God ignored me!

As I was put into the ambulance, the rescuers/bystanders said they would follow the ambulance and bring my car to the hospital. There were many blessed ones, who never met me before or after.

The ambulance ride to the nearby small town of Barton was not very long, and the Barton Emergency Room medical professionals started working on me immediately. A few moments behind were the Good Samaritans who brought my car keys to me and let me know where my car was parked. More blessings! All these helpers and I never lost consciousness.

After a brain scan, the doctor said, "It is serious. You have a brain bleed." He said they could *not* fix it, and they were transferring me to Reno via a medevac helicopter. I thought, *God's lifesaving plan for me has a lot of moving parts and blessed people!*

I hope that you do not know this, but those helicopters are *very* small, and they push you on your stretcher into the helicopter through the tail. This seemed funny at the time, but now (as I write this) maybe it is a sign of a new birth—the smallness and leaving many things behind (car, dignity, etc.).

Over the very high mountain, we went to Reno. As with the Barton Hospital, I was treated immediately. The neurologist explained that they would treat this with blood-clotting medicine and observe me. When the bleeding stopped, I could be dismissed. He also answered my main concern: "There is no brain damage that can be seen." I need to have that made into a poster to carry around and show current doubters.

What he said was correct, and I was ready to be dismissed the next morning. I had called my friends and coworkers at the conference to alert them of my situation. And they were coming to rescue me when I was dismissed.

Now, remember that my rental car could not ride in the helicopter, so it was still parked at Barton.

And, I forgot to mention that they had cut off the garments I was wearing on the top half of my body. They insisted that nothing could be pulled over the top of my head. An outstanding and creative nurse, with a container of safety pins, helped me fashion a "privacy blouse" so I would not need to leave the hospital in a lovely hospital gown.

The escape from the blessed lifesaving place began: Reno to Barton to Walgreens for pain meds and antibiotics and back to the Reno resort hotel.

It was quite a shock to see myself in the hotel suite mirror! I took a cell phone photo, which many friends said I should destroy. I looked like Herman Munster. But I wanted a record for my second or next life.

Cusco, Peru, Plane Crash

To say that I love to travel would be an underestimation of my life plan. My travel to 110 countries (at this writing) has provided me with many adventures. This is an understatement!

For ten-plus years, I had planned this trip to Peru. I was on a Princess cruise ship and reserved a shore excursion for an overnight trip to Machu Picchu. I have taken several of these extended shore excursions off Princess cruise ships. This was high on my travel bucket list.

And it turned out to be more of an adventure than I had planned!

There were two hundred of us on the excursion to see the ancient site of Machu Picchu. I had planned this for decades, and it was in the top five on my bucket list. Maybe I am up to a Top 10 bucket list?

We left the cruise ship and flew to Cusco for an overnight stay. It was a beautiful resort with wonderful accommodations.

The next morning, we took a chartered train to Machu Picchu. I was so pleased to see this historic site. It was great to fall back in time, hundreds or maybe thousands of years, and view how the people of that day lived. I felt honored to walk on their trails.

The important part was that we were walking in the footsteps of this ancient tribe of people. I have had similar feelings in Jerusalem, Egypt, and Jordan.

That day we were seeing this site, we were with others from all over the world, which is one of the great benefits of travel—meeting other travelers who have the same wanderlust as you do, but who have different views of how all these sites were created.

Other life forms, including many llamas, climbed up and down the innumerable rock steps. For a short-legged person, there were stresses at every giant step.

I carried with me my sister Annette's Maori walking stick from New Zealand. It was both to remember Annette, to figuratively take her with me to Peru, and to provide support for walking up and down the many, many steps. This stick also helped me push away the llamas, who thought I was on their trail instead of vice versa! While you are reading this, realize that there were no handrails or ramps or accessible areas.

I made the Machu Picchu climb fine and would recommend it before you get too old to do this trek.

That evening I reviewed my day at the resort and thought that the adventure was complete, and we would fly back to the ship tomorrow. How ill-informed I was!

There were two hundred tourists on this excursion; 140 of them flew to meet the ship on an 8 a.m. flight out of Cusco. The rest of us were on the 10:00 a.m. flight with other guests not from the cruise ship. I had the aisle seat in row fifteen.

With my extensive travel, I have created a personal plan that includes a small string wallet with my medicine, identification, passport, money, etc. I wear it around my neck and over my shoulder, enabling me to leave the plane quickly with all I need to survive any event, including an emergency evacuation.

The plane began to accelerate, and I could feel the plane begin to leave on time. Early on all went well, but then there were terrible noises as we were lifting off. The pilot aborted the takeoff and locked down the brakes. I did not know at the time, but the Cusco airport has a *very* short runway before falling off a cliff.

Miraculously, the pilot got the plane stopped before we went off the end of the runway. Praises! But the tires were on fire, so we had to complete an emergency evacuation of the plane. The oxygen masks fell from overhead. When cleared to do so, I stood up immediately and instructed the two people in my row to get into the aisle. I insisted that they leave everything in the overhead bin. "Go home to your grandchildren!" It was not because I was brave. It was because I was scared and getting people to exit ahead of me delayed my exit time. Our row was to exit through the back of the plane.

Unfortunately, I had to hurry other passengers and close their overhead bins to keep them from getting their belongings. Not because I was brave but because I was scared, I insisted that *everyone* go first. I said, "Get off the plane! Go to your grandchildren."

Then, it was my turn at the airplane emergency exit door. I admit to not knowing exactly how high off the ground an airplane is. (And, this was only a Boeing 737, not really a big plane.) The flight attendant was helpful but insistent. And, as he had said to others, he said to me, "*Jump!* Jump into the chute! The plane is on fire" (which was true).

I could *not* jump. I just could not leave my feet. Finally, I sat down on the airplane floor and scooted into the chute. Wow, gravity is a mighty force! I was immediately on the ground with firemen lifting me up and quickly escorting me to safety.

Do *not* try this, but if you must, know that all the other passengers will have photos of you as the last passenger exiting the plane. Many of these travel friends have shared our story on Facebook. Yes, these are the Facebook times, so our "crash group" has its own Facebook page!

Know, also, that if you are at a small airport and your plane crashes on the only runway, you have closed the airport for you and all others coming and going.

Also, know that the cruise ship with three thousand-plus passengers will sail on! I worried at the time, but the rule should always be safety of the larger group. I had an interesting experience in Cusco for three days. As you see, it created an entire book chapter.

Activities included handwashing the clothes I was wearing since the luggage for all tour members had gone on the 8:00 a.m. plane. Again, the clothes that I was wearing were the only clothes I had. I created a laundry room in my luxury hotel room. I put on the luxury hotel robe and washed my clothes in the bathroom sink, wringing out as much water from the clothes as I could.

Next, I wrapped the clothes in the luxury towels, placed them on the floor, and walked on the towels repeatedly. In the "rinse and repeat" process, I changed from soaked towels to dry towels and repeated.

Touring the small town for toiletries and underwear, I acquired something I never expected to claim that I owned: Peruvian panties!

The hotel was great, and all our expenses were covered by the travel group.

The airport opened in three days, and we were to board

a different plane. You would think after this event, we would have been worried about getting on the plane, but off we went, boarding the plane. If you can count it as an advantage, when the airport was opened, we were flown to Ecuador, an additional country for me to visit! The ship picked us up there.

Thank you, God, for the additional granted time on earth to serve you and others. This is a daily goal and promise.

Life in College Station, Texas

My move to College Station occurred on May 1, 1997. I have worked in and out of College Station since 1972 as county extension agent of Gaines County, 4-H specialist, and district extension director, so I was familiar with the city and the Texas A&M University System.

The adjustment was both joyful and stressful. While looking for a house to buy and waiting for my house in Amarillo to sell, I lived in an apartment. Because of the significant student population (with Texas A&M University and Blinn College, whose main campus was located in a nearby town), the real estate agent suggested that I live in a "professional" apartment complex in the adjoining city of Bryan. This was comfortable.

My Amarillo house sold in three months, and I began to look for a home in College Station. There were several to choose from with the population growth in this city. As we toured homes, I found one that had been on the October Home Show, and I was ready to buy.

Everything went great with the support and assistance of my friend and real estate agent, Linda Richardson. I was going to move into my new home. This happened on November 3, 1997 (my sister Annette's birthday).

It took a bit of time for my furniture to arrive from Amarillo, but this was a small problem. One day, during lunch, I invited the 4-H faculty members, who were at a meeting in town, to visit my new home. They saw all of the house, including the attic, sat in the empty garden tub, and gave full approval.

Acceptance by Mother was more hesitant. She could not believe that I was moving even further from her. Later, she learned to embrace this special opportunity for me with my new position.

The Advantages—Annette lived in Dallas, which was only three hours away. This meant that I was also only three hours from Dallas Cowboy home games. Other friends and cousins were closer, too, since they lived in the metroplex area.

The biggest advantage was the opportunity to lead the largest state 4-H program in the United States. Every day was a blessing, a challenge, and a surprise. I focused on this opportunity every day and challenged everyone to make a difference in the lives of our 4-H youth and families. Our citizens and our future depended on this.

Many long-term friends lived closer to me now that I was in College Station. I also have many friends in the Houston, San Antonio, and Dallas areas. It was a good thing that they were closer since I needed to drive to them. Air service from College Station to the rest of Texas and the world was more limited than in Lubbock and Amarillo.

I have detailed many other advantages that occurred during my tenure as the Texas State 4-H leader in other chapters.

Retirement—On August 31, 2008, I retired. I had planned for this, and I was looking forward to retirement. I had a life plan that included leaving a job or position at the top. I felt like I successfully accomplished this goal and still feel this way in 2019!

Plans to Move to the Dallas Area—Because Annette lived in Dallas and the Dallas Cowboys played in Dallas, I planned to relocate to the metroplex. I made several trips to Dallas so Annette and I could tour homes for sale in that area. We toured many homes on the south side of the metroplex. There were several possibilities, and I was energized by this plan.

Screeching Halt—All of you reading this will clearly remember the market fall during the fall of 2008. The only choice was to pray, watch, and wait.

It took me until the spring of 2019 to begin to regroup. I took a part-time job with the Texas AgriLife Extension, Department of Family and Child Development. In that department, I managed a grant to develop training materials for childcare providers.

This opportunity was a blessing to me. I have completed several curriculum development projects throughout my career and have always loved it. As a part of the grant, we trained childcare providers across the state of Texas.

Even though this was a part-time position, I was able to take a great amount of time working on this project. Making our Texas children safer was a strong personal mission that I have. So I was satisfied and pleased with the important work that I was doing.

Christ United Methodist Church—I began to believe that this was all in God's plan.

Mother died in March 2000 and my ties to West Texas

changed. With her death, I did not feel I had to remain a member of Luther Bethel Baptist (our home church). My permanent home had moved to College Station. That was *my* home now!

I joined Christ UMC and quickly became very involved. I have detailed that involvement in another chapter.

College Station Has Become a Blessed Home for Me—I find now that I love it here. Besides being involved in Christ UMC, I love the fact that the George H. W. Bush Presidential Library Complex, which includes the library and the Leonore Annenberg Presidential Conference Center is located here in College Station. We are invited to events there almost every week. These enlighten and promote strong involvement in our country.

After Hurricane Harvey, the community and the George H. W. Bush Presidential Library organized a concert that included Lady Gaga, Alabama, Lee Greenwood, the Gatlin Brothers, Lyle Lovett, Robert Earl Keen, Rock and Roll Hall of Famer Sam Moore, gospel legend Yolanda Adams, Cassadee Pope, and more than twenty other artists.

I have great friends here, who daily strengthen and support me. I have learned that God's plan for me is a great plan. And, that plan is to be here in College Station, Texas. It is and continues to be a wonderful plan. Thank you, God.

Now, I find that accidentally College Station has become the place that I have lived the longest. I have lived here for twenty-two years, outlasting my family home of nineteen years. Who would guess that this West Texas woman could become a southeast Texas woman?

Travel to the African Continent
—The Holy Land, South Africa, Botswana, Zaire, and Namibia

The Holy Land—As time for the millennium approached, I began to plan my trip to the Holy Land. This was a big goal since, as you know, I lived in Lubbock, Texas, during this time. Lubbock was half a world away, and to say it was landlocked would be accurate.

We loved traveling via a cruise ship and found a trip offered by Princess that included the Holy Land. A plan was created, and we were scheduled.

There was much concern about being away from our family, and the "this is the end of time" conversations were at a high level.

We took a flight from the United States to Istanbul, Turkey, to join the ship. The terrain, the architecture, and the dress were so exotic. I loved it. During the city tour of Istanbul, we visited the Blue Mosque and the Hagia Sophia (which is currently a museum). While standing in the Blue Mosque, I silently recited the Lord's Prayer.

First we went to Egypt and stayed at a luxury hotel from which we could see the pyramids and the Sphinx. Wonderful and fascinating would describe the entire tour. Because we were there on New Year's Eve, a musical program was presented, and a light show on the pyramids was a highlight.

On January 1, 2000, we were in Jerusalem, exactly where I wanted to be since I'd had an epiphany in the Albertson's Supermarket! I promised myself that I would *not* be in an ordinary place when the millennium began.

We saw all of the significant Christian sites—the area of the stations of the cross (where Jesus carried the cross), the Crucifixion site, and the tomb. It was wonderful, but I had to focus on finding quiet in my mind to worship.

Also, we went to the Jordan River and the location of the Sermon on the Mount. Every place and every moment was precious, memorable, and a blessing to have the privilege to travel here..

We boarded the ship the next day and began to sail across the Mediterranean to fly home. Fortunately, every trip seems like a trip of a lifetime, but I knew that I must return to spend more time in Israel.

In 2015, I returned to the Holy Land for an entire week. We took a land trip and flew into Tel Aviv. Currently, there's controversy surrounding the capital. Israel and the United States recognize Jerusalem as the capital, and the other countries of the world recognize Tel Aviv.

We landed in Tel Aviv and had a two-night stay. The best part of this was a panel discussion with a Jewish rabbi, a Christian minister, and a Muslim leader, who were in a Rotary Club together. What a blessing to meet these men, who represented these three religions, and listen to them share how they worked together in the community.

The blessing of the weeklong journey was that we had more time at the religious sites. One change was that we had to go through airport-type security at the Wailing Wall. On my earlier trip, we just passed by the crucifixion area, but on this trip we had time to stop and pray.

The site of Jesus's birth was a real blessing because we had an appointment, so we were the only ones there at our time. Solitude is such a rare event in this holy place and a blessing when it occurs. It is hard for Christians to imagine that these are loud, bustling places when, as Christians, we desire quiet.

It was the best decision to make a second trip. This significant place for me and my faith is not to be seen in a rush. Time for worship and contemplation is important and necessary.

Lifetime Trip (yes, another lifetime trip) to South Africa, Botswana, Zimbabwe, and Namibia—I knew that I needed to make this trip in 2018 because it was a strenuous trip and I was advancing in age. From College Station, it was a twenty-hour flight (there is no direct flight, and this was the time in the air).

We landed in Botswana and stayed at a beautiful resort on the river that flowed into Victoria Falls. We could see the mist of the falls from our room. Seeing Victoria Falls was high on my priority list because I had already seen two of the other big three falls: Niagara and Iguazu. We rode the train from the resort to the falls with a wonderful historic storyteller on board.

Victoria Falls is on the border of South Africa and Zimbabwe. Several of the other travel members walked into the falls wearing rain gear, but I just wanted to look for as long as I could.

We then moved from the beautiful resort to safari-style living arrangements. We were at several camps, which we traveled to via helicopter, small plane, or jeep. The camp style was what we would call shabby chic, but comfortable and beautiful. Do not misunderstand. These camps were styled this way to get the feel of the country. We were always safe and ultimately comfortable.

As anyone who travels to Africa desires, we wanted to see the "big five": elephant, lion, tiger, rhino, and Cape buffalo. This goal was accomplished. I had forgotten about the meercats. This was a surprise to me—not the meercats, but the fact that grown Americans let these critters sit all over them and especially on their *heads*! Not me, of course!

A highlight was meeting native families and children, who performed for us and allowed us to purchase some of their local crafts. Our jeep would not start at the end of this segment of the tour, and the native men pushed us off to get the engine going.

As stated earlier in this story, Africa is a long way away, but I would make the decision to make this trip again and my new view of the world.

"4-H: The Entire Couch Family Was Involved"

Professor and Extension Associate Director Emerita*

Getting young people to join 4-H is easy—as I have been known to tell new county extension agents and volunteers—but keeping them as members is *hard*.

At my elementary school in the rural Luther community, the principal, Mr. Archer, called us to a meeting in the gym-a-torium. In small rural schools in 1959, we did not have an auditorium *and* a gymnasium, but a gym-a-torium.

Well, back to the story. We were gathering the first through eighth grade students for a presentation on 4-H by the assistant county agricultural agent. He showed us a *filmstrip*. For anyone under the age of sixty, this was a small roll of pictures that was manually moved through a small projector to show on the wall. Proving that youth want to join, the filmstrip was about starting a gardening project. More shocking than the idea that a gardening project would interest me was the fact that I was thirty books into reading all fifty of the Nancy Drew Mystery novels inside the house, and in the *shade*. That evening at our house, two miles from the school, I told my parents that I wanted to join 4-H and have a gardening project. I know that they were surprised, but Mother was in the Home Demonstration Club, so she knew about the county extension programs.

Off we went in 4-H, which after ten years included programs in gardening, clothing, bedroom improvement, citizenship, leadership, food and nutrition, and public speaking. My sister joined when she was nine. Mother and Dad served as volunteers in several projects and activities.

Both Annette and I went to the National 4-H Congress with winning 4-H record books, which Dad typed. I was pleased that the time needed to work on record books got me out of doing dishes.

Seriously, this base of knowledge, leadership, and public speaking contributed to the career that I loved and celebrated for thirty-eight years. Plans for their children to be the first in their families to go to college was the goal for all returning World War II veterans. My parents and Grandmother Phipps (my mother's mother) bought savings bonds from Hereford calves sold each year to start our college funds.

Early on, I knew I was going to college—to Texas Technological College in Lubbock, Texas. All of our District 2 4-H events were held on the campus. But what to major in was the question, and that was decided by my experiences in 4-H and my admiration for my county home demonstration agent, Dr. Catherine Crawford. Even her influence by the time we were coworkers at the District 2 office to encourage me to complete my PhD is not to be measured. Significant mentors are everywhere among the extension employees at every level of the agency.

To go from a small gardening project behind the farmhouse

in Luther to being appointed as associate director of 4-H and Youth Development for Texas was an impossible dream for a nine-year-old girl, but it happened, and it happens in counties, districts, regions, and states all across our nation. Growing leaders is at the core of 4-H and Youth Development. The 4-H project is just the venue of interest. Getting youth to set goals, accomplish them, and succeed through the guidance of extension employees and volunteers across our nation is really the American way.

This is the end of the first section, which is serious and official. Now we begin the humorous events and stories that occurred during the forty-nine years of my life in 4-H and County Extension

When I was eleven, I had been recruited to do a method demonstration—mine was a speech and a set of posters. Later we called them illustrated talks. Of course, I was presenting my talk for practice at one of the Home Demonstration Clubs. (They were and still are very supportive of 4-H, giving youth opportunities to report and demonstrate what they have learned.) I had three-by-five-inch note cards in my hands and was ready to go. I can see my easel and the eleven women sitting in a semicircle around me. Less than thirty seconds into my report, I forgot my memorized talk, and all I could say was "Oh, Mama!" The club president softly said to me, "Why don't you start again?" That was the answer. So I started from the beginning and made it all the way through the second time. I count this moment as seminal to the love and joy I find in speaking to groups all over our country. Most recently, I spoke to the International 4-H Youth Exchange in Reno, Nevada.

It's shocking, I know, but a year or two later, I won district for a method demonstration, and the prize was a trip to the Texas

4-H Roundup. Several cars were going from Howard County, where Luther was located, and I was to ride from Big Spring to College Station in a car with others from my county. As far as I can remember, this was the first time I traveled any distance (seven hours) with people other than my family. Off we went. I guess, because I was the youngest and the most uncertain, I rode in the middle of the back seat. When it is announced that we were stopping in Gatesville for gasoline, the girl next to me took something out of her purse that was wrapped in a tissue. She showed it to me, but I did not know what it was.

As we were slowing down to turn into the gas station, she shoved me aside, made a retching noise, and threw the object down on the seat. Well, from this angle, I now could see that it looked like vomit! The driver skidded the car into the gas station. My seat companion dashed out of the car and raced into the gas station restroom. (You can tell how long ago this was because she would have had to get a key for those outside restrooms.) I threw the tissue over the object and tried to make a small target. There was pacing, calling on the 4-H member in the restroom, and some general panic. Our adult volunteer saw no humor in this situation.

I did not know that day, but I know now that this incident was preparing me for my work as a county extension agent, extension 4-H specialist, district extension director, and associate director of 4-H and youth. You may think my statement is a stretch, but I now know there is no way to plan, think, or believe what highly motivated young people can create or try to accomplish during camp, leadership events, Roundup, Congress, and all of the other events and activities! I've seen it all does not even begin to describe the stories I *cannot* tell.

Regarding the diversity of our great state of Texas, we should have offered special training for 4-H members and families who traveled from West Texas to College Station for Roundup before the late 1970s. Survival in the unair-conditioned corps dorms at Texas A&M can best be described as "set your alarm for every two hours to turn your hot pillow to the cool side." Many of you reading this will know exactly what I mean.

By 1965, I was a junior food and nutrition leader, having gone through the junior leader training. I was leading six boys and girls in a food group meeting in the Luther community. During the lesson, which was held at the dining room table, one of the boys stood up on his chair and walked across the table to go elsewhere in the house. As you can guess, nothing to prepare me for this was taught at junior leader training. Life lessons and working with different ages and stages of people is another one of the great life lessons. That boy is now the farm manager for the couple who operate the Couch family farm property for me in Luther, Texas.

Camping is a tradition in Texas 4-H, from the Texas 4-H Conference Center at Lake Brownwood to local and district camps throughout Texas. The Panhandle (districts one and two) has a sixty-five-year tradition of electric camps. These camps are advertised as learning about electricity and safety, but they are really learning leadership in a forested environment near Cloudcroft, New Mexico. It is quite a challenge to move 120 or so youth and adults from the Texas Panhandle to the mountains of New Mexico. Another purpose is spending uninterrupted time with industry professionals in electrical and energy careers. I attended electric camp twelve or fifteen times during my career in the Panhandle. The setting with no internet, no television, and no radio allows participants to focus on learning about electricity, leadership, cooperation, survival, and challenges.

The only challenge I could not survive was "no see ums," small flying insects that you cannot see before the biting begins. The first notice I would have of them would be the red welts all over my arms and legs. It is bad to be kept from your goal by insects, but the allergist asked me, "Who do I need to write a letter to in order to get you free from this event?" I said, "Me!" So, even with this trouble, many favorite memories of 4-H youth from the Lubbock and Amarillo area are times of learning and dancing and dancing and learning at electric camp.

During the seventy-fifth anniversary of 4-H in Texas, Preston Sides organized a press tour of Texas. A team of 4-H members was trained to present 4-H successes and issues to the entire state. The press tour went to Dallas, Fort Worth, Austin, and Houston. In each location, we held a press conference to update local political and media leaders. Upon completing this tour late on Friday, I flew back into Lubbock to pick up an extension-owned station wagon and drive to Palo Duro Canyon to a Methodist camp, where Moore County was holding a leadership event for youth at risk. I arrived at the Lubbock airport about 11:00 p.m., secured the vehicle, and loaded my luggage and teaching materials for the ninety-minute trip to Palo Duro Canyon.

Probably based on my travel schedule and my lack of good judgment, I started out for the camp. About five miles from the highway turnoff to the camp, I dozed off, allowing the car to veer onto the grass between the north- and southbound lanes. When the station wagon came to a stop, I was alive and wide-awake. Then, of course, I continued on to the camp. A few miles after turning off the highway, a tire blew out on the right side of the car. Before I could get completely stopped, the other tire on the right side also blew out.

I drove five miles an hour on the two left tires (saving one of the rims seemed a low priority at two o'clock in the morning). As I approached the camp at about 6:00 a.m., I unpacked some luggage, changed to a fresh outfit, and freshened my makeup. I sat in the car and waited for the camp breakfast crew to come by on the way down into the canyon. I decided that the car would not be safe on the decline. In a few minutes, people arrived and reported my plight to the Moore County Extension agents, and to the rescue they came!

In hindsight, I do *not* recommend my behavior, but I was always committed to making every effort to follow up on my appointments, even when there were challenges. But this sixty-four-year-old is now committed to using better or improved judgment during such times.

Even with the above event behind me, I loved teaching, traveling to counties to conduct trainings, and sharing what other 4-H programs were doing. One of these experiences provided me with another unplanned experience. For a volunteer meeting in Levelland, I wanted to use helium-filled balloons for the recognition event. On the way out of Lubbock, I stopped at a balloon shop and filled the back of the extension's station wagon with the balloons.

Traffic was unusually heavy, and I was passing a large number of cars, which I thought was very unusual, but I was watching the large bunch of colorful balloons and everything seemed OK. Of course, then I realized that I was passing a funeral procession. This dawned on me when I *finally* saw the hearse. I have always thought that balloons at a funeral were quite a nice, symbolic touch.

Among the other great events that Texas 4-H members have the opportunity to attend is the National 4-H Congress. I have worked this event ten times. Probably my second trip to the event, as a chaperone (first time as a 4-H member), gave me one of the best perspectives I can remember. We were on the fifth floor of the Conrad Hilton in Chicago, and a Texas 4-H member from Moore County said to me, "Dr. Couch, there are more people on this floor of the hotel than live in my town of Sunray, Texas." Now, that said it all for me in the fifty-nine years I worked in 4-H. This broad world perspective is what 4-H membership and leadership activities give our youth. They see the world from a new, lofty, innovative, and wide-eyed perspective.

You have seen others detail their experiences when the Texas 4-H and Youth Development Program was honored at the White House for the one-hundredth year of our program. For this rural farm girl, this was an unbelievable thought even to have. Forty-seven of us representing youth, volunteers, parents, industry partners, extension employees, and extension administration went to the White House. President Bush spent twenty-five minutes with us, talking directly to the youth. I could not have imagined this event any better in my mind. At least by this time in my career, I was experienced enough not to wear my standup dress with my sit-down shoes!

From the view of someone who is nearly five years retired from extension, I am so pleased that the Texas 4-H and Youth Development Program is a strong as ever and continues to reach and teach the young people of the State of Texas. Please join them in the youth development pursuits by contacting your local County Extension Office.*

This chapter has some repeats from other stories. This version is from a one-hundredth anniversary of 4-H in Texas report.

Beulah Lennis Phipps's
Personal Journal 1937–1941

January 1, 1937–December 31, 1937

January 1–5, 1937—No entry.

Wednesday, January 6, 1937—I went to see Miss Cook at Lawn. That afternoon I walked to the girl, and we rode around for a while. Made ice cream for supper.

Thursday, January 7, 1937—Next morning the ground was covered with snow. We pulled ice off the trees to melt for dishwater. Made snow ice cream. Mary, Jon, and I cut out paper dolls.

Friday, January 8, 1937—Still very cold and Mrs. Cooke told me to go to the gin to get the mail. I had to "skate," so I hit the ground with a bump.

Saturday, January 9, 1937—Mucho cold, so I had to go to the gin after the mail again. The Haynes boys scared me nearly to death. We played some more dolls.

Sunday, January 10, 1937—I had hopes of coming home. But there was still a lot of ice on the ground. I couldn't stay any longer, so they brought me home to get rid of me.

Saturday, February 20, 1937—I fixed up Helen's package for her. The package contained a scarf and a lot of thread.

Tuesday, February 23, 1937—Helen's birthday.

Friday, March 26, 1937—Helen and Virgil came over to see us. Old man Walhburg had to come. Of course, he made Virgil return home to get the old gripy home safe and sound.

Saturday, March 27, 1937—Cleaned up the house, and in the afternoon, we went to town with the rest of the Negroes. Had a grand time walking around the streets.

Sunday, March 28, 1937—The Cooks came over and spent the day. Late that afternoon, we went home with the Cooks, so Helen could meet the train much more easily.

Monday, March 29, 1937—It was raining the next morning. We bought tickets about ten minutes before the train came. The train arrived, and she nearly forgot her suitcase. The Cooks brought us home.

Saturday, April 1, 1937—Dark, then we went after R. E. Charles. Thought maybe we would have to go to Moore after Juanita. Went to town and rode around. Juanita drove home. Charles told me a thing that broke my heart. I thought if I lived over it, I might not look like anything. I really worried about it.

Wednesday, April 7, 1937—Dady carried me to Uncle Sid's to stay for a few days.

Thursday, April 8, 1937—A sheep had butted Effie. Weak and cooking.

Friday, April 9, 1937—We ... in the morning. May Lee was planning my party. Went fishing. I went to the show and saw *School of Explosion*.

Saturday, April 10, 1937—Went to the cemetery working. Then, went home with Oma Lee. She was planning my party. So, you see, we had it. Saw James Sproits, Joe Lee Cooper. We broke the porch in.

Sunday, April 11, 1937—Went to church and after dinner Arlis and I, Jessie Ray, and Oma Lee came over to Winters. Went to the show. Saw Grady Baker. Arlis rode around with Mozelle Periphery and them.

Wednesday, April 28, 1937—*My birthday! I received my package from HWelen*—two beautiful handkerchiefs.

Friday, April 30, 1937—Aunt Doris, Uncle Jim, and Marian spent the day with us. Mr. Lamberth came to see me, and I could work for Maria.

Saturday, May 1, 1937—Went over to Mrs. Lamberth's to find out about my job. I didn't much want to work, but I needed the money.

Sunday, May 2, 1937—I packed my clothes ready to start to work right away. I didn't dread my work, but I hated the old lady.

Monday, May 3, 1937—Just about seven o'clock, here comes Bernice and Marie. We arrived and, of course, the first thing was to clean the house and, of course, it took me all day.

Tuesday, May 4, 1937—Up again and working all day. The job I hated the most was washing dishes. It took me two scours to wash the dishes. I never saw so many dishes!

Wednesday, May 5, 1937—Today, I again washed the dishes and mopped the whole house and cleaned up real good. I also helped plant some in the beautiful garden.

Thursday, May 6, 1937—My household job continues, and I had to do a big ironing. I always had to help with the cooking and carry water from the lot. Ha! Ha!

Friday, May 7, 1937—Again, I am cleaning up the house and mopped and dusted the front room, so wouldn't have so much to do the next morning.

Saturday, May 8, 1937—Oh! Boy! Saturday morning and I am up at 5:00 a.m. to clean and mop the rest of the house, and I cleaned up so that I could be ready to come to town with Mr. and Mrs. Gardner.

Sunday, May 9, 1937—Glad to be at home. I slept nearly all day and packed some more of my china to go back with me to work in the coming week. I sure dreaded it.

Monday, May 10, 1937—I went to the Hardley Sandler Show [A West Texas showman, oilman, and Texas legislator, Harley Sadler was also an actor and tent show owner. He traveled through the United States in tent shows during the period from 1910 to 1944, primarily in Texas and the Southwest. Elected to the Texas Senate in 1943, he served until his death in 1954.]

Dady carried me back to work, and it was sure muddy from the Gardners' house to Bernice, and we slide off the ditch. Marie sure was glad to see me.

Tuesday, May 11, 1937—Up early and began to gather up the clothes to wash. Carried them up to Mrs. Gardner's, and boy do I mean we really had the washing, and I was sure tired.

Wednesday, May 12, 1937—Went to Mrs. Gardner's to iron. I had two bushel baskets of clothes. I had a real good iron. I am sure I had a lot of fun out of Jim Gardner. I sure do like old Jim.

Thursday, May 13, 1937—Marie was sure mad today. She fussed at every one and even the cats. I happened to break an iced tea glass, and I thought we were going to have a war.

Friday, May 14, 1937—Cleaned all the house and hoed a little in the backyard and packed my clothes to come home the next morning.

Saturday, May 15, 1937–May 20, 1037—Mother and I went to town. Finished up all the work and was worn out. I ate some cucumbers for dinner, and they sure made me sick.

Sunday, May 16, 1937—Stayed in bed all day because of my trouble.

Thursday, May 20, 1937—Mother and I went to town. We met the Cooks going to Mr. and Mrs. Reed's to make ice cream. We went with Mrs. Cook. Mr. Cook carried the car back.

Friday, May 21, 1937—We sent Helen's … this morning. Came home early and we went to Garland Foster's funeral. And I rode home with the Hagers.

Saturday, May 22, 1937—Stayed all night with Elese. We went to town. Then, we rode around with Albert Palim. I learned to drive, but we went back roads part of the time—reverse!

Sunday, May 23, 1937—Stayed at home all day by myself.

Saturday, May 29, 1937—Rained. Lane was muddy. We had a date with Albert and Alvin. Had a grand time. Told them goodbye because I was leaving for Tarleton. I bought me a new suitcase.

Sunday, May 30, 1937—I went over to Strother to tell them goodbye.

Monday, May 31, 1937—I packed my clothes and was glad I was going to school, but still I hated to leave the Hagers. But, I would see them by and by. The judgment peace.

Tuesday, June 1, 1937—Up early, left about 6:30 a.m. for Lawn. Mr. and Mrs. Cook carried me. I cried most all the way. I couldn't find any place, so I returned the same day. Came a big rain.

Wednesday, June 2, 1937—It was good to be at home. I hung out all my clothes. In the afternoon, I went to the Hagers'. Of course, I had to tell them all about my trip and enjoyment.

Saturday, June 5, 1937—Spent the afternoon in town.

Tuesday, June 8, 1937—We went to Guion to gather berries. Dad and I picked 1½ gallons of berries. Canned berries in the afternoon, and Dady worked for Mr. Burton in the afternoon.

Wednesday June 9, 1937—We washed, and in the afternoon, we dug onions for Mr. Burton. I never got so tired of working with onions. We smelled like onions!

Thursday, June 10, 1937—We still dug onions and smelled more like them all the time. I was sure glad when we got through with the onions.

Friday, June 11, 1937—I helped Mother with the butter, but I carried Dady to work. Then, I came back to work on the onions again.

Saturday, June 12, 1937—We had to dig onions all day Saturday, and I was sure tired. More onions. The boss came over. We hoed tomatoes in the morning but dug onions in the afternoon.

Sunday, June 13, 1937—Glad to get out of the onion patch. Rested most all day, and slept a lot, too. We went over to Kay's and left and went on to town.

Monday, June 14, 1937—Back at the onion patch. Mr. Burton went with us, and we had to do a lot of work that day.

Tuesday, June 15, 1937—Dug more onions but not as many as we did the day before. We dug thirty or more bushels.

Wednesday, June 16, 1937—We dug onions. We thought that maybe we would get through, but we didn't.

Thursday, June 17, 1937—Dad and I went back again, and we sure had to work hard to get the rest of the onions done. We got our own pay. I made $12.25 for digging onions.

Friday, June 18, 1937—We started hoeing for Graver Davis. There was sure a bunch of workers, about fifteen or sixteen. Some of them sure did blab.

Saturday, June 19, 1937—Sonny Boy hoed that morning. We worked for him again. We worked up until Saturday noon. He fired a bunch of them, but we got more work to do!

Sunday, June 20, 1937—I rested most all day and slept a lot of the day. I had to work all week, and I was ready for rest when Sunday came around.

Monday, June 21, 1937—Hoed again for Gruver Davis. We had a lot of fun hoeing Sudan (Johnson grass).

Tuesday, June 22, 1937—Again to the cotton patch and it was sure hot. I wish I was in the icebox; it was so hot (the weather).

Wednesday, June 23, 1937—It was hot (the weather) again, and I had to be in the cotton patch.

Thursday, June 24, 1937—Again, to the cotton patch and I was so tired when night came. I was always ready to hit the bed and go to sleep.

Friday, June 25, 1937—Carried Dady to hoe and then came home to help Mother after dinner. I went back to the field, and we finished hoeing for Grayer Davis. I got our pay.

Saturday, June 26, 1937—Got up ready early and did the biggest washing in the morning, and I went to town in the afternoon to see all the people.

Sunday, June 27, 1937—Stayed at home all morning and afternoon. Elese, Thelma, Sonny Boy, and I drove around and went to the schoolhouse and made some pictures.

Monday, June 28, 1937—We started hoeing for Bog Lewis. We had a lot of work to do because there was a lot of weeds in the cotton.

Tuesday, June 29, 1937—Up early again. Fixed dinner. Then went to hoe again for Bob Lewis. Worked hard again, and it was sure hot out in the field.

Wednesday, June 30, 1937—We worked hard, so we could get through Maurice Davis. Came to see if we could hoe for him the next day. We did get through early.

Thursday, July 1, 1937—Went to Mancie Davis to hoe the next day. No one was hoeing but Dady and I and a little Negro boy. We had lots of fun with the colored child.

Friday, July 2, 1937—Carried Dady to the field. Came home and went to town. Went back to the field in the afternoon and hoed for Maurice David. Uncle Sid came back from Temple and stopped by.

Saturday, July 3, 1937—We hoed up until Saturday. Got our pay. Elese, Thelma, and the rest of us went to town. We were supposed to go to town that night. Travis Woods came after me, broke the lock on the church door. Went to the Knapps' for dinner. Mr. and Mrs. Knapp weren't at home for dinner. Drove around in the pasture in our slips. Saw R. R. coming, so we ran back to the house. We got ready and went. Richard came by the store, and Pauline wanted to go to Clayton Flat, so we went. L. B. Fields, Urpy Mundom, and Wayne Brown followed us. We really had fun. Clifton and Paul met us, so we went to town. Clifton and Paul met us coming back for us to go to Vealmoor, if they could get the car.

Francis and Joe Ella ran off, so I got to go to Vealmoor by myself with Paul and Clifton. Lucille came back with us. We really had fun.

Sunday, July 4, 1937—Elene went to Abilene. I went to the show and over to Strather. She showed me "The Woman I Love." I started home and saw the "Kirby Girls" with Albert and Alvin close to where Bill Moore parked.

Monday, July 5, 1937—We hoed for Mr. Newsome out north of town. No one hoed but Mr. Thorpe, Dady, and I. Had lots of fun.

Tuesday, July 6, 1937—Hoed again for Mr. Newson. All of Stephens hoed, and also two smart gentlemen hoed. They tried to blab to me, but I just hate them.

Wednesday, July 7, 1937—We hoed again, but we finished for Mr. Newsom about noon. Came home and ate our lunch. It started raining about night.

Friday, July 9, 1937—Went to town with Mother. I felt bad the rest of the day. In the late afternoon, I went to Elese for her to read the "silly letters" and also gathered some peas.

Saturday, July 10, 1937—The lane was sure muddy … [could not read, runny ink] guitars and musical instruments.

Sunday, July 11, 1937—Home early. Elese and Thelma came home with me. In the afternoon went to town, (Saturday). Then went to hospital. Borrowed money to get into the show.

Monday, July 12, 1937—We were up early and fixed the water to wash. We sure had a big washing. Bought a new pair of shoes. Also, bought thirty cents [worth] of candy. Came after Johnson grass over at Elese's.

Tuesday, July 13, 1937—Moved all the canned stuff on the other side of the room. Aunt Lillie Dietz, Alta, and Woodrow came over to see us. Wanted us to go over to them, but we could not.

Wednesday, July 14, 1937—Spent the night with Oma Lee. Went with Arlus and Robbie Lou. We drove … into the house at Oma Lee.

Thursday, July 15, 1937—Oma Lee and Aunt Annie and I went to church. Then I went home with Marion Marie. Brought us home late that afternoon. Helen came about sundown. Alma came with West about sundown. Came with West's folks. We were supposed to go to church.

Friday, July 16, 1937—Went to town in the morning. Then ate dinner. Went to Crews. Then, we went to church that night. Stayed all night with Uncle Pay and Leona.

Saturday, July 17, 1937—Came home early in the afternoon. Then ate some dinner and went to town in the afternoon with Elena and Thelma. Then for the night we went to Hagers'.

Sunday, July 18, 1937—Aunt Thelma came down and told Helen that Momma was going home on the train. So Helen left that morning. Afton, Elese, and I went to town. Saw everybody. Thelma and Katherine sure was mad as us.

Monday, July 19, 1937—Bright and early the next morning I went to Hagers' to spend the day. I helped them wash. We went swimming in the afternoon.

Tuesday, July 20, 1937—We washed that morning and in the afternoon. Mother and I got ready and went to town. I helped Dady get everything ready and went to town. I helped Dady get everything ready so Dady could go to Big Spring the next day.

Wednesday, July 21, 1937—Dady left about 6:30 a.m. I had to do all the milking, and I sure was tired. Elese and Thelma came over to see me. We had a grand time.

Thursday, July 22, 1937—I had to get the milking done. I went over to Elese and Thelma. They came home with me. We sure had lots of fun.

Friday, July 23, 1937—I had to help mother with the butter and get off to town. Made candy at dinnertime. Afternoon went to Elese to get my hair set but forgot to take my hair set outfit. We worked the cows and talked CJ into going with the Whittingburg boys. We came in. We were in a sad condition.

Saturday, July 24, 1937—Helped can peaches up until about 12:45 p.m. Then took a bath, went to town with Thelma and Elese. Saw Joe E. Brown in *Riding on Air*. Elese came home with me. We went back to town in the Model T after vinegar. Had lots of fun.

Sunday, July 25, 1937—Up real early and went to Elese's to spend the day. Ate dinner. Then went to a baptizing. Then went swimming after they left. Oh boy, we sure had fun hopping like frogs!

Monday, July 26, 1937—Up real early and ready to go to hoe for Mancie Davis. Came home, ate watermelon, and I also watched the cows and chickens. Sure was tired. Took a bath. Present to bed.

Tuesday, July 27, 1937—Up early and ready to hoe for Mancie Davis. It sure was hot, and I really did work. Came home about six and watched the cows.

Wednesday, July 28, 1937—Up early again and hoed for the same man again. We didn't go back to hoeing until about 2:30 because we only lacked about eighteen rows. Watched the cows again when I came home.

Thursday, July 29, 1937—Washed all my clothes and packed them, ready to go to Oma Lee's. Slept some in the afternoon. Uncle Charly came and went back with them. We supposed to ride the bus. Pulled a joke on Oma Lee. Ate watermelon and went to the store. Ate supper, washed my hair with the hose. Went to Crews' with Arlie. Had lot of fun. We parked. Went in the new Plymouth.

Friday, July 30, 1937—Up early and went to San Angelo. Bought the town out. Ate lunch in the park. Came home about 1:30. Slept some after got home. Had a water fight. James Spences wanted Oma Lee to go to Crews', but she wouldn't go because I was there.

Saturday, July 31, 1937—Up real early, cleaned up the house, and cooked dinner. Took a bath and went to town. Oma Lee and I went to the show. The name was Three Musketeers—a good show. We thought maybe James Pratt wanted Oma (her thought). We had a lot of fun. I nearly laughed my sides out. Fun.

Sunday, August 1, 1937—Up early and Oma Lee, cousin from Miles, came over. All the rest of them, except Oma Lee, her two cousins and me stayed here in the afternoon, and the rest of them went to Mr. Tounget's.

Monday, August 2, 1937—Felt kinda bad in the morning but worked on my scarf and also whipped some lace on one scarf. I slept some. Picked some beans. Took a shower bath in the early night. Mr. and Mrs. West came by.

Tuesday, August 3, 1937—Picked peas in the morning. Started on my vanity set. Phanel did not come after me until Wednesday. Had another water fight. Mrs. West came over.

Wednesday, August 4, 1937—Packed my clothes. Started to the club, but Dad came, so I came home. Ellen came over. Went to town in Model T. Rode around. Got our dresses. I went over there, and we cut our dresses out. Dad went after watermelon.

Thursday, August 5, 1937—Up early. Went to Elese's and started on our dresses. Helped wash. Worked on my vanity set. Elese and Joe Anne came home with me. Joan went back with Mr. Greenhill.

Friday, August 6, 1937—Elese went home early in the morning. After dinner I went to Elese to make my dress. The Jobe boy was there, and he threw water on us. I didn't get my dress done.

Saturday, August 7, 1937—I felt bad. So I went down to get Elese to help finish my dress. After Joe Anne and Elese came up here. We went to town in the afternoon and again that night. Elese and I went with some …

Sunday, August 8, 1937—Stayed at home in the morning. In the afternoon, Thelma, Afton, Joe and Sonny Boys, and I went to Pokes Flat to take some pictures. We saw Arlis and Jessie Ray in town.

Monday, August 9, 1937—Up real early so Dady could go to Big Spring. Elese headed maize. I saw her in the late afternoon. Joe Anne and Afton spent the night with me.

Tuesday, August 10, 1937—Afton and Joe Anne went home real early. Cleaned up and went after the mail. And got a new pair of hose in town. Worked on my scarf. I had to do all the milking in the evening.

Wednesday, August 11, 1937—Stayed at home all day. We saw Dad was gone, so I had to help do a lot of the work. I went to sleep in the afternoon and slept for about two hours.

Thursday, August 12, 1937—We washed in the morning, and boy was I tired. I was so tired. I couldn't sit up. Went to Elese's in the afternoon. They all came over here, and we played some. Had fun.

Friday, August 13, 1937—Helped Mother get off to town. In the afternoon I stayed at home and worked on my scarf. I finished it and then worked on my vanity set. Had lots of fun.

Saturday, August 14, 1937—Ironed in the morning. Went to town in the afternoon. We thought we were going to get to talk with Irene Greenhill. Went to the show with Elese. I spent the night with them. Had a lot of fun eating Jennings's watermelons.

Sunday, August 15, 1937—Came home real early and Thelma came home with me. After dinner Thelma, Afton, Joe Anne, Alfa and kids, Ed, Elese, and PJ went to town and went to the funeral. Had a chance to go with them.

Monday, August 16, 1937—Up real early and started to head maize for Mr. Stanley. I made $1.75. But sure was tired in the afternoon. I had to milk in the evening. Glad to get to bed.

Tuesday, August 17, 1937—Up early and headed maize again. I was sure sore, and I couldn't hardly move because I was so sore. I made $1.50. A good day's work.

Wednesday, August 18, 1937—Headed maize all day. We got through for Mr. Stanley. We received our pay. I made $4.75. It rained some before I went to bed, but still I got a good night's rest.

Thursday, August 19, 1937—It rained so we couldn't hoe maize. Dady went up to Mr. Pass so he could go to Big Spring. Went to town after mail. Went to Elese's afterward. Lane was muddy and bumpy. T. J. Jennings headed creek bank.

Friday, August 20, 1937—Up early so I could help Mother with the butter. I asked Elese to stay until after dinner, and I would go and cut feed. Had a grand time cutting feed.

Saturday, August 21, 1937—Ironed my dress so I would have it ready to wear. Went to town after Elese had already gone, but I saw them.

Sunday, August 22, 1937—Went to Aunt Mary's to a reunion. Sonny Boy and his dad, Ellen and husband, Samson, Aline Lucile were there. We saw Pattet from Throckmorton. Had a grand time. Had ice cream.

Monday, August 23, 1937—Up early and fixed my sock, ready to pick cotton. Didn't pick. Mother and Dady went to Lawn to get the cash from Mr. Coole. Elese, Thelma, Afton, and Joe Anne spent the afternoon.

Tuesday, August 24, 1937—Went to pick cotton in the afternoon. Didn't pick very much. Mrs. Cooke brought the fifty dollars down here. We had lots of fun picking cotton.

Wednesday, August 25, 1937—Picked cotton for Mr. Stanley again. Didn't do very much, but still we had lots of fun. The Hager bunch was sure funny.

Thursday, August 26, 1937—We started for Francis "Khold." I picked ninety-eight in the morning. It was sure hot, and it came up a shower of rain in the afternoon. We quit about three or four o'clock.

Friday, August 27, 1937—Went to Hagers' to see if they were going to pick cotton. They were washing, but we went about one o'clock. Didn't pick so much. Thelma and Geneva came by that night because Mr. Harrison died.

Saturday, August 28, 1937—Went to town and bought my slacks for rather I was going to get some to wear. We cooked our supper on the creek. Had a grand time.

Sunday, August 29, 1937—Stayed at home all day and took some medicine. I sure felt better after I got through.

Monday, August 30, 1937—We still picked cotton, and it was raining some, so we brought Joe Anne home. We had lots of fun over there at Francis's.

Tuesday, August 31, 1937—I went back to pick cotton. Did very well today. I sure worked hard. It showered around today. Didn't rain much.

Wednesday, September 1, 1937—Went back to pick cotton. I picked 120 in the morning. Then, I went to town after the Delbert house caught afire. Mr. Hager was over at Miller Secondhand Store.

Thursday, September 2, 1937—I was sick, but Thelma, Geneva Mae, Afton, Elese, and I started to walk, but we couldn't make it. Mr. Hager wouldn't let Chevy go. Sonny Boy went in the afternoon on his horse.

Friday, September 3, 1937—I was determined to pick (cotton) at Delbert's, so I walked. Just got over there, and it rained. Came back to the Hagers' and pickled in the afternoon there. We had lots of fun down there.

Saturday, September 4, 1937—Elese, Afton, Joe Anne, Thelma, Geneva, Sonny Boy, T. J., and I all went to town. We saw a show at the new show. I forgot the name of it, but it was sure good.

Sunday, September 5, 1937—Up real early and went to Greenhill to phone Koehler to see if I could pick cotton on Monday. Went to Grandma's and today was the day we had the fun. Ate dinner with Oma Lee.

Monday, September 6, 1937—I went to Koehler's to pick cotton. The dogs ate my dinner up, and what wasn't ate Buggers stole. So I didn't have dinner. I picked 270 pounds.

Tuesday, September 7, 1937—Picked again. But still had a great day. I picked 259 pounds, and it rained about five thirty. We got our pay. We were supposed to do more the next morning but didn't.

Wednesday, September 8, 1937—Went to town and paid down our dresses. Elese went over to pick cotton with me so she could pay for her dress out. Arlis and Uncle Charlie came over here.

Thursday, September 9, 1937—I picked cotton all day. I sure had lots of fun out there picking cotton with a bunch of Mexicans.

Friday, September 10, 1937—Dady carried me over there to pick cotton. I was sure glad because it was Friday, and boy was I helped because just one more day until we get our dresses.

Saturday, September 11, 1937—We didn't pick cotton because I was too tired and Dady had some work to do. Went to town with Elese. Went and saw Buck Jones in *Empty Saddles* (maybe *Feather Your Nest*). Got our pay and got our dresses.

Bought our new dresses. Elese and I went after slacks and a yellow dress. About dark, Arlis and James Sprout, James Fowler, and PJ went to Ballinger. We went to the Texas theater and saw Glen Autry in *Round-Up Time in Texas*. We sure had a high-heel time.

Sunday, September 12, 1937—Grandma, Aunt Doris, Evelyn, Ira, Jesse Ray, and Marion all came over here for dinner. Elisa also came over here for dinner. Elese came over, and we took some pictures.

Monday, September 13, 1937—Up again and started picking cotton. I picked for Bill Mayo. This was right after Thelma and Afton got mad at Elese and me.

Tuesday, September 14, 1937—I picked again for Bill Mayo. This was the day that I met the Phipps boy. We sure had lots of fun.

Wednesday, September 15, 1937—This day I seared for another man. By night I was sure tired.

Thursday, September 16, 1937—Today I picked 270. I was sure tired when night came. I was ready for the bed.

Friday, September 17, 1937—Again I picked cotton. I didn't pick quite so much. The Phipps boy came after me. I was so tired, I wouldn't go.

Saturday, September 18, 1937—Picked cotton until about eleven. Came home and went to town. Went back late that afternoon. Saw Bill and invited him to the party. He came and wanted me to go somewhere else.

Sunday, September 19, 1937—Slept in the morning. About one o'clock Elese, Thelma, Geneve came after me. We went to the show. Saw Shirley Temple in *Wee Willie Winkie*. Rode around with G. J. and Sonny.

Monday, September 20, 1937—We picked here by the house on Pirking's place. We got through by dinner and moved west of town. I picked 223.

Tuesday, September 21, 1937—Again I picked cotton. I picked 239. We got to wave at Bill when I came back home. He sure is cute.

Wednesday, September 22, 1937—Don't have much to say only I picked more cotton. Today I picked 250. That was real good for me to be so small.

Thursday, September 23, 1937—I picked cotton again. I picked 237. I sure hate to pick cotton, especially when it was nearly all dead.

Friday, September 24, 1937—Again I picked cotton. I was so tired when I came home. Bill came after me to go to the show, but Dady wouldn't let me go. Poor Bill. I guess he thinks he has a hard time.

Saturday, September 25, 1937—It was sure cold. I went to Elese to get my hair set. It was afternoon, and I went to town. After four I went to Oma Lee's. Oma Lee and a bunch of kids came back to Winters and rode around.

Sunday, September 26,1937—Went to church at Blanton. In the afternoon went to Ballinger after tennis balls. Came home and went to church that night. Ted White brought me home.

Monday, September 27, 1937—Picked cotton all day. Made $1.78 picking cotton. I sure hate to pick, but I must pass away the time.

Tuesday, September 28, 1937—Dady found out that we could move to Big Spring. We started packing our things. Went and told Bill goodbye. He sure hated to see me leave.

Wednesday, September 29, 1937—Left about nine after we got the truck loaded. Wore my slacks. Stopped and bought a laundry bag at Woolworths in Big Spring and pot holders. Arrived here about 2:00 p.m.

Thursday, September 30, 1937—Worked hard all day trying to get all the things unpacked. Stayed at home all day and worked.

Friday, October 1, 1937—Things looked just a little bit better. We got nearly everything straight. Went over to Helen's. Then painted the mailbox and met the postman.

Saturday, October 2, 1937—Up early. We went to town. Carried our washing. Bought Mother a hat. It was nearly night when we came home. Sure was tired. But wish I was in Winters.

Sunday, October 3, 1937—Went to Sunday school with Page Murry. Had a grand time. Slept some in the afternoon. Then rode around. Ate watermelon over at the Raineys'. Enjoyed it.

Monday, October 4, 1937—Worked around here to try to get everything ready so I could go to Winters with Dady.

Tuesday, October 5, 1937—Up real early. Left about eight for Winters. I was sure tired when I reached Winters. Dady wouldn't go by Big Spring. Went to see Elese and boy was she proud to see me.

Wednesday, October 6, 1937—Up real early and began to help tear down the shed. I pulled so many nails I couldn't see nothing. Went to town and found out Bill was out at Vealmoor. Close to home.

Thursday, October 7, 1937—Came home early and began to work. We loaded the truck. Spent the night with Elese. Grandma had a stroke of paralysis. We phoned Mother about it.

Friday, October 8, 1937—Up about four o'clock and started home. Elese liked to cry. I really did. Ran off in the ditch. Mother went on the Uncle Pat's. Grandma died about four o'clock. Went to the gin.

Saturday, October 9, 1937—Rained most all day Wanted to go to the funeral but couldn't go. Went to Helen's in the afternoon so Dady could have some water.

Sunday, October 10, 1937—I was nearly sick with a cold. I slept some in the morning. Went to see Page in the afternoon. Then came home and went to Helen's. Woodrow came to tell us that Mother was in.

Monday, October 11, 1937—It was raining this morning, and I stayed in bed until about 10:30 a.m. Embroidery in the afternoon. Page came about four o'clock and stayed awhile.

Tuesday, October 12, 1937—Up early and we all went to Helen's to spend the day. I embroidered some and ironed. Went to the store. Saw Warren's car but not him. Ate a watermelon.

Wednesday, October 13, 1937—Rained again today but not so much. Embroidered some more. Mother went to town with Mr. and Mrs. Rainey. Sure was lonesome. Got a letter from Elese.

Thursday, October 14, 1937—Embroidered in the morning. About 12:30 p.m. went to Helen's. Dady came after me. Was sure cold and rained some more. Wrote to Elese at night.

Friday, October 15, 1937—Mother and Dady went to Big Springs. Stayed at home by myself and made some candy. Had real good luck with it. Paid Uncle Jim Worls (sp).

Saturday, October 16, 1937—Cleaned house. Went to town in the afternoon with Mr. and Mrs. Rainey. Went to the fruit supper with Dub Lewis, Page, and Charles [first mention of Charles]. Had a grand time.

Sunday, October 17, 1937—Went to Sunday school with Page. In the afternoon went to Ted Fields's, then to Helen and Virgil's. Then brought Jersey home and went to Page's when I got home.

Monday, October 18, 1937—I picked cotton. Sure was tired when night came.

Tuesday, October 19, 1937—Up again and picked cotton. I was tired. I was always glad when night came so I could hit the bed.

Wednesday, October 20, 1937—Helped pick cotton. I pulled 386. The most I have pulled this week.

Thursday, October 21, 1937—Picked cotton. Helen came over about noon. She wanted me to go over there and stay all night with her. I did and had lots of fun. Got a letter from Oma Lee.

Friday, October 22, 1937—Picked cotton all day, and then Dady carried me over to Helen's to spend the night. Virgil came home about 5:10. Sure early to get in.

Saturday, October 23, 1937—Pulled bales until about 10:30 a.m. I pulled 109. Then came to the house and got ready to go to town with the Raineys. Had a good time.

Sunday, October 24, 1937—Up real early and pulled bales. Didn't pick so much because we had sorry cotton to pick in. Spent the night with Helen and Virgil.

Tuesday, October 26, 1937—Came home real early and started to pull bales. I pulled 321. Sure worked hard.

Wednesday, October 27, 1937—Ethelyne helped me pull until dinner. The Raineys went to town. Mother & Dady went to Helen's to work on the well. I pulled by myself. I pulled 316. Real good.

Thursday, October 28, 1937—Pulled cotton all day. I sure hate to pull cotton, but I had to. I pulled 303.

Friday, October 29, 1937—I pulled cotton. I pulled 414. I had to pull part of the day by myself. Mr. Rainey helped Dady pipe the well.

Saturday, October 30, 1937—Mother and Dady went to town early in the morning. I went to town with Mr. and Mrs. Rainey. Bought my trunk. I paid $9.90 for it.

Sunday, October 31, 1937—Went to Sunday school with Page and went home with her for dinner. Then went to the Knapps' and then rode around. We went to town in the afternoon.

Monday, November 1, 1937—Up early and ready to go pick cotton. That was all I had got to do. I pulled 322 today. A lot.

Tuesday, November 2, 1937—I pulled cotton again in the morning. Then I went to Helen's to see the windmill raised, but we didn't get it up.

Wednesday, November 3, 1937—Went to Helen's again. I gathered up a bunch of men to help raise the windmill.

Thursday, November 4, 1937—Rained some in the early morning, so I didn't make cement to fix the windmill around the bottom.

Friday, November 5, 1937—After so long a time, I started pulling bales again. We wanted to get the bale out, and we would be caught up.

Saturday, November 6, 1937—I pulled 97 and quit so I could get ready to go to town with Mr. and Mrs. Rainey. I brought my shoes and hose. Had a good time in town.

Sunday, November 7, 1937—Baked a cake and went to Sunday school with Page. Page came home with me for dinner, and then we went to see Juanita Hamlin.

Monday, November 8, 1937—Went to Murry to see about picking cotton, but it was too wet. They went to town. I embroidered all the day, and it rained some in the afternoon.

Tuesday, November 9, 1937—It rained some more, but I couldn't pull bales so I embroidered some on my scarf.

Wednesday, November 10, 1937—We went to Helen's to work. Virgil and Dady went to town. I did some needlework. I spent the night with Helen.

Thursday, November 11, 1937—Came home from Helen's and then went to pull cotton for Murry. We sure had lots of fun.

Friday, November 12, 1937—We pulled cotton again over at Murry's. We got our pay. I made $3.08.

Saturday, November 13, 1937—I didn't pull cotton, but I washed my hair and got ready to go to town. Bought me a new purse.

Sunday, November 14, 1937—Up really early and cooked two cakes for the birthday dinner. We sure had a nice time and a large crowd.

Monday, November 15, 1937—Up early and ready to pull for Murry again. I made $1.25. We quit because they were nearly through. Web Nix came for us to haul and pull cotton.

Tuesday, November 16, 1937—We started pulling for Web Nix. Dady was to haul cotton for him for a dollar a bale. I pulled 480.

Wednesday, November 17, 1937—I pulled for Web Nix again. I pulled 400 today, not very much but pretty good for me.

Thursday, November 18, 1937—I pulled 441 today. A little bit better but we had real good cotton to pull in.

Friday, November 19, 1937—Pulled again. I pulled with Paul Biffer. He pulled 419, and I pulled 418. Boy, I say, he sure is cute.

Saturday, November 20, 1937—Pulled cotton up until about three o'clock. I pulled 300. When we got the bales out, we quit. I went to the gin with Dady

Sunday, November 21, 1937—Went to Sunday school with Page and then went home with her. Had a nice time. Made candy in the afternoon.

Monday, November 22, 1937—I started to pull bales, but it was so cold I quit and came home. I sure like to have frozen.

Tuesday, November 23, 1937—Up real early. We went to town. I bought my dress and a lot of other things too.

Wednesday, November 24, 1937—Dady and I went after wood in the morning, and in the afternoon we started pulling bales for Mr. Rainey.

Thursday, November 25, 1937—I pulled bales again today. Helen and Virgil pulled for Mr. Rainey too. Wrote to Elese. Went after Ethelyne.

Friday, November 26, 1937—Pulled bales again. We finished the bales so Mr. and Mrs. Rainey carried it to the gin at Lawn.

Saturday, November 27, 1937—It was too cold to pull so I went to town. I bought my brown hat and got my dress. Had my coat cleaned at the tailor's shop.

Sunday, November 28, 1937—Up early and got ready to go with Page to church and Sunday school. Wore my new outfit. Had lots of compliments on it.

Monday, November 29, 1937—Pulled cotton all day. I forgot how much I pulled. Page Murry came to see if she could pull. Helen and Virgil went to Mr. Little's.

Tuesday, November 30, 1937—I pulled cotton again, and I forgot the amount that I pulled. Page came to see if we would tend to their things.

Wednesday, December 1, 1937—We pulled cotton again. We finished the bale so Mr. Rainey could carry it off. I went and cut off the windmill. I received a letter from Elese.

Thursday, December 2, 1937—It was damp. I went to town with Mr. and Mrs. Rainey. Got the material for Mildred's elephant. Had a grand time.

Friday, December 3, 1937—Started on Mildred's elephant. Mother and Dady fixed the gatepost over our place and got some wood.

Saturday, December 4, 1937—Washed my hair and got ready to go to town. I saw Raymond Milliarn in town and talked to him a long time.

Sunday, December 5, 1937—Up early and ready to go to church at Big Spring with Mr. and Mrs. Rainey. We ate dinner with Mr. Rainey, Mother, and Dady.

Monday, December 6, 1937—I pulled bales again for Mr. Rainey. I didn't pull very much, but I made over a dollar.

Tuesday, December 7, 1937—I pulled cotton again. It sure was a pretty day.

Wednesday, December 8, 1937—Turned cold, and we didn't pull any cotton because it was so cold. Mother went to town with Mr. and Mrs. Rainey.

Thursday, December 9, 1937—It was cold again. So I didn't go to pull bales.

Friday, December 10, 1937—Dady and I went to town with Mr. and Mrs. Rainey. I bought Mary Jon a present.

Saturday, December 11, 1937—Stayed at home all morning and then went after wood over at Helen and Virgil's.

Sunday, December 12, 1937—Went to Sunday school with Page, and then went home with her for dinner. Then went to the Hamlins'. Page and I went to church that night. I went with a Lewis boy.

Monday, December 13, 1937—Pulled bales all day.

Tuesday, December 14, 1937—It was cold and icy all over. I did needlework.

Wednesday, December 15, 1937—I stayed in and did needlework, and I went to town with Mr. Rainey, Dady, and Virgil. I mailed Mary Jon a Christmas package.

Thursday, December 16, 1937—Cooked a fruitcake, and when I finished I went to Page's, but she was not at home. She had gone to Juanita Hamlin's in town to spend the night.

Friday, December 17, 1937—Mother and I went over to Helen's to spend the day, and Dady went to town to see about a place.

Saturday, December 18, 1937—Mother, Dady, and I went to town. We carried our washing to do, and we bought our Christmas.

Sunday, December 19, 1937—Went to Sunday school with Page and Juanita. Then we went to town to watch Gay Hill broadcast over the radio. Had a grand time. Went to sing that night at Layfield's.

Monday, December 20, 1937—I felt bad so I stayed in bed awhile and then did handwork some in the afternoon.

Tuesday, December 21, 1937—It was misty some. I went over to Page's in the afternoon and did some needlework.

Wednesday, December 22, 1937— Again, I went over to Page's in the afternoon and did some needlework.

Thursday, December 23, 1937—Went to town, then came home and ate supper, then went to the Christmas tree with Page. I saw C ... Lockhart over there and was introduced to him.

Friday, December 24, 1937—Went to the mailbox to meet the mail carrier. Then pulled bales in the afternoon. I pulled 174. That is good for me.

Saturday, December 25, 1937—Cleaned up the house and pulled some bales in the afternoon. Cooked some that night for Christmas.

Sunday, December 26, 1937—Up early and cooked some more. Helen and Virgil came over for Christmas. We had a lot to eat. Went to Ray Keel's party. Fell off the back of the porch.

Monday, December 27, 1937—After dinner I went to Page's and then went to Juanita's to spend the afternoon. Pulled some cotton, and it started raining. I pulled 80 pounds.

Tuesday, December 28, 1937—Sat around because it was too wet to pull cotton. I did some handwork.

Wednesday, December 29, 1937—I went to town with Dady to peddle the butter. Had a nice ride over the muddy road.

Thursday, December 30, 1937—I did some more handwork today. I tried to finish my laundry bag, but I could not get it done.

Friday, December 31, 1937—We rode around and hunted for a house to live in. We went to the Hamlins'.

January 1, 1938–December 31, 1938

Saturday, January 1, 1938—I went to town with Dady to take the stuff off. Mother and I went up to the Murrys' to listen to the radio. Juanita was there.

Thursday, January 6, 1938—It faired off. Page and Mrs. Murry came down. We went down to Elbert and stayed awhile. We watched them ride two of the horses.

Friday, January 7, 1938—Up early. Dady and I went to town. We found out that we could get the Oliver house. Bought some stuff to clean it with.

Saturday, January 8, 1938—Up early and we all went over to the house to clean up some. Then late in the afternoon we went over to Helen's after wood.

Sunday, January 9, 1938—Went to Sunday school with Page. Then Page came home with me for dinner. Helen and Virgil was there too. Rode around some. Page, Elbert, and I went to church Sunday night.

Monday, January 10, 1938—Dady went to town after papers. We would own the room until Dady came home when we started papering.

Tuesday, January 11, 1938—Up early so we could get started papering. We finished that room and started on the other one. Boy, I was sure tired when night came.

Wednesday, January 12, 1938—Finished papering and then scrubbed all the house and put one of the rugs down. Went over to Helen's to see if they could help us move.

Thursday, January 13, 1938—Packed up and moved all our household goods that day. I sure was tired when night came. We had a lot to do after dark.

Friday, January 14, 1938—Was finished moving. We also moved our cows and chickens. Rested when night came. I was sure tired and ready to hit the bed.

Saturday, January 15, 1938—Up real early and got ready to go to town with Dady. It was late when we got back. I was so tired.

Sunday, January 16, 1938—Page came by after me to go to Sunday school. I was so tired, I didn't want to go. Stayed at home until dinner when we went to Helen's.

Monday, January 17, 1938—Dady and I hauled some feed. Then I went to Murry's after the label. Worked around the house trying to get things straightened up more.

Tuesday, January 18, 1938—Dady went to Winters, and I started pulling bales for Ted Fields. I pulled 229.

Wednesday, January 19, 1938—Up early and pulled bales until about one, and then it rained some. I fixed the fence and did some other work, too.

Thursday, January 20, 1938—Up early to pull bales until late in the afternoon. I worked some in the yard.

Friday, January 21, 1938—We went to town, and it rained nearly all the way to town. I was sure glad to get back from town.

Saturday, January 22, 1938—It rained all day. I worked around in the house. Page came by to tell me that she was going to Littlefield for a visit with her sister.

Sunday, January 23, 1938—Went over to Helen's for dinner. Came home kinda early, and I was tired so I went to bed early.

Monday, January 24, 1938—Helped Dady haul some wood and do odd stuff around the house.

Tuesday, January 25, 1938—Up early so we could haul feed. We hauled 500 bundles today. I was sure tired when night came.

Wednesday, January 26, 1938—Dady and PJ hauled one load of feed, then quit and started pulling bales. I pulled right close to 200. Real good for scattering cotton.

Thursday, January 27, 1938—Pulled bales all day and was kinda tired when night came. I went to bed real early.

Friday, January 28, 1938—Went to town with Mother and Dady. I bought my window curtains from Montgomery Ward in town. We did a big washing.

Saturday, January 29, 1938—Up early so we could finish hauling feed. We got through about four. Then I helped clean up and make up some Jell-O for dinner Sunday.

Sunday, January 30, 1938—It was sure cold. Stayed at home all day. I tried to keep warm.

Monday, January 31, 1938—Helen came over to spend the day. Was cold in the morning, but I pulled bales in the afternoon.

Tuesday, February 1, 1938—Up early so we could get an early start pulling bales. I pulled 287. I went to the mailbox in the late afternoon.

Wednesday, February 2, 1938—Pulled bales of cotton. My, I was so tired, and I was sure glad when all the bales were out.

Thursday, February 3, 1938—Pulled bales again. Late in the afternoon I went to the mailbox. Boy! I was so tired.

Friday, February 4, 1938—Pulled bales again. I went to the store and bought bananas and got the mail.

Saturday, February 5, 1938—We went to Helen's, and then we went to town. Bought our new gasoline iron. I was sure proud of it. Charles came after me to go to the singing.

Sunday, February 6, 1938—Cooked dinner. Then we went to Helen and Virgil's. Then we went to the Puckett's after greens. Stopped at Sowell's to visit for a while.

Monday, February 7, 1938—Pulled bales for Ted Fields. I pulled 198. Mr. Oliver came after us to pull bales for him.

Tuesday, February 8, 1938—We pulled bales for Mr. Sid Oliver. I pulled 200. It was so thin, and I walked a lot. I was so tired.

Wednesday, February 9, 1938—Pulled bales again for Mr. Oliver. I was so tired when night came.

Thursday, February 10, 1938—I helped Dady put in two windows. I painted the woodwork for the south room. Then I went to the store after curtains.

Friday, February 11, 1938—Helped Dady and Mother off to town. Cooked dinner for Helen and Virgil. Handwork for chair cushions. Worked around the house cleaning it up.

Saturday, February 12, 1938—Cleaned the house. Ironed some. Then went to the store after the mail. Page came to see me. She wanted me to go home with her, but I didn't.

Sunday, February 13, 1938—Went to Sunday school with Page. Then went home with her for dinner. Tried to go on top of the house. Went to Dalton's house and played in cottonseed. Went to church services with Page and Elbert. Boy, we had fun.

Monday, February 14, 1938—Helped do up the work and then went to the mailbox. Did handwork on a pillow part of the day. Also made some candy. Helen and Virgil went to Mr. Little's.

> Newspaper article: Miss Margaret Jackson, teacher of the senior Sunday school class, entertained her pupils with a Valentine party in her home at the teacherage Saturday night. Served to the following ...Mr. and Mrs. Virgil ... Miss Lennis Phipps ... Page Murray ... Sybil Harrison ... Lena Mansfield ... Charles Mundant ... John Brasher.

Tuesday, February 15, 1938—Stayed in bed part of the time. Did needlework. Then read awhile.

Wednesday, February 16, 1938—The same old thing. It rained all day. I also did some handwork. I worked on my pot lifters. I finished them today.

Thursday, February 17, 1938—Worked around the house. Then I got out and got some wood. I started some handwork on one of my towels.

Friday, February 18, 1938—Helped Dady get off to town. Then the rest of the day I did handwork. Helen and Virgil came in from Mr. Little's. They spent the night with us.

Saturday, February 19, 1938—Went to Helen and Virgil's. Came back. Cleaned up the house. Then went over to Page's. Page came home with me. We spent a night that will always be a memory.

Sunday, February 20, 1938—Dady carried Page and I over to the house. We went to Sunday school. Page came home with me for dinner. Late that evening I went home with her to stay all night.

Newspaper article: Miss Lennis Phipps and Charles of this community attended Center Point church services.

Monday, February 21, 1938—We had planned to visit school, but snow was all over the ground, and we didn't. I stayed over at Page's until late. We went over to Daltina's to get something to read.

Tuesday, February 22, 1938—Made a lot of ice cream. Then went to the mailbox in all of this slop. I like to have fallen down two or three times.

Wednesday, February 23, 1938—We went to town. I bought me a bunch of junk. We did our washing. And boy was I tired when night came.

Thursday, February 24, 1938—It rained nearly all day. I did handwork on my cup towel set.

Friday, February 25, 1938—Helped Mother and Dady get off to town. Did handwork and some work in the yard.

Saturday, February 26, 1938—Helped Dady put in the window. In the afternoon, we went over to Helen and Virgil's. I went with Page and Elizabeth to Mansfield's that night.

Sunday, February 27, 1938—Got ready to go to Sunday school with Page and Elbert. Had lots of fun. We went to Clanton for the afternoon.

Monday, February 28, 1938—Mother and I went to Mr. Sewell's to spend the day. I received a letter from Elese through the mail.

Tuesday, March 1, 1938—Went to the mailbox. Then went over to Page's. We had lots of fun. Stopped by Edna's and stayed awhile.

Wednesday, March 2, 1938—Up real early and went to Helen's to spend the day. I helped Mother do the ironing. Got the check from Uncle Dink.

Thursday, March 3, 1938—Helen came and spent the day. I helped Dady on the cow lot. Then we went after the cow at Buck Olinair's.

Friday, March 4, 1938—Helped Mother and Dad off to town. Went up to Hammer. Washed some. Finished my cup towel set and did first one thing and then another. I mopped.

Saturday, March 5, 1938—Cleaned up the house and washed my head. Took a bath. Then went to the mailbox. Started over to Page's and met her in the car, so I went to the store with her.

Sunday, March 6, 1938—Went to Sunday school. Then went to Bliss for dinner. B. E., Edward, and Charles came over. We really got mad. Charles skinned up my hand. Knocked into the bumper. We had lots of fun.

Monday, March 7, 1938—Helped do up the work. Then went to Hanner's after some magazines to read. I read until late that night.

Tuesday, March 8, 1938—It rained nearly all day. I finished reading one magazine and carried it home.

Wednesday, March 9, 1938—Went to Helen's to spend the day. I took cold, and boy, did I really feel bad. Went to bed when I came home.

Thursday, March 10, 1938—I helped Mother do the churning. Then I did some handwork on my scarf.

Friday, March 11, 1938—Helped Mother and Dady get off to town. Then went to Hanner's and stayed awhile. Page and I went to visit Juanita Hamlin for the afternoon.

Saturday, March 12, 1938—I went to town with Page. We walked all over town. We saw Francis and Elbert. There was going to be a party Saturday night, but I couldn't go.

Sunday, March 13, 1938—Mother and Dady and I went to Center Point to church. Went home with Mr. and Mrs. Daniels. Page and a bunch came after me, but I couldn't go. Then Elbert came but didn't go.

Monday, March 14, 1938—Dady went to town. Mother and I went over to Helen's to spend the day. I had to watch the sheep.

Tuesday, March 15, 1938—Helped clean up. We ironed some. Then Mother went to Mrs. Scott's to spend the afternoon. I pieced my quilts.

Wednesday, March 16, 1938—Helped Mother move bed in the back room. Hanner came and stayed awhile. Then Helen came also.

Thursday, March 17, 1938—I helped churn. Then went to the mailbox. I saw Lorena Procter and talked to her for a while.

Friday, March 18, 1938—Mother and Dady went to town. I went to Helen's to spend the day, and I also watched the sheep.

Saturday, March 19, 1938—I had to go back to Helen's because Mother and Dad went back to town after the cow. Came home real early and mopped.

Sunday, March 20, 1938—Went to Sunday school with Page. Then went home with her for dinner. We sure had a good time. We stopped at Dalton. Wayne and Billie Mack was at home.

Monday, March 21, 1938—Helped do up the work. Helen came over and sewed some handwork on her scarf. Let me tell you, I will sure be glad when it is finished.

Tuesday, March 22, 1938—Page came over and stayed awhile. I walked home with her. I also made some soup for supper.

Wednesday, March 23, 1938—Up early and went over to Helen's to watch the sheep. I did handwork on Helen's scarf. We had a real good time.

Thursday, March 24, 1938—Helped Mother and Dady churn. Then went over to Helen's about ten to watch the sheep. I worked again on Helen's scarf.

Friday, March 25, 1938—Went to town with Mother and Dady. I bought my dress, shoes, and hat at Burr's. Saw Georgie, Nell, and Pauline Clanton in town.

Saturday, March 26, 1938—Cleaned up all the house and cooked a cake. I thought maybe a bunch of kids would come, but it rained all Saturday. And I was sure they wouldn't come.

Sunday, March 27, 1938—It rained again. I stayed at home all day. And I tried to read to entertain myself but couldn't.

Monday, March 28, 1938—Up doing the same old thing. Went to the mailbox. We got lots of mail. I got a letter from Peanuts (Oma Lee)!

Tuesday, March 29, 1938—Mother and Dady and Helen went to town. I went over to Helen's to watch the sheep. Mother washed in town.

Wednesday, March 30, 1938—Went to Page's to spend the day. Her sister from Littlefield was there. Saw Elbert. Then went over to Helen's late and helped her with the cows.

Thursday, March 31, 1938—Went over to Helen's to spend the day. Came home at dinner. After some lard. I stayed until after we penned the cows about sundown.

Friday, April 1, 1938—Helped clean up the house. Then went over to Helen's. Helen made some cookies. They were sure good.

Saturday, April 2, 1938—Cleaned up the house. Mopped all the rooms. Then about three o'clock we went over to Helen's, and I brought her cup towels to hem. Also baked a cake.

Sunday, April 3, 1938—Went to Sunday school with Page. Then Page and Sybil came home with me. I drove Page's car home. We had lots of fun.

Monday, April 4, 1938—Helen came over to sew on my dress. Mother and Dady went down to Baker's. Also the two Mrs. Hamlins came.

Tuesday, April 5, 1938—Mother and Dady went to town. Helen and I went to the club at Mrs. Scott's. Hanner brought us home, and then we went over to see Helen for a while.

Wednesday, April 5, 1938—Went over to Helen's to see if she would come and sew. A cloud was coming up, so we went over to my house. Boy! It was really cold.

Thursday, April 7, 1938—It sure was cold. I sat by the fire and tried to keep warm. I did some handwork, too. I wanted to make ice cream, but the snow was dirty.

Friday, April 8, 1938—It was too cold for Mother and Dady to go to town. We went after wood in the afternoon. I sure did get cold.

Saturday, April 9, 1938—Mother and Dady went to town. I mopped and cleaned up. And I went over to Helen's to get my hair cut. She also set it.

Monday, April 11, 1938—Worked around and cleaned up. I also read some and tried to go to sleep but couldn't for the wind.

Tuesday, April 12, 1938—I worked around and went up to Hanner's to help for the musical coming the next night.

Wednesday, April 13, 1938—We went to Helen's to get her to come and sew. Page and Mrs. Murry came over. I went to Hanner's—a musical that night. Had a real good time.

Thursday, April 14, 1938—Up early and went over to Helen's to spend the day. I did handwork on my pillows. Rain came up after dinner.

Friday, April 15, 1938—Mother and Dad went to town. I went over to Helen's for her to come over here. She didn't come until after dinner.

Saturday, April 16, 1938—Went to Sybil's to see if she could spend the night with me. Then I went over to town with Dady after the cows were fed.

Sunday, April 17, 1938—Went to Sunday school with Ted and Hanner. Thelma went to the Easter egg hunt with Knop A. Haynes. Wore my new dress. Had a real good time.

Monday, April 18, 1938—Went over to Helen's to spend the day. Helped watch the sheep.

Tuesday, April 19, 1938—Went to Hanner's club. Had a real nice time. Helped Hanner serve cake and cocoa. Page was there.

Wednesday, April 20, 1938—Went over to Helen's. After we got home, we ironed. We also went to see Mrs. Blythe. I also went over to the musical at Roy Keel's. Had a good time.

Thursday, April 21, 1938—Went over to Helen's to spend the day. I did needlework on my pillow and finally finished it. I did some handwork for Helen, also.

Friday, April 22, 1938—Mother and Dady went to town, and Hamby came down to sew some. We really had a good time.

Saturday, April 23, 1938—Went over to the Knapps' to spend the night. Ed and R. E. came over to the Knapps'. We really had a good time.

Sunday, April 24, 1938—Went to Sunday school with Ed. Then went to the ball game, and Ed, Joe Ella, Francis, and R. E. came home with me. Went with "Pinky"!

Monday, April 25, 1938—Went over to Helen's to spend the day. Came home real early and read some of my magazine that I got from Francis.

Tuesday, April 26, 1938—Cleaned up and helped Mother and Dad get off to town. Page came over to spend the day. Had a real good time. Dady bought me a Bible for my birthday.

Wednesday, April 27, 1938—Helped clean up and then went over to Helen's about dinner. She came back with me to sew some. I read some after I went to bed.

Thursday, April 28, 1938—Went over to Helen's to spend the day. Helped her wash and then went to clean up the house. Today was my birthday. I am sure getting old.

Friday, April 29, 1938—Helped Mother and Dady get off to town. They cleaned up real good. Then read some. Late in the afternoon went up to Hanner's. Then we went to the store. Saw L. B.

Saturday, April 30, 1938—Worked around. Then went to Helen's to get my hair set. I went with L. B. friends that night. We went to the wiener roast and then to Baker's. Had lots of fun with Pinky Fields.

Sunday, May 1, 1938—Roy Keel came after me. Went to Sunday school with Sybil, R. E., Francis, Ed, and Joe Ellen came home with me for dinner. We made some pictures that afternoon. Went with Sybil, Curtis, and Hollis to church (we were supposed to anyway). Had a good time.

Monday, May 2, 1938—Went over to Helen's to stay while she went to Mrs. Blyers, and I stayed there. Came home real early and brought the cows home.

Tuesday, May 3, 1938—Helen, Mother, and Dady got off to town. Then cleaned the house and went to the mailbox. A really bad cloud came up. Peg and Mrs. Murry came. Helen came too.

Wednesday, May 4, 1938—Went over to Helen's to see if she wanted to sew some. She couldn't come until after dinner, so I came on home. Went back after the cows in the afternoon.

Thursday, May 5, 1938—Helped with part of the churning. Then went over to Helen's. Dady took the truck and hauled some rock. I went over there and came back in the truck.

Friday, May 6, 1938—Went up to the Harris' about 10:00 a.m., and she was going to the mailbox so went with her to get our mail.

Saturday, May 7, 1938—Helped do the work. Then we washed some. Mrs. Blythe came and wanted me to come to the musical at her house. I got to go. Came back with Curtis Hood.

Sunday, May 8, 1938—Dady carried me to Sybil to go to church, so I went. Went home with Francis and Joe Ella. We went to the ball game at Vincent. I went with Merle Hayney.

Monday, May 9, 1938—Helped with the churning. Helen came over to sew, and I had to go back with her to get the cows.

Tuesday, May 10, 1938—Helped Mother and Dady get off to town, and Helen came over to sew. She spent the day. I went and got the cows out of the pasture.

Wednesday, May 11, 1938—Went to the store real early to get some thread. Then in the interim went to Page's, and she brought me home when she went to the way.

Thursday, May 12, 1938—Helped with the work so Dad could help Virgil with the garden fence. They finally got it up after so long a time.

Friday, May 13, 1938—Helped clean up and bake some pies. Then went to the store. Helen came over to sew some in the afternoon.

Saturday, May 14, 1938—I had to iron. Boy was it hot. Joe Ella, Eddy, Francis, R. G., and Charles came over. I was supposed to go to Helen's but went to the party at Eding in Center Point. Oh, that Charles!

Sunday, May 15, 1938—Went to Sunday school with Sybil. She came home with me for dinner. I drove their car. Boy, we really had fun today.

Monday, May 16, 1938—Helped churn. Then went over to Helen's. She had to iron. I stayed for dinner. Then I came home to get them, so we could select the spot for our house.

Tuesday, May 17, 1938—I mopped and cleaned up real good. Then went to the club with Hanner, Mr. Coleman, and Keuka. Had a real nice time.

Wednesday, May 18, 1938—Went over to Helen's, and she came back with me to sew. Virgil came and ate dinner with us. A real bad cloud came up.

Thursday, May 19, 1938—Helped visit. Worked later that afternoon for events over to Sybil. We had more fun than a barrel of monkeys. Ha-ha.

Friday, May 20, 1938—Cleaned up the house. Then went to Hanner's to stay for a while. Made some ice cream. Had more fun.

Saturday, May 21, 1938—Helped vaccinate the cows. Then cleaned up and went to Sybil's to spend the night. We sure had lots of fun. We went to sleep about 1:30 a.m.

Sunday, May 22, 1938—We went to Sunday school and then ate dinner. Went to a ball game. Had a lot of fun and went to singing.

Monday, May 23, 1938—Helen came over to sew. I went to the mailbox. Had lots of fun. This is what we always have. What a team!

Tuesday, May 24, 1938—Tried to sleep some but couldn't because it was so hot. Helen came back to sew.

Wednesday, May 25, 1938—Tried to sleep but could not. Went to Sybil's to get her to stay all night with me so we could go to the play. Boy! We really had a time and enjoyed it.

Thursday, May 26, 1938—Carried Sybil home. Then came back and worked around the house at my usual work.

Friday, May 27, 1938—Mother and Dady went to town. Then I went over to Helen's real late. Sure came up an awful storm. Blew the house about ten feet.

Saturday, May 28, 1938—Cleaned up. Went to Sybil's and a party at Center Point. Then to town. Had two flats in Charles's car.

Sunday, May 29, 1938—Went to Sunday school. Then went to the park in town with Charles.

Monday, May 30, 1938—Back at the same old job. Boy, I was really tired when night came. I finally went to sleep a little in the afternoon. Boy was I glad.

Tuesday, May 31, 1938—Cleaned house really good. Then went to the store after the mail. I saw Pauline. Boy, she sure is funny.

Wednesday, June 1, 1938—Helped wash and iron some. Went after the cows.

Thursday, June 2, 1938—Went over to Helen's and stayed all day. Helped her work in the garden and some in the yard.

Friday, June 3, 1938—Linda came over and spent the day with me. We went to the store about 4:00 p.m. Then she went after the cows with me later.

Saturday, June 4, 1938—Went to Helen's, then home. Washed and ironed and cooked a cake for Sunday. Went after the cows late.

Sunday, June 5, 1938—Went to Sunday service with Sybil. She came home with me for dinner. I had a grand time. Pete Reed sure gave us a good scare. Boy, I say!

Monday, June 6, 1938—Back at the same job. Went over to Helen's and stayed awhile. Came home after dinner.

Tuesday, June 7, 1938—Mother and Dady went to town. Went over to Helen's after the cows. Also made two trips to the store, one after the mail and another one with Helen.

Wednesday, June 8, 1938—Helen came over to sew. Boy, it came up a really bad cloud. Was I scared.

Thursday, June 9, 1938—Went to Helen's to see about the sheep. Came home just as soon as dinner was over. I finally got to sleep some.

Friday, June 10, 1938—Mother and Dady went to town. I stayed by myself. I mopped and cleaned up.

Saturday, June 11, 1938—Mother and Dady went back to town. It came up a real storm. I still was scared. Went to the pasture after the cows and went to Hannah's to stay awhile.

Sunday, June 12, 1938—Cleaned up and went over to Helen's to watch the sheep.

Monday, June 13, 1938—Went over to Helen's and stayed awhile. Then came home. Went to the mailbox. Saw L. B. Fields.

Tuesday, June 14, 1938—Cleaned up. Then went over to Helen's to watch the sheep.

Wednesday, June 15, 1938—Worked all day long, ironed some and cleaned house. Went to the mailbox.

Thursday, June 16, 1938—Went to Linda's after my patterns. Then went to Helen's and stayed awhile. Tried to sleep but couldn't.

Friday, June 17, 1938—I did some work around here. Then went over to the place to see about things. Wanted to go to the mailbox but could not go.

Saturday, June 18, 1938—Cleaned real good and cooked a cake. Went to Vealmoor that night. Truman made a date with me for Sunday night. We had fun.

Sunday, June 19, 1938—Went to Sunday school with Sybil. Went home with her for dinner. Clifton and Truman came, so we went after Francis, Joe, and Sybil. We had more fun cutting up.

Monday, June 20, 1938—Went to town with Dady and went over to Helen's and stayed awhile. Watered the sheep. Sure had fun.

Tuesday, June 21, 1938—Cleaned up and went to Hanner's and stayed awhile. Then came home. Went to the mailbox. They brought out our lumber for our house. Boy was I glad.

Wednesday, June 22, 1938—Went to see Sybil, and we went over to see their place. We went to a cakewalk. We had a grand time.

Thursday, June 23, 1938—Went over to Helen's and came home real early and tried to sleep, but I couldn't. I went to the mailbox.

Friday, June 24, 1938—The same old thing. It came up a cloud toward night, and boy was I scared.

Saturday, June 25, 1938—Wanted to go to town with Dady but couldn't because I had so much work to do.

Sunday, June 26, 1938—It rained so I slept all day. Boy was I glad it rained so I could sleep. I was just tickled pink.

Monday, June 27, 1938—Boy, the same old thing. I sure hit high places. Let me tell you, I was sure glad when night came. Sybil came over here.

Tuesday, June 28, 1938—Boy! We made ice cream just as soon as the old hens laid. It sure was good. Sybil stayed all day with me. Ha, ha, ha.

Wednesday, June 29, 1938—Went over to Helen's and watched the sheep. They wouldn't know just what to do if Lennis was there.

Thursday, June 30, 1938—Went to the store after mail. Then went over to see Helen.

Friday, July 1, 1938—Went to Helen's real early, and lo and behold if Francis, Sybil, and Joe Ella didn't come. Made ice cream. Went to the store and had more fun than a barrel of monkeys.

Saturday, July 2, 1938—Cleaned up real good. Washed my hair and worked around here, not doing anything that I could get out of.

Sunday, July 3, 1938—Broke the lock on the church door. Went to the Knapps' for dinner. Drove around in the pasture in our slips. Saw R. E. come back to the house. We got ready and went to Richland. Came back by the store, and Pauline wanted to go to Clayton Flat, so we went. L. B. Fields, Jim Mundom, and Wayne Brown followed us. We really had fun.

Clifton and Paul met us so we went to town. Clifton and Paul were coming back for us to go to Vealmoor if they could get the car. Sybil, Francis, and Joe Ellen ran off, so I got to go too.

Monday, July 4, 1938—Stayed at home. Was supposed to go to the rodeo if Clifton came, but he didn't make the ride.

Tuesday, July 5, 1938—Mother and Dady went to town. Cleaned up what I could.

Wednesday, July 6, 1938—Went over to Helen's. Boy, we really had fun. Had ice cream for dinner.

Thursday, July 7, 1938—Stayed at home and did not do anything that I could account for.

Friday, July 8, 1938—Sybil, Joe Ella, and Francis came over and spent the day. We made ice cream. Boy, we really had fun. Saw Elbert Dalton.

Saturday, July 9, 1938—Stayed in bed all day. Boy, I was really sick. I finally caught up with my sleep.

Sunday, July 10, 1938—Didn't go to Sunday school with Sybil because I felt bad. Clifton, Sybil, R. E., Francis, and Paul came after me. We went to town. Had more fun.

Monday, July 11, 1938—We started moving some in the afternoon, and boy was I tired when night came.

Tuesday, July 12, 1938—Mother and Dady went to town. I tried to sleep but couldn't for the flies.

Wednesday, July 13, 1938—Cleaned up our new house and moved some. Boy, I was really tired when night came. I was ready to go to slumberland.

Thursday, July 14, 1938—I watched the sheep. That is always my job. Straightened up some or tried to. Didn't make much of an out of it.

Friday, July 15, 1938—Back at the same old job—sheep herding. Cleaned up around some more. Tried to clean up the yard.

Saturday, July 16, 1938—Cleaned up. Then went with Paul to a rodeo in Ackerly to dance. Got more fun out of two little boys about cold drinks.

Sunday, July 17, 1938—Went to Sunday school with Jimmy and Opal. Francis came home with me for dinner. We walked around in the afternoon. Saw a crazy man. Saw Elbert and ate supper with all.

Monday, July 18, 1938—Monday was going to help move some more, but it rained so we couldn't.

Tuesday, July 19, 1938—Stayed at home and made some ice cream. Had to do all the milking by myself.

Wednesday, July 20, 1938—Tried to finish moving but it rained, so I got to sleep.

Thursday, July 21, 1938—Watched the sheep and was going to get some moving stuff. We got it loaded, and it came a real hard rain. We just got soaked.

Friday, July 22, 1938—More rain but looked like it would fair off.

Saturday, July 23, 1938—Rained some more. Ironed most of the day. Boy, really had an ironing.

Sunday, July 24, 1938—I slept some. Clifton and Paul came. It was too muddy to go anywhere. We went to Helen's to make ice cream. We sure had fun.

Monday, July 25, 1938—Tried to sleep but couldn't and then I ironed some. Read awhile. Then I helped milk.

Tuesday July 26, 1938—Watched the sheep. Then slept some and had to do all the milking by myself. Boy, I was sure tired when I got ready for the bed. Joe Ella came over.

Wednesday, July 27, 1938—Went to Knapps' and spent the day. Boy, we sure had fun. They walked part of the way home with me. I really had fun. I killed a little snake with seven rattlers.

Thursday, July 28, 1938—Back at the same old job. Went over to Page's after the eggs.

Friday, July 29, 1938—Stayed at home and made ice cream. It sure was good. Tried to sleep but couldn't.

Saturday, July 30, 1938—Washed my hair. Got it set. I was lonely for Sybil, but she would not come home.

Sunday, July 31, 1938—Went to Sunday school with Neil. John Brasher rode home with us. I slept a lot in the afternoon.

Monday, August 1, 1938—Stayed at home and watched the sheep. Cleaned up in the afternoon.

Tuesday, August 2, 1938—Page came over and spent the day. Helen came and ate dinner with us. Chased all the cows. Had more fun. Curtis came after me.

Wednesday, August 3, 1938—Helped Helen can beans. I never saw so many beans.

Thursday, August 4, 1938—Cleaned up and watched the sheep. Tried to sleep but here came Sybil and Arlene, and they stayed awhile.

Friday, August 5, 1938—Sybil and Arlene came over and stayed awhile. Then they came back that night. We sure had a lot of fun. We went to Ruby's and stayed awhile.

Saturday, August 6, 1938—Lucille, Cawk PA, and W. Roe came, and I went with them. Had more fun than a barrel of monkeys. Would have had if they had been in a barrel.

Sunday, August 7, 1938—Went to Sybil's for the day. Paul and Clifton came. We went to Gail's after some horses. I fell on the floor. Shot a gun. Sure had a lot of fun.

Monday, August 8, 1938—Went to Sybil's and she went with me after the eggs over at Page's. Sure had a lot of fun.

Tuesday, August 9, 1938—I had to do the milking, as usual. Tried to make some ice cream but couldn't. Made a failure of it.

Wednesday, August 10, 1938—Lucille, Cawk, and W. Roe came but couldn't go. Sybil went with A. W. I know they had more fun, don't you?

Thursday, August 11, 1938—It rained. P. E. wanted to go to Sybil's but couldn't go until after dinner. She didn't come until after 4:00 p.m.

Friday, August 12, 1938—Stayed at home and Sybil did not come.

Saturday, August 13, 1938—Sybil over and stayed all night. Saw a show at the called *Utah Grail*. Had trouble with the car. It was twelve.

Sunday, August 14, 1938—Went to church at Center Point. Sybil came home with me for dinner. Weldon and Uncle George came. Clifton and Marie Clayton came, too, so we all went riding. Went to Vealmoor.

Monday, August 15, 1938—Stayed at home and tried to sleep but couldn't.

Tuesday, August 16, 1938—Laid off Ruby's pillow slips. Then went to Sybil's after noon. Francis and Joe Ella came over here. They came over to Sybil's and stayed awhile.

Wednesday, August 17, 1938—Tried to sleep some. After dinner, I ironed some.

Thursday, August 18, 1938—I did handwork on Ruby's pillowcase.

Friday, August 19, 1938—Sybil came over to spend the day. We made ice cream. It sure was good. I worked on my pillow slips and helped Sybil start hers.

Saturday, August 20, 1938—Had to do all the work because Mother was sick. I ironed some, and boy was I tired when the night came.

Sunday, August 21, 1938—Went to Sunday school with Sybil. Stayed all day over there. Went to a baptism with them. Went to church with Ruby that night,

Monday, August 22, 1938—Finished Ruby's pillow slips. Then read some and tried to go to sleep.

Tuesday, August 23, 1938—Stayed at home all day by myself and went to the mailbox.

Wednesday, August 24, 1938—Cleaned up real good and ironed some and slept some and read some stories.

Thursday, August 25, 1938—Went to Sybil's to spend the day. She had to wash, and I helped her do the washing.

Friday, August 26, 1938—Stayed at home all day by myself. I worked on my vanity set. Helen came over in the afternoon.

Saturday, August 27, 1938—Ironed some and cleaned up the house real good, mopped, cooked two pies, and helped milk.

Sunday, August 28, 1938—Sybil came over for dinner. She and I went to the Edens' for dinner. Jeff, Shorty, and Penny ran a race with them. Sybil, Conley, Elbert, plus two went riding after church. Ate watermelon.

Monday, August 29, 1938—I slept some.

Tuesday, August 30, 1938—Sybil came over in the afternoon, and we made some ice cream. We sure had a good time.

Wednesday, August 31, 1938—Worked around the house.

Thursday, September 1, 1938—Helped milk and worked around the house. Went to the store and Sybil, Morrene, Don, Neil, Odell, Pauline, and Dan went with me. Went after eggs.

Friday, September 2, 1938—Charles came. Penny and Sybil in the afternoon. Wanted her to come home with me, but she couldn't come.

Saturday, September 3, 1938—Cleaned house and washed the buckets. Then ironed some and read and slept.

Sunday, September 4, 1938—Started to Sunday school, but Sybil wanted me to go to the park where we had a real good time.

Monday, September 5, 1938—Did handwork. Worked on vanity set, read some, and slept some.

Tuesday, September 6, 1938—Stayed at home by myself. Worked on my vanity set some.

Wednesday, September 7, 1938—Helped wash the buckets and ironed some too. Ruby gave me my scarf.

Thursday, September 8, 1938—Worked some on my scarf and slept some.

Friday, September 9, 1938—Went to Ruby's after a bucket of water, so she wanted me to stay for dinner. Which I did. *Writing different!*

Saturday, September 10, 1938—Cleaned up the house real good. Baked a cake and ironed some.

Sunday, September 11, 1938—Stayed home and cooked dinner. Mr. and Mrs. Eden came over for dinner. We went to Moore to a singing. Morris Clanton came over.

Monday, September 12, 1938—Worked on my scarf. Went with Mother after the eggs. Saw Sybil Harrison.

Tuesday, September 13, 1938—I went to the mailbox. Ate dinner with Ruby. Mother bought Sybil's pillow.

Wednesday, September 14, 1938—Went with W. O., Carager. Sybil teased me. She only got the best of me several times but went on every unknown road in the county. Next went through the bump gate and parked in the pasture. Sybil and Penny had to get out ...

Thursday, September 15, 1938—Helen came up to the house to get the eggs.

Friday, September 16, 1938—Went to the mailbox. Thought Page and Juanita were coming, but they did not come.

Saturday, September 17, 1938—Went to Sybil's house. She came home with me and stayed all night. We drove down through Clayton Flat in our old Model T. Saw Paul, liked to run into us ...

Sunday, September 18, 1938—Went to Sunday school with Neil. Went to Sybil's for dinner. Rode horses and went to a ball game. Dub came, but I was with L. B. So he went with Sybil.

Monday, September 19, 1938—Stayed at home all morning. Then went with Mother after eggs. Saw Sybil. We had more news.

Tuesday, September 20, 1938—Stayed at home, washed my hair, and Helen set it. Pressed my dress so I could wear it to school.

Wednesday, September 21, 1938—Left for school at sunup. Road to the store with Melvin Anderson. Met Margaret Collet. Had more fun. What do you think? Stayed all night with Nell E.

Thursday, September 22, 1938—Back to school again. Sybil and I went to town at noon and bought some things. Billie Max and I bought some candy when we got back to Luther.

Friday, September 23, 1938—Stayed at home by myself. I went to the mailbox. Handwork, slept some, too.

Saturday, September 24, 1938—Cleaned up the house. Went to the mailbox. Rode back with Odell and Clifton. Went to Sybil's to get my hair done. Penny Proctor, Lebert, and Page came over after me.

Sunday, September 25, 1938—Went to Sunday school and church. Then went to Sybil's for dinner. We sure had lots of fun, didn't we. Boy, I say we did.

Monday, September 26, 1938—I read some. Then worked on Sybil's pillow. We sure had lots of fun around here.

Tuesday, September 27, 1938—I cleaned up. Then mopped the floors and went to the mailbox. Then to Ruby's. We made some ice cream. It sure was good. Boy, I say.

Wednesday, September 28, 1938—Helped with the work. Then did handwork on my scarf.

Thursday, September 29, 1938—Tried to sleep some but couldn't. Boy, I say, I was sure tired when night came.

Friday, September 30, 1938—Made some ice cream. Got old "mully" from Tom and nearly blistered my hands. They were sure sore. Did the milking.

Saturday, October 1, 1938—Cleaned up and went to the mailbox after the paper. Started to Sybil's to get my hair set, but she was pulling bales, so Helen set it.

Sunday, October 2, 1938—Went to Sybil's to go to church, but she was sore about the wreck. So, she wouldn't go. Page and Elbert came, so we went to the show in town.

Monday, October 3, 1938—Fixed my sack. Then went to pull bales for Tom. I pulled 140. I was sure tired when night came.

Tuesday, October 4, 1938—Helped with the work. Then fixed my lunch and went to the field. Boy was I tired when night came.

Wednesday, October 5, 1938—Pulled some and we finished pulling for Tom. Boy, I was sure glad.

Thursday, October 6, 1938—Stayed at home. I ironed some and then went after the eggs.

Friday, October 7, 1938—I finished Mother's scarf. Then, I did the milking. Boy, I was sure tired when night came.

Saturday, October 8, 1938—Cleaned up the house. Washed my hair and got it set. Then went to Helen's. Page and Elbert came after me to go to Morgan's for a party.

Sunday, October 9, 1938—Up real early and went to Center Point to church, Then went to Edens' for dinner. Then to the singing at Moore. I went to church at night.

Monday, October 10, 1938—It rained just a light shower, just enough to keep from picking cotton.

Tuesday, October 11, 1938—Stayed around home. Went to the mailbox. Then read some. And tried to sleep but could not.

Wednesday, October 12, 1938—Went to pick cotton again, Boy was I tired when night came.

Thursday, October 13, 1938—Pulled (cotton) again, and boy, I sure did get a lot too. I made myself rich.

Friday, October 14, 1938—Cleaned up the house. Then went to pull bales. Quit real early and had to do the milking.

Saturday, October 15, 1938—Cleaned up the house. Then cooked a cake and fixed things because we were going to have company the next day.

Sunday, October 16, 1938—Went to Sunday school with Sybil. Then they all came over here for dinner. Had a grand time.

Monday, October 17, 1938—Finished pulling cotton for Tom. Boy was I glad. I pulled 301. I was sore and tired when night came.

Tuesday, October 18, 1938—Handwork on Mother's scarf. Then had to do the milking because Mother and Dady had gone to town.

Wednesday, October 19, 1938—Up early and went to town to look for a coat. I bought my coat at Montgomery Ward.

Thursday, October 20, 1938—The weather was so cold until I like to froze, but didn't you see.

Friday, October 21, 1938—Went to the mailbox. Then worked on Mother's pillow slips all that I could. Wanted to go to Carlsbad Caverns.

Saturday, October 22, 1938—Did some ironing and mopped some and cleaned up around the house.

Sunday, October 23, 1938—Went to Sunday school with Neil. Then stayed at home and read some in the afternoon. I really felt bad, you see.

Monday, October 24, 1938—Pulled more cotton today.

Tuesday, October 25, 1938—Cleaned up the house. Then had to do the milking by myself.

Wednesday, October 26, 1938—Pulled more cotton. Boy, I sure was tired when night came.

Thursday, October 27, 1938—Tried to pull more, and I was sure tired when night came.

Friday, October 28, 1938—Cleaned up the house and then pulled 30 pounds. Had to do the milking.

Saturday, October 29, 1938—We had to do all the work because Dady went to O'Donnell to see the place.

Sunday, October 30, 1938—Went to Don's for dinner. Made a birthday cake for Don. Ate some watermelon.

Monday, October 31, 1938—Pulled some more bales. I sure was tired when night came.

Tuesday, November 1, 1938—Stayed at home and cleaned up the house. Pulled 30 bales of cotton.

Wednesday, November 2, 1938—Went back to the field. Pulled 119 all day, but of course it was late when I got out there.

Thursday, November 3, 1938—It was cold because a hard rain came the night before. It was cold.

Friday, November 4, 1938—Some warmer and I went to the mailbox with Mother and Dady.

Saturday, November 5, 1938—Cleaned up the house. Then ironed some. Went to the mailbox after the Enterprise. Cooked a cake.

Sunday, November 6, 1938—Mr. Frank Simpson came and ate dinner with us. Went to Helen and Virgil's after dinner. Then milked.

Monday, November 7, 1938—Boy, it was cold. I finally got warm after a long time.

Tuesday, November 8, 1938—Went to the mailbox with Mother and Dady. Washed and ironed the pillow slips.

Wednesday, November 9, 1938—Pulled bales for the day. Pulled 121. Pretty good for the time that I had out there.

Thursday, November 10, 1938—Pulled 10 pounds. Then we started picking. I picked 93 and had to stop and go after the eggs.

Friday, November 11, 1938—Did some work and had to milk the cows.

Saturday, November 12, 1938—Went to town with Jimmy and Opal. Bought a coat. Then to the shower. Carried AE home. Then Charles brought me home. We had fun.

Sunday, November 13, 1938—I was so tired that I did not pull any cotton. Helped with the milking.

Monday, November 14, 1938—I was so tired that I did not pull any cotton. Helped with the milking.

Tuesday, November 15, 1938—Helped Mother and Dady get off to town. Went to the mailbox for the mail.

Wednesday, November 16, 1938—Went to the bale patch. Pulled 203. Pretty good for such spotty cotton.

Thursday, November 17, 1938—I was sure tired. I was sick with a bad cold. I stayed in bed all day. Then I helped milk.

Friday, November 18, 1938—Went to the mailbox. Little bit better, but we had real good time.

Saturday, November 19, 1938—Did up the work and then got ready, thinking Charles would come and get me, but he didn't. Poor me. No date.

Sunday, November 20, 1938—Went to Sunday school with Sybil. She came home with me. We went to a movie. Saw *Tropic Holiday* with Bob Burns. ("A Hollywood screenwriter looking for inspiration for his next film goes to Mexico, where he runs into a beautiful Mexican girl who sets her sights on him … Bob Burns, Dorothy Lamour, Ray Milland. …" wrote Charles.)

Monday, November 21, 1938—Stayed at home. Helped with the churning. Read some.

Tuesday, November 22, 1938—Got a magazine from Ruby to read. Did some handwork.

Wednesday, November 23, 1938—Helped Dady work at the house. Tried to stay awake but couldn't.

Thursday, November 24, 1938—A nice Thanksgiving for me. Went to the mailbox. Then ironed some.

Friday, November 25, 1938—Sybil came over, and then we went to her house to see if she could go with me. She did. Boy, did we have a good time.

Saturday, November 26, 1938—Went to the mailbox. Received a letter from Charles. I was glad to hear from him.

Sunday, November 27, 1938—Went to Sunday school. I went to town. I bought my brown hat and got my dress. Had my coat cleaned at the tailor's shop.

Monday, November 28, 1938—Did a big ironing. Boy was I tired. Mailed a letter to my dear Charles in La Mesa. Wore my new outfit. Had lots of compliments on it.

Tuesday, November 29, 1938—Went to the mailbox as Dady went to town. Had to do the milking.

Wednesday, November 30, 1938—Went to the mailbox after the mail. Received a letter from Elese.

Thursday, December 1, 1938—Cleaned up. Went to the mailbox. Hoped I would get a letter from dear Charles but didn't. I wonder why.

Friday, December 2, 1938—Went to the mailbox. Hoped I would get a letter from dear Charles but didn't. I wonder why.

Saturday, December 3, 1938—Charles came down. We rode around. Sybil went with us. Boy, we really had fun. I was sure to see Charles.

Sunday, December 4, 1938—Came home from Sunday school. I tried to get Sybil to come over, but Mrs. Jackson came over. And, Leonard Hodnett came over.

Monday, December 5, 1938—Worked around the house. I did handwork, ironed, and helped milk.

Tuesday, December 6, 1938—Cleaned the house and mopped. Then went to the mailbox. Did the work early so I could spend time with Sybil.

Wednesday, December 7, 1938—The bus left us. Visited school. Bought some Christmas presents. Got Charles a military set. I also got a letter from him.

Thursday, December 8, 1938—Went to the mailbox. Mailed Charles a letter. I sure was hoping that he would come home for the weekend, but he did not.

Friday, December 9, 1938—Went to the mailbox as Mother and Dady went to town. Cleaned up the house. Then I milked.

Saturday, December 10, 1938—I started to go to Sybil's but didn't. Went with Ruby to the fire closet at the church.

Sunday, December 11, 1938—Sybil came home with me for dinner. Page and Ellen came over in the afternoon. I drove my Model T over to Sybil's and went by PV at night.

Monday, December 12, 1938—Went to the mailbox. I received a letter from dear Charles. Boy was a glad to hear from him. I wrote to him and sent it by Neil Spencer.

Tuesday, December 13, 1938—Wrote my order out for my cedar chest, but Dady forgot to mail it. Boy was I sore.

Wednesday, December 14, 1938—Went to Luther to mail my order and some letters. I ironed a lot when I got home.

Thursday, December 15, 1938—Boy, I really felt bad but was able to work.

Friday, December 16, 1938—We went to Ackerly and La Mesa. Saw a show at the Mesa in La Mesa. Buck Jones was in it.

Saturday, December 17, 1938—Sybil fixed my hair. Charles came. Boy, we had some fun. The Model A wouldn't run because Sybil chopped it so much. I had a swell time.

Sunday, December 18, 1938—Mother, Dady, and I went to Center Point to church. Came home for dinner. Went by PO with Neil. Saw Sybil and Truman were over there.

Monday, December 19, 1938—Went to meet the mail carrier to get my package. We really enjoyed it and my cedar chest.

Tuesday, December 20, 1938—Made some candy. Went to the mailbox. Wayne Dalton came by and visited until the mail came.

I got a letter from Charles. Poor Charles was going to Dike, Texas.

Wednesday, December 21, 1938—Did up my work and started for the schoolhouse. Sybil and I took the present of the tree. We sure had lots of fun over there.

Thursday, December 22, 1938—Went to the mailbox. Went to the funeral for Ted and the Hamlin baby. My, it was sad!

Friday, December 23, 1938—Went to the mailbox but did not get much. Made some divinity candy. Sybil came over. She helped me with my work, and I fixed her fingernails. Went to the Christmas tree at Richland.

Saturday, December 24, 1938—Cooked a cake. Went with Neil to Sybil's to shoot some firecrackers. Went to town after Euell and Loyle. We sure had lots of fun.

Sunday, December 25, 1938—Christmas Day at home with Mommy and Dady.

Monday, December 26, 1938—Cleaned up the house. I started to go to Sybil's. Stopped for stamps at Luther. Also, looked in the mailbox.

Tuesday, December 27, 1938—Sybil came over here to spend the night. Made cookies and candy. I declared that she would help me milk.

Wednesday, December 28, 1938—We went to Luther to mail a package to Mrs. Cook. Made some date loaf candy. Sybil is it.

Thursday, December 29, 1938—I did the milking. It was cold and crazy.

Friday, December 30, 1938—Went to the mailbox. I mopped and carried water and wood. I milked early.

Saturday, December 31, 1938—Went to Luther to send mail.

January 1, 1939–December 31, 1939

Sunday, January 1, 1939—Went to Sunday school with Sybil, and then we went to Page's for dinner. Elbert, Page, Billie Mayes, Sybil, and I rode around some and met … [could not read].

Monday, January 2, 1939—Went to the mailbox. Did some handwork and helped with the milking.

Tuesday, January 3, 1939—Went to the mailbox. Then went to Sybil's with Neil. Then Sybil came home with me. We had fun.

Wednesday, January 4, 1939—Sybil and PJ went to the mailbox in a real bad sandstorm. Then we went over to her house.

Thursday, January 5, 1939—Went to the mailbox. Then cleaned up the house. And, behold, I did the milking as usual.

Friday, January 6, 1939—I helped with the churning. Then Mother and I had to do the milking because Dady went to Colorado, Texas.

Saturday, January 7, 1939—It misted nearly all day and then about night it rained some. Sybil and Odell came after Neil and me. We went after Conley, but he wasn't at home. Miss Jackson went with us. It rained, and we slide off into the ditch.

Sunday, January 8, 1939—Stayed at home all day. Just worked around.

Monday, January 9, 1939—Helped with the churning. Then that night we went to practice the play. Boy was it going to be good.

Tuesday, January 10, 1939—Cleaned up the house, as usual. Then I be Johnnie if I didn't have to milk.

Wednesday, January 11, 1939—It rained all day so I just sat around and studied my part in the play.

Thursday, January 12, 1939—Helped with the churning and then went to the practice for the play. Boy, we really did not on it.

Friday, January 13, 1939—Went to the mailbox, and I really did get a letter from Charles. Boy was I proud. I began to think that he had forgotten about Lennis Phipps. I wrote him back and then milked.

Saturday, January 14, 1939—Went to town. Hoped maybe I would see R. E. but didn't. My, I was sad. I was afraid he would leave me.

Sunday, January 15, 1939—Went to Sunday school and then to Ruby and Tom's, and to see Bonnie Puckett, Truman, and Morris. Clanton came so I was very disappointed about being gone. Went to the PO. Pauline Scott ate supper with me.

Monday, January 16, 1939—Did my usual work and then went to the mailbox, and behold, I had to milk the cows. John Brasher came to Helen's, and I declined if he didn't want the life out of me.

Tuesday, January 17, 1939—I helped Virgil haul feed.

Wednesday, January 18, 1939—Boy, we really had fun, and behold, I had to go and practice the play at Gay Hill. Saw P. E.

Thursday, January 19, 1939—Hauled more feed and we had to go practice the play again. Oh, such nonsense some people do make up.

Friday, January 20, 1939—Worked around the house and then went to the mailbox and did some handwork, too.

Saturday, January 21, 1939—Hauled some feed. Then dear Charles came. We had to practice the play. Charles and I rode around. Boy, he is a honey and just so dear to me. Went to town. He gave me a perfume set.

Sunday, January 22, 1939—Went to Sunday school with Neil, then came home. I changed. Maybe I will get to go to Big Spring with Charles to carry his grandmother to the bus.

Monday, January 23, 1939—Didn't do nothing but study the play. Then we went to practice the play. Behold, it was really going to be good.

Tuesday, January 24, 1939—I went to practice the play. I really did get a ride with Connelly Lockhart. It was late when I got home. Received a letter from Charles.

Wednesday, January 25, 1939—Practiced the play again. It sure was getting old with me.

Thursday, January 26, 1939—Helped with the churning. Then practiced the play. We really did good that night.

Friday, January 27, 1939—Went to the schoolhouse and practiced the play about noon. Then came home and milked and went to the play. Saw R. R. Our plan turned out to be good.

Saturday, January 28, 1939—Cleaned up the house and then went to the mailbox. And behold, I received a letter from Charles. Kinda surprised.

Sunday, January 29, 1939—Went to Sunday school with Sybil and Pauline. Scott came home with me for dinner. We went to her house in the afternoon. Sybil and Clanton came.

Monday, January 30, 1939—Helped with the churning. Then went to the mailbox. I wrote to Charles and went to Luther to mail it.

Tuesday, January 31, 1939—I mopped and did handwork and went to Ruby's after water. Had to do the milking by myself.

Wednesday, February 1, 1939—Mother and Dady went to town, and I stayed at home. Boy, I was really tired when night came.

Thursday, February 2, 1939—Received a letter from C. W. Worked around the house and did some handwork. Then studied my play. Went to bed and wrote Charles a letter about twenty times.

Friday, February 3, 1939—Baked some pies. Then milked and went to Vincent to put on the play. What a mess we made of it. I will never forget this event.

Saturday, February 4, 1939—Cleaned up the house and Charles came, so we went places. Did we have fun. I really did. Penny and Sybil was with us.

Sunday, February 5, 1939—Sybil, Penny, Charles, and I went to Sunday school. We really had more fun. I really like old Charles.

Monday, February 6, 1939—Cleaned up the house and, behold, I had to churn. Boy, I was really tired.

Tuesday, February 7, 1939—I really felt bad but made no difference how I felt. I had to go on with the work.

Wednesday, February 8, 1939—Went over to Mrs. Harrison's to spend the day. We sure had lots of fun over there.

Thursday, February 9, 1939—Went to the mailbox. I really did get a letter from Charles. I sat down and wrote to him. Boy, it was a honey.

Friday, February 10, 1939—Went to the mailbox and then tried to sweep out some of the West Texas sand. And I did some handwork.

Saturday, February 11, 1939—Cleaned up the house and then helped Dady load some feed. Went to the social and came back with Charles. We really have good times together.

Sunday, February 12, 1939—Went to Sunday school with Charles. He and I went to Ed and Joe's for dinner. We really had fun. I will always remember this day. Went to the post office with Neil and Ruby.

Monday, February 13, 1939—Sat around and tried to keep out of trouble but couldn't. Did some handwork.

Tuesday, February 14, 1939—Stayed home by myself. I really did get a letter from Charles. I answered it, and boy was it a good one. I say so. Also got a letter from Peanut.

Wednesday, February 15, 1939—Went to town. I absolutely bought myself a new coat. I mailed Charles a letter.

Thursday, February 16, 1939—I did a big ironing, and boy was I tired when night came. I really went to bed early.

Friday, February 17, 1939—I really had to stay at home. Mother and Dady could not go to town because it was so cold.

Saturday, February 18, 1939—Cleaned up the house Then milked. Thought maybe Charles would come but didn't. Stayed at home. Boy, it was lonesome.

Sunday, February 19, 1939—Charles came, and we went to Center Point. Boy, we really had fun. It was two o'clock when we got home. Found a dime. Went to … with Morris, Truman, Sybil, and Sylas.

Monday, February 20, 1939—Cleaned up the house. Then went over to Sybil's after the school bus run. Today was the birthday of Curley Top, my calf.

Tuesday, February 21, 1939—Joe Ella came, and we went to the mailbox. Boy, I really did get a letter from my dear Charles. Was I glad.

Wednesday, February 22, 1939—Cleaned up the house and went to the mailbox, but I didn't get any letter. Mailed one to Charles.

News clipping: Mr. and Mrs. Edward Haney and Mr. and Mrs. W. H. Haney attended church at Center Point Sunday. Mr. and Mrs. Robert Dalton and son, Elbert, and Miss Lennis Phipps and Charles Mundant of this community also attended.

Thursday, February 23, 1939—I really had a bad cold and really felt bad. Went to the mailbox and on to Luther to mail a letter.

Friday, February 24, 1939—Went to town to the mailbox and waited for the mail carrier a long time. Then here came Tom with the mail, so I got a ride back. I had to milk.

Saturday, February 25, 1939—Washed my hair and then went over to Sybil's to spend the night. We really had fun. I wore my new coat. We went to bed real early.

Sunday, February 26, 1939—Went to Sunday school. Then ate dinner with Sybil. Pauline came home with me and stayed until BYPO. We rode Neil's bicycle and had more fun than a barrel of monkeys.

Monday, February 27, 1939—Cleaned up the house. Then did handwork. My, it was lonesome. We really had a bad sandstorm.

Tuesday, February 28, 1939—Stayed a home by myself. Tried to sleep but couldn't much because I felt so bad.

Wednesday, March 1, 1939—Mother and Dady went to town to do the washing, so I was alone. Really had a lot of fun.

Thursday, March 2, 1939—Helen and I went over to Joe Ella's. She wasn't at home, so we went over to Haynes'. Received a letter from Charles. Joe Ella went to Luther to mail a letter to Charles. We were really busy.

Friday, March 3, 1939—Stayed at home like I usually do. Behold, I mopped and cleaned the house, but what is the use with so many sandstorms coming?

Saturday, March 4, 1939—We had the worst sandstorm. I thought maybe Charles would come but didn't. Thomas and Lucille and a boy from Coahoma came, but I didn't go.

Sunday, March 5, 1939—Went by Sybil's and went to Lawrence's and stayed awhile. Went to the funeral with Sybil. Saw Truman, Silas, and Morris. Went to Sybil's with Truman to see if Sybil could come home with me.

Monday, March 6, 1939—Boy, I was lonely and wondered why. Because two weeks had passed and me not seeing my dear Charles. I just dragged around because I felt bad.

Tuesday, March 7, 1939—Stayed at home and I just knew that I was going to get a letter from Charles, but never did. I did get kinda sore.

Wednesday, March 8, 1939—Went to the mailbox, but no letter. I couldn't imagine what happened to my dear one. I thought of everything. Maybe he was sick.

Thursday, March 9, 1939—Went to the mailbox and finally got a letter. Went to Ted and Hanner's. Then went over to Page's. Didn't get to read my letter until I got home.

Friday, March 10, 1939—Went to the mailbox and really did get a letter from Oma Lee. Made two pies. Boy, I was tired when night came.

Saturday, March 11, 1939—We had a real bad sandstorm, and boy, I was afraid that Charles wouldn't come. But he did. We had more fun. He was driving a new car or rather his uncle's.

Sunday, March 12, 1939—He and I went to Sunday school. Then P. E., Charles, and I all went to La Mesa. Francis and R. E. had a fuss. My! I had lots of fun. I really hated to leave old Charles. R. E. and PJ got home about sundown.

Monday, March 13, 1939—Sat around and tried to sleep some but couldn't for thinking of old Charles (the dear one I love).

Tuesday, March 14, 1939—Cooked two pies and did up the work and went to the schoolhouse for the big supper. Really had a good time.

Wednesday, March 15, 1939—Cleaned up the house as usual. I really did get a letter from Charles. Carried a letter to him back to the mailbox and met the mailman.

Thursday, March 16, 1939—Helen and I went to Joe Ella's. Mrs. Haney was there. We sure had lots of fun.

Friday, March 17, 1939—Cleaned up the house real good and went to the mailbox. I had to milk. Boy, I was worn out when night came.

Saturday, March 18, 1939—Charles came, and oh boy, we really had fun. Went over to Ed and Joe Ellen's and stayed awhile, then rode around and came home. I couldn't sleep for thinking of my dear Charles.

Sunday, March 19, 1939—Had to do all the work by myself because Mother and Dady was sick. Went to Center Point to church. Saw R. E. If I could only be with Charles longer. Came home and went to bed.

Monday, March 20, 1939—Stayed in bed until kinda late; then got up and cleaned up the house. I began to feel better. Wrote a letter to Charles and mailed in Luther.

Tuesday, March 21, 1939 – Went to the mailbox and really did get a letter from Charles. Boy, I was proud of it. Did some handwork and then did the milking.

Wednesday, March 22, 1939—Cleaned up the house and then tried to sleep some but couldn't. I wonder why.

Thursday, March 23, 1939—Went to the mailbox and received a letter from Charles and Juanita. Boy was I proud to hear from Charles.

Friday, March 24, 1939—Stayed around the house and did the work. Boy, I was really tired when night came. Ironed some but not much.

Saturday, March 25, 1939—Cleaned up the house real good, and Charles came with Page, Elbert, Penny, and Sybil, but we never went with them. Went to Ed and Joe's in our Model T. Ran into a mailbox.

Sunday, March 26, 1939—Charles came really early, and we went to the Stevenson's in Moore. We really had lots of fun. I hated to see old Charles leave. I wonder why.

Monday, March 27, 1939—Stayed at home all morning, but went over to Helen's in the afternoon for a while. Also went to the mailbox and I received a letter from Indiana.

Tuesday, March 28, 1939—Stayed at home by myself. I thought maybe I would hear from Charles but didn't. I sure wanted to hear. Dern his hide.

Wednesday, March 29, 1939—Went to the mailbox but still didn't hear anything from Charles. Received a letter from my girlfriend Elese.

Thursday, March 30, 1939—Went to the mailbox and, behold, I received a letter from Juanita and Charles. What a surprise! But really, I was glad.

Friday, March 31, 1939—Juanita Stevenson came to Ruby's, and then she stayed all night with me. We really had the fun. She is one more sight. It was late when we went to bed.

Saturday, April 1, 1939—Went by Moore so Juanita could get ready to go to town. Walked the whole town over. Bought two new pair of shoes. Saw Charles and R. E., talked a lot to them. Then Charles came about.

Sunday, April 2, 1939—R. E., Juanita, Charles, and I went to Center Point to Sunday school. Then we went to Mary and Finis's for dinner. We intended to make some pictures, but we didn't. Came home about two thirty. Really enjoyed myself.

Monday, April 3, 1939—Went to the mailbox. Then did some handwork. Tried to sleep but couldn't. I wonder why. I suppose thinking of the past.

Tuesday, April 4, 1939—Joe Ella and I went to the mailbox in the T before Mother and Dady went to town. Didn't hear from Charles. Boy, I was really downhearted. Went to the club at Helen's.

Wednesday, April 5, 1939—We went to the maize, and boy, I received good news. Boy. My, I was happy. Why shouldn't I be? I sat down and answered it. My, it came up a bad cloud.

Thursday, April 6, 1939—Went off to Luther to mail a letter. It was really cold. It sleeted and snowed a lot, too. But one thing I did get my letter off.

Friday, April 7, 1939—Stayed at home by myself. Boy, I really wanted to go to the play at Richland but didn't. A bunch of Claytons came and really gave me a scare.

Saturday, April 8, 1939—Cleaned up the house real good. Washed my hair, and above all I had to meet the mail carrier. Charles came, and we rode around.

Sunday, April 9, 1939—Waited for Charles until late. Went on with Ruby and Tom. Went to the Easter egg hunt. Had a good time. Charles and Sis came, but I wasn't at home. Went to … with Maurine. Came after church.

Monday, April 10, 1939—Up early and did handwork. I read some and tried to sleep, but I couldn't because I was all broken-hearted about Charles. I sometimes wonder why. I couldn't sleep for thinking of him.

Tuesday, April 11, 1939—Went to the mailbox really early hoping I would get a letter but didn't. I was really disappointed about it. I guess it is enough to worry a person to death.

Wednesday, April 12, 1939—Stayed at home again by myself. The rest went to wash. Went to the mailbox but still no letter. Gosh, I was disappointed more than ever.

Thursday, April 13, 1939—I went to the mailbox and really did get a letter. Boy was I proud but disappointed about Charles not coming home. I sat down and wrote four letters to my honey.

Friday, April 14, 1939—Went as far as the mailbox as they went to town. I walked back. Boy, it was really lonesome. If I could only have seen Charles.

Saturday, April 15, 1939—Hauled rock. Then went to Sewell's and by the mailbox. Hauled water and then went to Juanita's to spend the night. Walked to town and a bunch of kids went out to the park. We really had fun. A night to be remembered.

Sunday, April 16, 1939—Helped Juanita clean up the house. Then, in the afternoon, we went to the ball game. I came home with Mr. and Mrs. Osborne Truman, who came after me to go to Vealmoor.

Monday, April 17, 1939—I had to churn and then had a lot of other things to do. Boy, I was really tired when night came.

Tuesday, April 18, 1939—Went to the mailbox but no letter from Charles. Boy, I was really downhearted. I just knew I would hear from him but didn't.

Wednesday, April 19, 1939—Helped cook dinner for Virgil. Mr. Clanton and Shorty afternoon. I went to the mailbox but no letter from Charles. My, how sad I was. Also a card from Oma Lee about Allie Mai.

Went to the mailbox and I really received a letter from ["Charles" marked out] Elese. Gosh, I was tired when night came. Why should I be with so much work to do?

Thursday, April 20, 1939—Went to the mailbox and got a letter from Elese.

Friday, April 21, 1939—Juanita came over early on the ice route. We really had fun. Made ice cream. Virgil and Helen were here for dinner.

Saturday, April 22, 1939– Charles, Juanita, and I went to Sunday school. Then went over to see Mr. and Mrs. Osborn. Had a grand time. Rode around in the afternoon. Gosh, I really hated to see Charles leave.

Sunday, April 23, 1939—Went to the mailbox as usual. Gosh, we never get anything but a letter from my girlfriend Elese.

Monday, April 24, 1939—Went to the mailbox as usual. Gosh, we never get anything but a letter from my girl friend Elese.

Tuesday, April 25, 1939—Went to the mailbox. Then cleaned house real good. Boy, I really did feel bad. Didn't feel like doing nothing but I did. No letter from Charles.

Wednesday, April 26, 1939—Same old grind as usual. All went to town but me. Did all the milking by myself. Then Helen and I went to Luther after Virgil.

Thursday, April 27, 1939—Went to the mailbox and no letter from Charles. I couldn't imagine what was the matter that he didn't write.

Friday, April 28, 1939—Still no letter from Charles. Stayed at Ruby's for a while. I tried to sleep some but couldn't, so I did some handwork.

Saturday, April 29, 1939—Cleaned up the house and then Charles came, and he and I and Byron Conway all went to Moore. Then Juanita and Eva Mae went with us to town. Really had some fun. Oh, that Charles!

Sunday, April 30, 1939—Charles came about ten. We stayed here awhile and then went over to Helen and Virgil's. Carried them to the singing. Rode around. Had a real good time. Charles stayed here for a while. Went to Sybil's.

Monday, May 1, 1939—Went to the mailbox as soon as the road dried off but never got anything but the paper.

Tuesday, May 2, 1939—Went to the mailbox but no letter. I really did feel bad. I wonder why. Suppose you guessed. Tried to do some handwork and sleep too but couldn't.

Wednesday, May 3, 1939—Went to the mailbox as usual but still no letter. I received my package. Boy, I was glad.

Thursday, May 4, 1939—What do you know, but I really did receive a letter from La Mesa, Texas. I wrote two letters, one to Juanita and the other to Charles.

Friday, May 5, 1939—They worked on the cellar so I had to cook dinner. Helen helped me some. Boy, I was really tired when night came. I did some handwork.

Saturday, May 6, 1939—Up early and went to town. Bought me some lace and pillow slips. Helen gave me a dresser scarf. Boy, I was proud of it. Juanita came. Had to stay at home.

Sunday, May 7, 1939—Helped do the work and then we washed some. Mrs. Blythe came and wanted me to come to the musical at her house. I got to go. Came back with Curtis Hood.

Monday, May 8, 1939—Went to the mailbox early but didn't get a thing. Boy, I was really disappointed. Oh, I did get a letter from Oma Lee but none from Charles.

Tuesday, May 9, 1939—Bought me a vanity set. Went to the mailbox and walked back. We didn't get anything but the papers.

Wednesday, May 10, 1939—Cleaned up the house and the rest went to town. Boy, it was lonesome for me. Did some handwork and by not going I had to do all the milking.

Thursday, May 11, 1939—I ironed some and then helped with the work. Mr. and Mrs. Smith, Mina Jackson, John Brasher, and Helen and Virgil all came to practice a song.

Friday, May 12, 1939—Cleaned up the house and then went to the mailbox but no letter. Gosh, I really did wonder why Charles didn't write.

Saturday, May 13, 1939—Tried to sleep but couldn't because it was so hot. Then I did some handwork. Gosh, I was really tired when night came.

Sunday, May 14, 1939—Went over to Charles's about 9:30 a.m. Stayed for dinner. We really had lots of fun. Charles walked part of the way home with me. The Raineys came. Went to BYPV.

Monday, May 15, 1939—Tried to sleep but couldn't because it was so hot. Then I did some handwork. Gosh, I was really tired when night came.

Tuesday, May 16, 1939—The same old grind. Worked around and absolutely I slept some. Boy, I was so tired I went to bed early.

Wednesday, May 17, 1939—About noon I went over to Juanita's. She was taking state examinations, and I had to stay at the store with Mary and the kids.

Thursday, May 18, 1939—Did the work up early and went to the schoolhouse for our ball game. We really had fun. Boy, I really played ball and really enjoyed myself.

Friday, May 19, 1939—Did some handwork and read some, and behold, I really did sleep some. Helen came up to sew.

Saturday, May 20, 1939—Behold, the wonderful moment came when Charles came over. We had to stay at home because Clyde didn't bring the car in, but just the same we were together.

Sunday, May 21, 1939—Went to Center Point to church and then Charles came over. We went to Ed and Joe's and then went to BYPU. We really had lots of fun in our Model T.

Monday, May 22, 1939—Needlework. Went to the mailbox and then to Luther to mail a letter to Peanut. I ironed some.

Tuesday, May 23, 1939—Went over to Ollie's about one. Juanita was over there and also Eva Mae. Charles and Juanita came over about sundown, and we really had the fun. That is natural, isn't it?

Wednesday, May 24, 1939—The folks went into town to wash, and I tried to sleep some. Charles and Juanita came over. It came up a cloud. The kids really got scared. Charles went home early.

Thursday, May 25, 1939—Charles came by on the ice route headed to La Mesa. Juanita went back to Ollie's to spend the day. I ironed some more.

Friday, May 26, 1939—Cleaned up the house and went to the mailbox and received a letter from Oma Lee. Went over to Ollie's to see Juanita. Did some handwork too. Charles came by with my folks.

Saturday, May 27, 1939—Charles walked over here. I came upon an awful cloud. It really hailed. Juanita and Charles wore my overcoat home. He was quite a sight.

Sunday, May 28, 1939—Sis and I sat around. Then after we got the work done, we went to Helen's. Carried Sis home so she could get her clothes and go to work. Charles came, but I was not at home.

Monday, May 29, 1939—Went to town with Helen and Virgil. We picked up Charles at the store. Boy, I was glad to see him. Bought me some new handwork and some thread.

Tuesday, May 30, 1939—Worked around and tended to all things. I worked some on my vanity set, but gosh, I will never get it done.

Wednesday, May 31, 1939—I stayed at home as usual. I don't get to go nowhere except to the cow pen, but that is my regular stopping place.

Thursday, June 1, 1939—Worked some on my scarf, but nothing seemed to satisfy me because I didn't get a letter from La Mesa.

Friday, June 2, 1939—Went to Ruby's and stayed awhile. Then tried to sleep some but couldn't. I wonder why.

Saturday, June 3, 1939—Washed my hair and cleaned up. Thought maybe Charles would come, but he didn't. He spent the weekend at Afton/Spur.

Sunday, June 4, 1939 – Mother went to P. E. Jack and Mildred's. Stayed at home and cooked dinner. Then went over to Juanita's but she had gone to Moore, Texas.

Monday, June 5, 1939—Went to the mailbox and then to the store. Talked to Juanita. She really told me a lot of things. Slept some in the afternoon.

Tuesday, June 6, 1939—Had to milk by myself and do the other work. We had a sick cow. Spent the afternoon at Juanita's. Had a real good time.

Wednesday, June 7, 1939—Folks went back to town. I tried to sleep some, but Helen came so I couldn't. Did handwork. Had to milk by myself.

Thursday, June 8, 1939—Had to milk by myself and do the other work. We had a sick cow. Spent the afternoon at Juanita's.

Friday, June 9, 1939—Helen and Sybil came to spend the day. Had to cook dinner. Sybil, Pauline, Neil Spencer, Helen, and Virgil all went to the play in Richland. It was good. From Valley River.

Saturday, June 10, 1939—Charles came real early, and we went over to Juanita's. Then we went to the Dalwoods', and Sybil went with Juanita. We really got scared at something. I really had fun.

Sunday, June 11, 1939—Started to SS (Sunday school). Patsy was at Helen & Virgil's … [someone was late, cannot read] was late, and we did not go to Church. Went home with Charles for dinner. It was 4:00 p.m. when Charles left. The Lydles from town came.

Monday, June 12, 1939—I ironed some and slept some. Made some ice cream for supper. Boy, it was good. I should say so.

Tuesday, June 13, 1939—Went to the mailbox as usual. Then Helen came over and had to cook dinner. Boy was I tired when night came. Milked by myself.

Wednesday, June 14, 1939—Went to the mailbox as usual. Then Helen came, and we had to cook dinner. Carried her to the store. Boy was I tired when night came.

Thursday, June 15, 1939—Ironed so I could go over to Juanita's Saturday. In the afternoon, I slept some and worked on my dresser scarf. It was late when I went to bed.

Friday, June 16, 1939—Went to the mailbox and then went to town and walked back. Tried to read the paper, but it was so windy.

Saturday, June 17, 1939—Cleaned the house. Went to town with Helen and Virgil. Charles, Penny, Juanita, and I all went riding. Went to Hockley to a dance but didn't stay very long. Had a pretty good time.

Sunday, June 18, 1939—Charles and I went to church at Center Point. He wanted me to go home with him for dinner but couldn't. I wanted to go to La Mesa with him but couldn't. In the afternoon went to Helen's.

Monday, June 19, 1939—Finished ironing and handwork on my scarf. Wanted to go over to Juanita's but couldn't go. I give up doing anything because I am always disappointed.

Tuesday, June 20, 1939—Took a bath and then went to the club and shower (for Opal) with Ruby and Helen. Came home with Ruby and Helen. Milked. Went to bed early but couldn't sleep. No letter from Charles.

Wednesday, June 21, 1939—The folks went to town to wash, and I stayed at home. Helen came up to sew. Couldn't milk because we didn't have any feed.

Thursday, June 22, 1939—I cleaned up the house, and then after dinner, I went over to Simpson to see Juanita. Broke the crystal to my watch. Got a letter from Charles.

Friday, June 23, 1939—After the folks went to town, I tried to sleep some for a while. I couldn't because it was so hot.

Saturday, June 24, 1939—A day to always remember. Went to town to get my watch fixed. Sid and Charles came. Wanted to go to the rodeo but couldn't. My, I was really disheartened. I wonder why.

Sunday, June 25, 1939—Ironed some. Then slept some. Boy, it was really hot, so hot that no one could hardly sleep.

Monday, June 26, 1939—Ironed some and slept some. Boy, it was really hot, so hot that no one could hardly sleep.

Tuesday, June 27, 1939—Always on padding days, I have to cook dinner. That is the only time I have because I always have company.

Wednesday. June 28, 1939—Received a letter from Oma Lee. Boy, I was glad. Helen, Virgil, and I went to Jack and Mildred's. Helen really gave us a scare over in Pounce's pasture. Had a good time.

Thursday, June 29, 1939—Ironed some. Did some handwork. Then later I helped milk. Went to bed and read some until bedtime.

Friday, June 30, 1939—Pauline Scott came, and then we went to the mailbox in her car. Received a letter from Charles. Cooked dinner. Then milked all the cows.

Saturday, July 1, 1939—Worked around the house and helped fix up the mailbox. We didn't get our paper. Charles came, and we went over to Simpson's. Clouds came up, and we came home early.

Sunday, July 2, 1939—Stayed home by myself. Charles said he might come by after me to go to Moore. He and Sis came that night to be ...

Monday, July 3, 1939—Did a big ironing. It was really hot. Afternoon I slept some and then helped with the cows.

Tuesday, July 4, 1939—Cooked dinner for Helen and then slept awhile. Milked by myself. Clifton Clayton came after me, but I didn't go.

Wednesday, July 5, 1939—Mailed a letter to La Mesa. Afternoon I whitewashed the cellar. Boy. I was tired.

Thursday, July 6, 1939—Went to town. Bought me a pair of shoes and a hat and some other things. Went to Neil's birthday dinner.

Friday, July 7, 1939—Stayed down at Ruby's for a while and then came home. Finally did sleep some. Milked by myself.

Saturday, July 8, 1939—Charles came, and we went down to Helen and Virgil's to make ice cream. We really had a good time.

Sunday, July 9, 1939—Went down to Helen and Virgil's and went to Sunday school. Charles and Virgil went hunting. Took some pictures. Stayed at home all afternoon.

Monday, July 10, 1939—Same old grind. Handwork. Then some ironing. Slept some.

Tuesday, July 11, 1939—Went over to Olive's to stay awhile. They wasn't at home, so I went over to Lula's, and she went to the club. Went back home and milked the cows.

Wednesday, July 12, 1939—Cleaned up the house. Then did handwork and went to Ruby's.

Thursday, July 13, 1939—Did a big ironing so I could clean house. Helped with the milking.

Friday, July 14, 1939—After I got the work done, I slept some and went to the mailbox, and I received a letter from Charles.

Saturday, July 15, 1939—Made ice cream and went over to Jimmy's to the party. Had a lot of ice cream to eat. Sybil and Penny came back with us.

Sunday, July 16, 1939—Went to Sunday school and then to Moore to make some pictures in the afternoon. It was late when we got home, and I was really tired.

Monday, July 17, 1939—Cleaned up the house and mailed a letter to Charles. I received a letter from Oma Lee.

Tuesday, July 18, 1939—Up about two and started for the Littles' about four. We arrived there about ten. Virgil carried me over to Aunt Darcus. Spent the night there. Phoned Oma Lee.

Wednesday, July 19, 1939—Packed my clothes and went to Mildred's with Helen and Virgil.

Thursday, July 20, 1939—Stayed in Big Spring for a while. It was late when we went to bed.

Friday, July 21, 1939—Oma Lee came, and I went down there. After dinner, we went swimming at Brevard's. Went to church that night in Blanton. Met a lot of folks.

Saturday, July 22, 1939—Cleaned up the house and went to town. Went to the show, *The House of Baskerfield.* Went to church in Blanton. Had a real good time.

Sunday, July 23, 1939—Arlis and Oma Lee went over to Uncle Pat's with me. Oma Lee stayed and went to church in Crews. Went to Aunt Dora's for dinner. Helen and Virgil came after me. and I went back over to the Littles'. Mildred took sick.

Monday, July 24, 1939—Mildred was sure sick, but we started for home after dinner. Burned out the engine in the car. Spent the night with Mildred and Jack.

Tuesday, July 25, 1939—Left about seven for home but got in a storm, so we pulled over. Received a letter from Charles. Milked by myself. Cleaned up.

Wednesday, July 26, 1939—Worked around and cleaned up the house. Then Dawn and I went to the mailbox. Boy, we really had some fun.

Thursday, July 27, 1939—I ironed some and wrote some letters. One to Aunt Oma Lee and Elese. Stayed at Ruby's awhile.

Friday, July 28, 1939—Went over to the Osborns' and spent the afternoon. Took some pictures to them. Milked myself, but boy it was late when I got finished.

Saturday, July 29, 1939—Canned some peaches. Then took a cake and moved around. Charles came, but I could go nowhere.

Sunday, July 30, 1939—Stayed at home all morning. Then Charles, Sis, and Albert came. We went over to Clyde's, and my folks came after me. We went to a singing. Back to town.

Monday, July 31, 1939—Wrote a letter to Charles. Oma Lee sent me some pictures. Went over to the store. Then ironed some.

Tuesday, August 1, 1939—Stayed at home and slept some. Did handwork on my scarf. Really tired when night came and hit the hay early.

Wednesday, August 2, 1939—Stayed at home and did handwork and slept some. Started the milking. I did it all because they were late.

Thursday, August 3, 1939—Went to see Sybil and stayed the night. We really had a good time laughing and talking. Cooked some in the afternoon.

Friday, August 4, 1939—Went to the mailbox. Then Helen came over. We stayed at home, and I cooked dinner for her.

Saturday, August 5, 1939—Cleaned up the house real good. Then about four went to town. Received a letter from Charles, and they were quarantined again.

Sunday, August 6, 1939—Went to Sunday school with Sybil and there for dinner. Afterward went by to get Pauline Scott for the ball game. Pauline and Sybil came home with me.

Monday, August 7, 1939—Ironed some. Then Olive came over and stayed awhile. It rained some. I did handwork.

Tuesday, August 8, 1939—Did handwork nearly all day. Intended to go to Olive's but rained, and it was so muddy.

Wednesday, August 9, 1939—Just worked around the house. Received a letter from Charles. And I wrote him.

Thursday, August 10, 1939—After dinner I went over to Pauline's and mailed some letters in Luther. Had a real nice time.

Friday, August 11, 1939—Rode with ice boy over to Olive's. Came home about four and milked. Boy, I felt bad, and I wonder why.

Saturday, August 12, 1939—Boy, it was lonesome for me today because I had to stay in the bed. Then did handwork the rest of the day.

Sunday, August 13, 1939—Went to Sunday school and over to Pauline's for dinner. Then she came home with me for supper. We really had a good time.

Monday, August 14, 1939—Cleaned up the house and ironed some. Went to the mailbox and to church. We were late to church.

Tuesday, August 15, 1939—Helen came to sew, and I went over to Olive's to help her with sewing. Milked the cows and played with calves.

Wednesday, August 16, 1939—Canned some peaches and did first one thing then another. Boy, I was tired, and I didn't go to church.

Thursday, August 17, 1939—Received a letter from Charles, and boy was I glad. They were quarantined again. Went to church and was really on time.

Friday, August 18, 1939—Worked around. Neil Spencer took my picture, and we went to town. Kelly Brown's car burned up, and we went over there as we started to church.

Saturday, August 19, 1939—Poor little me. I had to stay at home again. Charles didn't come home, and boy was I lonesome.

Sunday, August 20, 1939—We all went to Center Point to church. Helen and Virgil ate dinner with us. We went back to church that night.

Monday, August 21, 1939—Went to Ruby's and then to Helen's to stay awhile. Did handwork for a while.

Tuesday, August 22, 1939—Helen spent the day with me, and we really had a good dinner. Walked to the mailbox. Received a letter from C. W.

Wednesday, August 23, 1939—Mailed a letter to La Mesa. Then ironed some and boy was I tired. Went over to Mrs. Osborn's awhile.

Thursday, August 24, 1939—Ironed some more. Then helped milk. Gosh, the cows got out, and I nearly walked my legs off after them.

Friday, August 25, 1939—Helen and I sewed on my quilt until late. Then I cooked a pie and milked.

Saturday, August 26, 1939—Cleaned up the house and then went to town with Ruby. Came home. Ironed and went to Pauline's and Sybil's. Charles and I went to Center Point.

Sunday, August 27, 1939—Charles and I went to Center Point to church. Then I went over to Mrs. Osborn's for dinner. Had a real nice time and lots of fun.

Monday, August 28, 1939—Wrote a letter to Charles and mailed it in Luther. Boy, I was really blue and downhearted, but somehow I managed to iron.

Tuesday, August 29, 1939—Worked on my quilt some, but I had the headache so bad I couldn't do anything. Boy, I was tired when night came.

Wednesday, August 30, 1939—They started painting the house, and I had to cook dinner or rather help. Boy, it was sure a job. Mr. Smith came over for dinner too.

Thursday, August 31, 1939—Worked some more on my quilt, and boy, I worked so hard that I was sure tired when I got ready to hit the bed.

Friday, September 1, 1939—Cooked dinner for the group again today, and by the time we finished, it was late. I cleaned house real good.

Saturday, September 2, 1939—Charles came. Penny, Sybil, Charles, and I went to Mary's to the party. Charles and I made plans for our future, and I was happy. Love Charles from the depths of my heart.

Sunday, September 3, 1939—Charles and I went to Sunday school. Then he and Sybil came home with me for dinner. We drove around and went over to the Osborns'. The Conway baby was born. Charles and I went to the singing, and I hated to see him leave.

Monday, September 4, 1939—Late in the afternoon, Mrs. Cook, Mary Jane, Mrs. Allen, and Ruth Baker came. Mrs. Cook and Mary Jane spent the night with us. We talked until late. Wrote to Charles.

Tuesday, September 5, 1939—We went to town and then to Coahoma to carry Mrs. Cooke and Mary Jane. Had a flat, and it was really late when we got home. I milked, and I was tired.

Wednesday, September 6, 1939—Mrs. Osborn came and spent the afternoon. Walked part of the way home with Ray. Then I had to do all the milking by myself. Did handwork on my quilt.

Thursday, September 7, 1939—Boy, I had a bad cold, and it really made me feel bad. I got up and worked on my quilt.

Friday, September 8, 1939—Still no letter from Charles. Boy, I was disappointed. Went over to Olive's and spent the afternoon. Carried the pictures over there.

Saturday, September 9, 1939—Ironed and cleaned house. Charles came, he and Weldon Perry. Stayed at home after we came back from Sybil's. Charles stayed here for a while.

Charles and I and Sybil went to Sunday school. Went to Sybil's for dinner. We went to the baptism in the late evening. I felt bad. Mr. and Mrs. Rainey and kids came. Went to bed early.

Sunday, September 10, 1939—Charlene and I and Perry and Sybil went to Sunday school. Went to Sybil's for dinner. We went to the baptism in the late evening. I felt bad. Mr. and Mrs. Rainey and kids came. Went to bed early.

Monday, September 11, 1939—Stayed in the bed all day. Boy, my cold was really bad. And I felt so bad anyway. But I managed to help with the work some.

Tuesday, September 12, 1939—Finished my sunflower quilt. Then I cut some quilt scraps for another quilt, and I pieced a few blocks.

Wednesday, September 13, 1939—Worked some more on my quilt. Dady and Mr. Harrison went to O'Donnell after corn, so I had to milk by myself. Received a letter from Charles and answered it.

Thursday, September 14, 1939—Started on my new quilt but didn't get very much done on it. Anyway got a little done. Mailed a letter to Charles. Then went to Murrys' and milked. I felt bad.

Friday, September 15, 1939—Worked some more on my quilt. But I had to make dinner for Helen. Tried to sleep some but couldn't too much. Milked by myself, and boy did I feel bad.

Saturday, September 16, 1939—Dad went back to O'Donnell, and we had to do all the work by ourselves. Goes to say that I was tired when night came, and I fell in bed.

Sunday, September 17, 1939—Went to Sunday school with Neil and Don. Sybil came home with me for dinner. Page, Elbert, and Croak came after Sybil went. Reverend Hollywell came, and Sybil and she went to the singing. Had lots of fun with the group.

Monday, September 18, 1939—Carried butter to Mrs. Smith and Juanita Hamlin some. Went to the mailbox too and then tried to sleep some but not much.

Tuesday, September 19, 1939—Worked on my quilt again and also cut some quilt scraps.

Wednesday, September 20, 1939—Helen and I went over to Olive's to spend the afternoon, and I worked again on my quilt. Mrs. Munden pieced on my quilt.

Thursday, September 21, 1939—Helen and I went over to Olive's to spend the afternoon, and I worked again on my quilt. Mrs. Munden pieced on my quilt.

Friday, September 22, 1939—Went to the mailbox but no letter from Charles. I was really disappointed.

Saturday, September 23, 1939—A letter from Charles came, and boy was I glad. I went to town and picked out my cloth. Saw a lot in town. Went to Pauline's. Patty had a good time.

Sunday, September 24, 1939—Stayed at home all morning and cooked dinner. Then went with Sybil to church and came back with Tom and Ruby.

Monday, September 25, 1939—Worked on my quilt. I nearly have it finished, but I am really getting tired of it now. No letter from Charles. I read some too.

Tuesday, September 26, 1939—Went to the mailbox but still no letter. Talked with the mail carrier for a while. Stayed at Ruby's for a while.

Wednesday, September 27, 1939—Went to the bale patch early and pulled 205. It came up a cloud, and I quit before night. Received a letter from Oma Lee and Charles. Olive came.

Thursday, September 28, 1939—Went over to Juanita's to help her with the shower for Page. Had a real good time over at Hamlin. Helped with the milking.

Friday, September 29, 1939—Worked on my quilt again and cleaned house real good. Then ironed some and wrote some letters. Saw Sybil Harrison for a while.

Saturday, September 30, 1939—Mother and Dady went to town, and I went as far as Olive's and spent the afternoon. Worked on my quilt and played with Larry Joe.

Sunday, October 1, 1939—Cooked a real good dinner and then went to sleep for a while. Truman and Clanton came, but I didn't go anywhere. Went to singing with Neil.

Monday, October 2, 1939—Pulled some more bales and then talked to the Dalton boys for a while. I pulled 152 in the afternoon. Ironed some after supper.

Tuesday, October 3, 1939—I felt bad so I stayed at home and in bed part of the time, but I was able to do the milking anyway. Finished my diamond quilt.

Wednesday, October 4, 1939—Started on my improved nine-patch quilt. I cut quite squares when I felt like it, nearly all morning. I really felt touch.

Thursday, October 5, 1939—Worked on my quilt some more. I cut forty-one blocks all day and part of the night. Ironed some, too, but I still didn't feel very good.

Friday, October 6, 1939—Stayed at home. I ironed some and then went after the eggs.

Saturday, October 7, 1939—Cleaned up the house real good. Looking for Charles. Mrs. Osborn came and talked to me about her trip to East Texas. I was really shocked.

Sunday, October 8, 1939—It rained some, but I wore my new clothes to Sunday school anyway. Ruby … Neil, Odell Euill, John B, and Wayne all went to town to see *Dodge City* (A Texas cattle agent witnesses firsthand the brutal lawlessness of Dodge City and takes the job of sheriff to clean up the town, starring Errol Flynn). We could not get in with such a crowd.

Monday, October 9, 1939—I read some and then worked on my quilt some too. Went to the mailbox and received a card from Charles. Was really surprised. Mrs. Munden, Olive, and Larry Joe came in the afternoon.

Tuesday, October 10, 1939—Cleaned up the house and went to the mailbox. Received a letter from Charles. I was really glad to hear from him.

Wednesday, October 11, 1939—Stayed at home and cooked a pumpkin pie for supper. The rest went to town to wash. Milked by myself. Worked on my quilt some too.

Thursday, October 12, 1939—Cleaned up the house, and I pulled bales for the Harrisons. Pulled 210 in the afternoon. Very good for me, if I must say.

Friday, October 13, 1939—Worked on my quilt and cooked a pie. Helen came and spent the day. Mr. Osborn came about two to see if I knew when Charles was coming home.

Saturday, October 14, 1939—Pulled bales all day. I pulled 846. Charles came. We went to the show. Saw Bob Steele in *Mesquite Buckaroo*. Had a flat. Clyde and Olivet intended to go with us, but they went to bed before we got there.

Sunday, October 15, 1939—Charles and Mother and Dady all went to church at Center Point. Charles and I went over to Ed and Joe's. Charles is really a sight. I can really have more fun out of him. I love him.

Monday, October 16, 1939—Pulled bales all day ... carried my dinner to the field. I pulled 251. I didn't work too hard for the first day.

Tuesday, October 17, 1939—Helen came up here and spent the day. I worked on my quilt and then did the milking. Read some.

Wednesday, October 18, 1939—Pulled bales all day. I pulled 339. Boy, I was really tired when night came and ready to hit the bed.

Thursday, October 19, 1939—Sold my calf. Received a letter from Charles. Pulled bales in the afternoon. I pulled 239. Boy, I was really tired.

Friday, October 20, 1939—Helen cut my hair. Went to the store by Olive's and then to Hanner's to get Helen's hair set. Went to the supper. I was auctioned off and brought fifty cents.

Saturday, October 21, 1939—Cleaned up the house and ironed. Charles came, and we were supposed to go to Lewis's, but we roasted some marshmallows. I really enjoyed myself. A night to be remembered.

Sunday, October 22, 1939—Sybil and Charles came home with me for dinner. We carried Charles to the highway. Sybil and I came back by ourselves. We had some fun.

Monday, October 23, 1939—Pulled bales in the afternoon. I pulled 239 from dinner on. I was really tired when night came, and I really beat Sybil a lot.

Tuesday, October 24, 1939—Pulled bales all day. I pulled 327. And boy, did I feel the effect of it about dark. It came a shower of rain, and was I glad because I wouldn't pull tomorrow.

Wednesday, October 25, 1939—Went to the mailbox as usual and didn't get a thing. I ironed some too.

Thursday, October 26, 1939—Went to the mailbox as usual and didn't get a thing. Ironed some too.

Friday, October 27, 1939—Went over to Mr. Osborn to see if I was pulling. Put my quilt together right. They helped me on it too.

Saturday, October 28, 1939—I went to Rainey's at home. Spent the night and we really had a time. A night to always be remembered.

Sunday, October 29, 1939—Did the work up and played Chinese checkers. Then after noon we came home. I was glad to get home. Mrs. Munden was here. Went to Sybil about hair set.

Monday, October 30, 1939—Pulled bales in the afternoon. I pulled 210 and quit. Boy, I was really tired when night came. I helped do the milking.

Tuesday, October 31, 1939—I felt bad, but I went to the mailbox anyway. Worked on my quilt with the spare time I had, and that wasn't too much.

Wednesday, November 1, 1939—Pulled bales all day. I pulled 303. Then we practiced our play. It was really cold, and if I could have gone to bed early, it'd been just fine.

Thursday, November 2, 1939—It was cold so I didn't pull bales. Tried to stay warm but couldn't. No letter from Charles. I wonder why he hasn't written.

Friday, November 3, 1939—Still no letter from Charles. Went over to see Mrs. Osborn as the folks went to town. Stayed until about three and then came home and milked.

Saturday, November 4, 1939—Worked around the house and ironed some. Really intended to pull some cotton but didn't think I would have time.

Sunday, November 5, 1939—Went to Sybil's for dinner. Woody and Marvin came over. We played dominoes. Sybil brought me home, and we went to the store. Went to singing and then went to Richland.

Monday, November 6, 1939—Pulled bales and then helped with the work. I also worked some on my quilt. No letter from Charles.

Tuesday, November 7, 1939—Studied my part in the play and milked. We could go to practice on it or rather read it over.

Wednesday, November 8, 1939—Helped with the work and went with Helen to Mrs. Smith's shower. We went and practiced the play again.

Thursday, November 9, 1939—It rained and was so cold that I didn't pull bales. I studied my part of the play.

Friday, November 10, 1937—No letter from Charles. I did the work, and we went to practice the play. I still didn't know my part.

Saturday, November 11, 1939—Went after Odell, then went to the store and to Mrs. Osborn's. Charles was in bed asleep. He came, and we went to Moore. Finally went to bed.

Sunday, November 12, 1939—Sis, Charles, and I all went to SS. They wanted me to go with them but couldn't. They came back after dinner. We had fun. Just rode around. Went to the church with Ruby.

Monday, November 13, 1939—Pulled some bales but I couldn't for Sybil and Juanita Hamlin. We really had fun and practiced the play. I will sure be glad when this is over.

Tuesday, November 14, 1939—Cleaned up the house, went to the mailbox, and then went over to Mrs. Osborn's for a while. Studied my play. I nearly had it memorized.

Wednesday, November 15, 1939—Went after Joe Murphy to work and then pulled bales the rest of the day. Practiced the play. We are really learning it too.

Thursday, November 16, 1939—I churned while Dady and Joe hauled feed. I had to help Paula and Joe haul feed. I had to keep hauling one load of water. Wrote a letter to Charles and studied my play.

Friday, November 17, 1939—Cleaned up the house and worked on my quilt. Milked, then went and we practiced the play. It was really late when I went to bed, and I was really tired too.

Saturday, November 18, 1939—Thought maybe Charles would come home, but he didn't. Worked on my quilt some but not very much.

Sunday, November 19, 1939—Went to SS with Helen. Boy, my foot really did hurt. I had to wear my house shoes.

Monday, November 20, 1939—Practiced the play, and I was really sleepy when night came. I knew my part pretty good.

Tuesday, November 21, 1939—Carried milk and butter as soon as I could before the roads got so slick.

Wednesday, November 22, 1939—No letter from Charles. We practiced the play. And I sure tried too. I was ready to hit the bed when I got there. Johnnie Osborn.

Thursday, November 23, 1939—I received a letter from Charles, and boy was I glad. I wrote one to him. Helped wash up and then churned things.

Friday, November 24, 1939—Cleaned up the house, then went to the mailbox and over to Mrs. Osborn's. Practiced the play. We were supposed to put it on but couldn't because Lester boy was on the grand.

Saturday, November 25, 1939—Cleaned up the house as usual, then took a bath and Charles came over. Boy was I glad to see him. Juanita and I went to the show.

Sunday, November 26, 1939—Charles and I went to SS, and I went home with him for dinner. It was Charles's birthday. Had a really nice time. Juanita Hamlin came by.

Monday, November 27, 1939—Helped with the churning while they hauled feed. Juanita stayed until after play practice. I really enjoyed her being with me.

Tuesday, November 28, 1939—It rained some, but we practiced the play anyway. I was really tired of it. No letter from Charles. I was really disappointed.

Wednesday, November 29, 1939—Worked around and I felt so bad that I didn't feel like doing anything. We put the play on. Not many there. No letter from Charles.

Thursday, November 30, 1939—Had to do the milking by myself.

Friday, December 1, 1939—Clifton Little helped me some, and then he finished out the day.

Saturday, December 2, 1939—Clifton helped me with the milking at night and morning too. No letter from Charles. We received a lot of mail.

Sunday, December 3, 1939—Mother and I went to town to make my picture. Came home early with the cow feed and helped with the milking. I was disappointed because Charles didn't come.

Monday, December 4, 1939—Worked on my quilt some and went to the mailbox, but I didn't receive a letter. Hauled feed.

Tuesday, December 5, 1939—Went to Mrs. Osborn's in the afternoon. I worked on my pot holder some too. Came home really early and did the work up.

Wednesday, December 6, 1939—Went to the mailbox as usual and didn't get a thing. I was really worried about Charles.

Thursday, December 7, 1939—Worked on my quilt some. I would really be glad when I had it finished out my dress.

Friday, December 8, 1939—Worked some more on my quilt. And I mopped really good and worked around some, and toward night I milked.

Saturday, December 9, 1939—I ironed some and cleaned house again. I cleaned up. Thought Charles might come, but he didn't.

Sunday, December 10, 1039—Went to SS and came home with Sybil for dinner. There was really a bunch there. Went to the bank building. I drove A. M. Simpson's car.

Monday, December 11, 1939—In the afternoon, I went over to Mrs. Osborn's and sewed on my dress. I did a right smart too. We practiced the play.

Tuesday, December 12, 1939—Went to the mailbox as usual, but we didn't get anything but the paper. No letter from Charles.

Wednesday, December 13, 1939—Went to town with Sybil. Did my Christmas shopping. Seen about my picture. Came home early and practiced the play.

Thursday, December 14, 1939—Just worked around the house and worked on my quilt some. Then started my luncheon set. Helped milk.

Friday, December 15, 1939—Walked around and went to the mailbox. Received a letter from Charles. We put on our play, and boy was I glad it was over.

Saturday, December 16, 1939—Worked around and cleaned up the house. Finished cleaning the house. Finished my dress and my quilt. Stayed at home. Didn't have a date.

Sunday, December 17, 1939—Went to Center Point for both services. In the afternoon, I went over to Ruby's to stay awhile. They had company.

Monday, December 18, 1939—Mailed a bunch of Christmas cards and a letter to Charles. Received a letter from him. Went to the Hamlins' to the quilting.

Tuesday, December 19, 1939—Went over to Mrs. Osborn's as the folks went to town. Came home early and milked and worked on my scarf.

Wednesday, December 20, 1939—Went to town with Helen and Mrs. Munden. Did some more Christmas shopping.

Thursday, December 21, 1939—Went to the Christmas tree at the school. Received a gift from Juanita Hamlin. Baked my fruitcake.

Friday, December 22, 1939—Worked all day. Baked a cake and pies. Went to Harrison to see the Christmas tree. Had a good time. Really enjoyed myself.

Saturday, December 23, 1939—It was cold, but I helped cook a real good dinner. Sat around and fixed dinner. Helped with the milking.

Sunday, December 24, 1939—Boy, it was cold and snow all over the ground. I had to get out, and I helped with the work. Boy, it was cold.

Monday, December 25, 1939—Laid around because I really felt bad. I helped with the inside work, but I never got outside for anything.

Tuesday, December 26, 1939—Virgil carried the folks to town. Helen stopped by here all day. I received a letter from Charles. Boy was I glad and how. I milked.

Wednesday, December 27, 1939—Went to town with Helen and Virgil. We washed. Charles didn't come. How I was disappointed. I really hoped he would come.

Thursday, December 28, 1939—Sat around after I got the mail. Cleaned up.

Friday, December 29, 1939—No entry.

Saturday, December 30, 1939—No entry.

Sunday, December 31, 1939—No entry.

January 1, 1940–December 31, 1940

Monday, January 1, 1940—Worked on my luncheon set some. Cleaned the house real good. Helped churn some too.

Tuesday, January 2, 1940—Went over the Olive's and stayed awhile. Boy, it was really muddy. Mailed a letter to Charles.

Wednesday, January 3, 1940—Worked on my luncheon set some and ironed. Dady went to town with Mr. Harrison.

Thursday, January 4, 1940—Washed my slips and ironed them, too. Also worked on my luncheon set.

Friday, January 5, 1940—Took my embroidery over to Helen's and stayed all day. Went to the mailbox in the mist. Ironed some.

Saturday, January 6, 1940—It was real cold, and I helped with the milking. Worked on my luncheon set.

Sunday, January 7, 1940—Laid around and slept some. Wrote in my diary. Churned some.

Monday, January 8, 1940—Helped churn and then hauled some feed. Worked on my luncheon set some.

Tuesday, January 9, 1940—Mopped the house and worked on my luncheon set and finished it. Boy was I glad and how.

Wednesday, January 10, 1940—Cleaned up the house, set a quilt together, and ironed some. Read some after.

Thursday, January 11, 1940—No letter from Charles. Did a big ironing, and was I tired. Embroidered some after dinner.

Friday, January 12, 1940—Went to town to wash some. I received my package.

Saturday, January 13, 1940—Still no letter from Charles. We had a real bad sandstorm. Took off my pillow slips and made a new scarf.

Sunday, January 14, 1940—Stayed at home all day and read some and tried to sleep. Went to church with Ruby and Tom and went home with them after church.

Monday, January 15, 1940—Still no hearing from Charles. I found out he came home and didn't come over. Mrs. Scott died about noon.

Tuesday, January 16, 1940—Cooked something to take over to the Scotts and went to the funeral. Embroidered on my scarf after I finished the work.

Wednesday, January 17, 1940—Hauled all day. Mr. Osborn came over. Worked on my scarf after dinner.

Thursday, January 18, 1940—I ironed some and helped with the milking also. Worked on my scarf.

Friday, January 19, 1940—Helped with the churning. It was really cold, and I had a bad cold, too.

Saturday, January 20, 1940—Cleaned the house real good and went over to Olive's. They had received a letter from Charles. I was happy and how.

Sunday, January 21, 1940—Stayed home and cooked dinner. John Brasher came to dinner. Helped with the milking. Got some books from Ruby for reading, and I loved it.

Monday, January 22, 1940—Worked on my scarf and carried the milk and butter. I ironed some too.

Tuesday, January 23, 1940—Received a letter from Oma Lee. Boy was I glad. Stayed at Ruby's awhile. I felt bad part of the day.

Wednesday, January 24, 1940—Hauled some feed. J. J. came out and stayed all night. Bought some pigs.

Thursday, January 25, 1940—Went with J. J. to sell the pigs. Sold three. Ate supper in town. I drove his pickup nearly all afternoon.

Friday, January 26, 1940—Spent the day at Helen's. Worked on my scarf some too. I got wet milking. J. J. left for home today.

Saturday, January 27, 1940—Went to SS. John Brasher came over. Juanita and I went to the Smiths'. Jay and us all and John Couch [first mention of John Couch, Martha and Annette's father] went to the singing. Remembered the corner post and how.

Sunday, January 28, 1940—Carried Juanita Hamlin home, then hurried home because it was so cold. Embroidered some, too.

Monday, January 29, 1940—Cleaned up the house and went to the mailbox.

Tuesday, January 30, 1940—Worked on my scarf some and milked.

Wednesday, January 31, 1940—Hauled some water and read some and finished up what I had to do.

Thursday, February 1, 1940—Cleaned up the house and went to the mailbox. We didn't get anything but circulars.

Friday, February 2, 1940—Embroidered on my scarf and read some too before the folks came home.

Saturday, February 3, 1940—Stayed at home and cleaned the house too. I was sure tired, and I read some too.

Sunday, February 4, 1940—Went to SS and came home for dinner. John Brasher came home with us for dinner. We had a good dinner. Helen and Virgil ate dinner with us.

Monday, February 5, 1940—Cleaned up the house real good and went to the mailbox. Stopped at Helen's and stayed awhile.

Tuesday, February 6, 1940—Hauled feed and was tired when night came.

Wednesday, February 7, 1940—Sewed on my vanity set some. First one thing and then another until it was late and then helped milk.

Thursday, February 8, 1940—Went to the mailbox as usual and received a letter from Oma Lee. Boy was I glad.

Friday, February 9, 1940—John Couch came over and Asa D. John and I all went over to Juanita's.

Saturday, February 10, 1940—Had a wiener roast. Saw Charles, too. We all went to the show.

Sunday, February 11, 1940—Juanita and I did not get up until late, and Sybil and Joy came over. That was after noon. Clinton, Juanita, and I all went to church, and I came home.

Monday, February 12, 1940—Worked on my vanity set some, but I was so sleepy that I couldn't do anything.

Tuesday, February 13, 1940—I felt so bad because of my cold, but I was still existing. But how?

Wednesday, February 14, 1940—I ironed some, and boy was I tired. We went over to Harris's after supper and stayed awhile.

Thursday, February 15, 1940—Carried the Smiths' butter, and Sybil came over to spend the night with me. We had more fun.

Friday, February 16, 1940—It was really cold and snowy. It snowed all day. We made some snow ice cream.

Saturday, February 17, 1940—Cleaned up the house real good and did some embroidery. We made some ice cream.

Sunday, February 18, 1940—Sat around all day and read some. Tried to sleep some. Made some pies.

Monday, February 19, 1940—Cleaned up the house real good. Did some embroidery. Helped milk.

Tuesday, February 20, 1940—Cleaned up the house and milked. Went to the party at Pauline Scott's for the Harrisons. Had a good time.

> Newspaper clipping found in journal: "Miss Lennis Phipps and Charles Mundant of this community also attended church."

Wednesday, February 21, 1940—Went to town to see about our car, but it was gone. I was really disappointed.

Thursday, February 22, 1940—Helped Sybil and then loaded up the butter. I really felt bad. She and Pauline spent the night with me. Boy, I really hated to see them leave.

Friday, February 23, 1940—Sybil and they left around seven thirty. Tried to work some on the vanity set, but I didn't feel like doing much anyway.

Saturday, February 24, 1940—Helped Helen and Virgil move. Boy, I was sure tired and felt bad too. Read some when I went to bed.

Sunday, February 25, 1940—Went to SS. Neil, Ann, Delbert, Marvin, Pauline Scott, John Brasher, Lois, Juanita, and I went riding and made some pictures.

Monday, February 26, 1940—Worked around the house, did some handwork, and cleaned up my room real good.

Tuesday, February 27, 1940—Went to the shower at Gertrude Puckett's for Mrs. Earnest Scott. I had a good time.

Wednesday, February 28, 1940—Finished feed hauling and ironed what ironing we had to do. Busy I was for sure and tired when night came and how.

Thursday, February 29, 1940—Worked on my vanity set. Carried some butter and talked to Joy for a while.

Friday, March 1, 1940—Went to the mailbox and did not get much mail. I tried to sleep some and cook a pie for supper. Worked on my vanity set.

Saturday, March 2, 1940—Mr. and Mrs. Smith came by, and I went to town with Joy and them. Really had a good time. Helen and Virgil went to the Littles's.

Sunday, March 3, 1940—Spent the day with Joy and went to town in Virgil's car. Went to the singing with John Couch at Richland.

Monday, March 4, 1940—Washed buckets and cleaned house. Mother came home with Clifford Woods, and Dady and Virgil went after her.

Tuesday, March 5, 1940—Cleaned up the house and hauled water. Cleaned up my room real good. I washed some too. Boy, I was sure tired that night.

Wednesday, March 6, 1940—Carried the Smiths' butter and hauled water. Cleaned up my room real good. I ironed some, too. But I was sure tired.

Thursday, March 7, 1940—Mother came home with Clifford Woods. Washed buckets and cleaned up the house. Dady and Virgil went after her.

Friday, March 8, 1940—Carried Smiths' butter. Hauled water. Cleaned up my room real good. I ironed some too. Boy, I was sure tired that night.

Saturday, March 9, 1940—Walked to the mailbox and walked back by Ruby's and stayed awhile. Then cooked two pies.

Sunday, March 10, 1940—Cleaned up the house real good. Went to town to see about our car. Bought it out. John Couch came, but I couldn't go.

Monday, March 11, 1940—Mr. and Mrs. Eden came, and I went to Ackerly to a Methodist meeting. Had a good time. Mr. and Mrs. Hamlin and Juanita came after some eggs.

Tuesday, March 12, 1940—I ironed some and laid down to take a nap. I felt better anyway.

Wednesday, March 13, 1940—Stayed at home. Did the work. Mopped and then went to the steward meeting.

Thursday, March 14, 1940—Received a letter from Sybil and boy was I glad. She is coming to spend the week.

Friday, March 15, 1940—Some handwork. Delivered the butter to the Smiths. Read some and then I ironed some too, and read some more after I went to bed.

Saturday, March 16, 1940—Dady was sick, and I had to drive the car and help mother deliver the milk and butter. We had to milk after we came in.

Sunday, March 17, 1940—Mother and I carried some feed to town, and we had to fix dinner for Mr. Clanton and John Couch.

Monday, March 18, 1940—Again carried some feed and eggs to town. I was tired.

Tuesday, March 19, 1940—Dady was still sick, and we had to do all the work. Did the churning too.

Wednesday, March 20, 1940—Went to town with the stuff, and Helen and Virgil helped with the work. I was sure tired when we got home.

Thursday, March 21, 1940—*Worked around the house and did the work*—most of it by myself too. Went to town after clothes for Easter.

Friday, March 22, 1940—Did the milking and churning too. Then delivered Smiths' butter and worked some with the ironing.

Saturday, March 23, 1940—Mother and I went to deliver the milk and butter. Boy, I was sure tired when night came. Dady had part of the milking done when we came home.

Sunday, March 24, 1940—Cleaned up the house real good and did the milking. John Couch came for me to go to the party at the Kilpatricks' in Richland. Did not go.

Monday, March 25, 1940—Wore my new clothes and went to church. Came home for dinner and then went back to the Easter egg hunt.

Tuesday, March 26, 1940—I ironed some and felt real bad until I could hardly do anything. I rested some of the time.

Wednesday, March 27, 1940—Delivered the milk and butter. Carried a trailer to bring back a calf. Boy, it was really a job.

Thursday, March 28, 1940—Helen and I went to do wash in our car. Left about twelve o'clock and got back about three thirty. I was tired.

Friday, March 29, 1940—I ironed most of the day and didn't get through, but I really did put in a full day of it.

Saturday, March 30, 1940—Helped deliver some stuff to town. Came home and helped Dady finish up with the work. I was really tired.

Sunday, March 31, 1940—Cleaned up the house. Washed my hair. Cooked a cake. John Couch came, and we went to the party at Layfield's. Really had fun.

Monday, April 1, 1940—Went after Joy, and she and I and Mother went to Center Point to the singing. We really enjoyed it.

Tuesday, April 2, 1940—I ironed some and helped with churning. Went to the mailbox but not very much mail.

Wednesday, April 3, 1940—Mother and I delivered the stuff to town. Bought our groceries and came home.

Thursday, April 4, 1940—Ironed some more but finally finished it. Wrote a bunch of letters to mail tomorrow.

Friday, April 5, 1940—The wind blew hard, but I managed to clean up the house. And it misted some in the night.

Saturday, April 6, 1940—Neil, Bonnie, Del, Delbert, Pauline, John Brasher, Joy, and all went and took some pictures.

Sunday, April 7, 1940—Went to SS, then to the picnic. Helped with the churning. Wrote some letters. Also did some handwork.

Monday, April 8, 1940—John and us went to the singing at Richland.

Tuesday, April 9, 1940—Worked around the house as usual. Milked. Churned some butter. Sure was tired. Getting hot.

Wednesday, April 10, 1940—Wrote some letters. Helped with the churning. Also did small sewing items.

Thursday, April 11, 1040—Mother and I delivered the stuff to town. Saw Charles Munden in town. Carried my pictures to the studio.

Friday, April 12, 1940—Fixed a flat and carried feed and washing to town. It was late when we got home, but we did the milking.

Saturday, April 13, 1940—I tried to dry some clothes but really had a time with them. Joy, Neil, Helen, Virgil, and I all went to the play at Richland.

Sunday, April 14, 1940—Mother and I went to town to deliver milk and butter. It was after sundown when we got home. We had the car.

Monday, April 15, 1940—John Couch came, and we went to the party at Eris Denton's. We really had a good time. Pauline, Neil, Snooks, Bonnie, Dell, and I all went.

Tuesday, April 16, 1940—Went to church. Pauline, Snooks, Jay, and John all came home with me for dinner. Played tennis in the afternoon. We all got mad.

Wednesday, April 17, 1940—Mother and I went to town to deliver the stuff. Saw a few people I knew in town. Boy, it was sure hot today.

Thursday, April 18, 1940—Went to Juanita Hamlin's after setting eggs. Went by myself. Stayed quite awhile.

Friday, April 19, 1940—Cleaned up the house and ironed some too. Did some handwork and worked on my vanity set.

Saturday, April 20, 1940—Mother and I delivered the produce in town. Sure was tired when night came.

Sunday, April 21, 1940—Carried feed to grind and went to the funeral of Mrs. Anderson. Uncle Jim and Aunt Dora came. John and I went to Cecil Mansfield's for a party.

Monday, April 22, 1940—John Couch came for me to go to the singing.

Tuesday, April 23, 1940—Helped with the churning and ironed some and slept some too. Boy, I really had a big ironing.

Wednesday, April 24, 1940—Mother and I went to deliver the stuff in town. Got my hair cut. It was late when we got home, but we still had some work to do.

Thursday, April 25, 1940—*I ironed some and slept some too. Did handwork on my vanity set. I declare, I will never get it done*—it seems like.

Friday, April 26, 1940—I ironed again, but boy was I tired. I read some too.

Saturday, April 27, 1940—Went to town to deliver our stuff. I bought some stuff for sandwiches for Sunday.

Sunday, April 28, 1940—Dady and I carried feed to town to grind. Dady was vaccinated for small pox. Juanita Hamlin came. John Couch came, and we went to Juanita's.

Monday, April 29, 1940—Joy, Juanita and I went to Coahoma to the singing. Really enjoyed it too. Joy and I went to church at Bethel.

Tuesday, April 30, 1940—Went to the mailbox as usual. Then came home, cooked dinner, and did handwork and looked at some magazines. I got a letter from Auby Spencer.

Wednesday, May 1, 1940—Mother and I delivered the butter and milk to town. Mother bought me a birthday present. It was a necklace. I was really proud of it.

Thursday, May 2, 1940—Washed me out some dresses and ironed them. Mr. and Mrs. Hollwell, Helen, and Joyce came over for a visit.

Friday, May 3, 1940—Finished my ironing and delivered the milk and butter. Stayed awhile and laughed and talked.

Saturday, May 4, 1940—Mother and I went to town to deliver milk and butter. I was really tired when we got home.

Sunday, May 5, 1940—Went to SS. Went with Juanita and others to lunch.

Monday, May 6, 1940—Took food to town and had a picnic. Went with John Couch. We really had fun. Got home. Ironed some.

Tuesday, May 7, 1940—Worked around the house a lot. I tried to sleep some but couldn't. I also ironed some.

Wednesday, May 8, 1940—We delivered the stuff to town. I was sure tired when night came. Got home about sundown.

Thursday, May 9, 1940—Helped with the churning and ironed some. Tried to sleep but could not.

Friday, May 10, 1940—Mother and I delivered the stuff. It was late when we got home. I ironed some and tried to sleep but couldn't.

Saturday, May 11, 1940—Cleaned up the house. Had to rest from the long week.

Sunday, May 12, 1940—SS, and visited with friends. Helen and Virgil and Mother went to Aunt Dora to see her. Cooked some pies and were real good.

Monday, May 13, 1940—I ironed some more today. Went to the mailbox as usual. No mail but the paper.

Tuesday, May 14, 1940—Mother and I delivered the stuff and bought my slacks and blouse for my fishing trip. Joy and Doris went to the steward meeting.

Wednesday, May 15, 1940—I went back to Mr. Daniels's and stayed awhile. It was late when I got home.

Thursday, May 16, 1940—Dady and I went to town to grind feed. Came back by Mr. Daniels's as usual. It was late when we got home.

Friday, May 17, 1940—Gathered up my clothes for the fishing trip. Ironed some too so I would have something to wear.

Saturday, May 18, 1940—We delivered the stuff and came home early, and I went on the fishing trip. Mr. and Mrs. Smith, Joy, Helen and Virgil, Juanita, Mrs. Underwood, and me. We got there about noon.

Sunday, May 19, 1940—Up early and cleaned up the house and went around in Bee car. Ate dinner. Then started home about eight. I had a lot of fun. Was tired.

Monday, May 20, 1940—We delivered the stuff to town and came home early. Joy and I went to the steward meeting at Edina. We had a good time;

Tuesday, May 21, 1940—I felt bad but managed to stay up some anyway. I laid around, slept some too.

Wednesday, May 22, 1940—We delivered the stuff to town. Came home early, and Joy and I went to a meeting at the church. We had a good time.

Thursday, May 23, 1940—We went to wash and carried some feed to grind. It rained on us some before we got home.

Friday, May 24, 1940—I ironed some, but I did not finish because we delivered the milk and butter at the Smiths'.

Saturday, May 25, 1940 – We delivered the stuff to town, and boy, I was tired when we came home early and helped Dady some.

Sunday, May 26, 1940—Went to church with Juanita and Opal for dinner. Went to the show and saw Errol Flynn.

Monday, May 27, 1920—Cleaned up the house real good and ironed some more. John came to visit, and he had brake trouble.

Tuesday, May 28, 1940—I ironed some more, but it looks like I can never get caught up with the ironing.

Wednesday, May 29, 1940—We delivered the stuff and came home real early. Helen, Virgil, Snooks, Joy, John, and I went to a picnic in town with young people at Center Point.

Thursday, May 30, 1940—Stayed at home and just worked around with one thing or another. I did handwork and milked the cows.

Friday, May 31, 1940—I ironed some and made butter too. Joy and I made our plans for the weekend.

Saturday, June 1, 1940—We delivered our stuff to town, and we got home about sundown. Sure was tired.

Sunday, June 2, 1940—Helen, Mr. Smith, and I went to where they were fishing. We had a great time. Went by Von Rogers.

Monday, June 3, 1940—I ironed some and slept some too. I was sure glad to get our ironing done.

Tuesday, June 4, 1940—We delivered the milk and butter. Came home by noon. I was tired and went to bed early.

Wednesday, June 5, 1940—We went to town and washed and had some feed ground. It wasn't too late when we got home.

Thursday, June 6, 1940—Helped with the churning and tended to the clothes. I tended to the cows. We had a light rain.

Friday, June 7, 1940—I delivered our stuff. Came home early and went to the play. It rained on us on the way home.

Saturday, June 8, 1940—Stayed home all day. Joy was fixin' to leave later. Hamlin was killed about 6:30 p.m.?

Sunday, June 9, 1940—Virgil came to tell us the news, and I was fixin' to leave. Worked on a puzzle. Also read some.

Monday, June 10, 1940—Ruby and I went to town about one for the funeral. My, it was a sad affair. The funeral was at 4:00 p.m.

Tuesday, June 11, 1940—We delivered the stuff, and boy was I tired when night came. Was supposed to go to Ackerly to a steward meeting, but it rained.

Wednesday, June 12, 1940—We went in and washed at the laundry. I hung out clothes when I got home. Then helped milk.

Thursday, June 13, 1940—I ironed some and tried to sleep too. Then Ruby and I went over to the Hamlins'. I helped Juanita mop, and Ruby ironed.

Friday, June 14, 1940—We delivered our milk and butter in town. We got home real early. I helped with the milking.

Saturday, June 15, 1940—John and Asa D. came, and we went to Tom and Ruby's for a while. We sure had a good time. I talked a lot.

Sunday, June 16, 1940—We went to church at Center Point. I really had a bad cold. John came after to go to singing, but I was too late.

Monday, June 17, 1940—I felt bad nearly all day and laid around. Cooked a pie for the cakewalk. Then went to the candidate rally. Had a good time.

Tuesday, June 18, 1940—We delivered our stuff in town. My, it was sure hot. We bought our groceries and stopped at the Edens'.

Wednesday, June 19, 1940—I ironed some today and cleaned up the house real good. Boy was I tired. Did the work up.

Thursday, June 20, 1940—Finished the ironing, and I was proud. Delivered the butter over to the Smiths because they were at her mother's.

Friday, June 21, 1940—Went to town as usual. It was really early when we got home. I really helped with the milking, too.

Saturday, June 22, 1940—Cleaned up the house real good. About sundown, John and Asa came over, and we went to Page's for a party. Had a good time.

Sunday, June 23, 1940—I mopped and cleaned up the house. Went to SS in our car. Came home and tried to sleep some. John came after me, and we went to church.

Monday, June 24, 1940—Cleaned up the house real good. I ironed some more and finished it and was glad.

Tuesday, June 25, 1940—We delivered our stuff to town. It was sure a hot day. We came home early, and I helped milk the cows.

Wednesday, June 26, 1940—We carried our wash to town. It was late when we got home, and I was sure tired.

Thursday, June 27, 1940—Slept some today and did some needlework on my pillow slips. It looked like I would never get them finished.

Friday, June 28, 1940—We delivered our stuff to town. It was late when we got home, and boy was I tired. I had to help with the milking.

Saturday, June 29, 1940—John and Snooks came over, and we went to Layfield's and made ice cream. Sybil was there. We sure had fun.

Sunday, June 30, 1940—I went to SS over here. Sybil came home with me for dinner. We went to the Andersons' for a picnic. Sure had a good time.

Monday, July 1, 1940—I ironed some today and hauled some water. Sybil came home with me for dinner. We went to the Andersons' for a picnic. Sure had a good time.

Tuesday, July 2, 1940—We delivered our stuff in town, and it was late when we got home. I was tired and how.

Wednesday, July 3, 1940—We carried feed to town. Also carried our washing. We sure had a big washing, and I was sure tired when night came.

Thursday, July 4, 1940—Worked all day around the house. I also worked on my pillow slips some. I don't believe I will ever get through with them.

Friday, July 5, 1940—Back to town again. We got in from town real early, but we had lots of work to do.

Saturday, July 6, 1940—Cleaned up the house real good and then went to Neil's birthday party. Sure had a good time and more fun, and how.

Sunday, July 7, 1940—Went to SS. Came home for dinner. John came, and we went to the singing at Richland. John was leaving the next week for the military, and was I sad.

Monday, July 8, 1940—I slept some, but it was so hot. Then I finished some handwork.

Tuesday, July 9, 1940—We went to town as usual. I was really getting tired of this job. Had my teeth fixed.

Wednesday, July 10, 1940—Finished the ironing and boy was I glad. I always get through in time to wash all dishes.

Thursday, July 11, 1940—Did the wash up and went to Juanita's to spend the afternoon. We started her a blanket, and we had fun.

Friday, July 12, 1940—Went to town as usual. It was really late when we got home. I was really tired.

Saturday, July 13, 1940—I absolutely stayed at home for the first time in a while. Slept some in the afternoon.

Sunday, July 14, 1940—Went to SS as usual. Came home and slept some. Then went back to church.

Monday, July 15, 1940—Back at the same old job. I was really tired too. I ironed some. I went to bed early.

Tuesday, July 16, 1940—We delivered our stuff to town. It was late when we got home. And, I was really tired.

Wednesday, July 17, 1940—Cleaned up our house real good and made punch for the stewards. Thirteen people were there.

Thursday, July 18, 1950—I ironed some today and carried Smiths' butter. Stayed awhile and played with John Dean.

Friday, July 19, 1940—Back to town again and carried Smiths' butter, Stayed awhile and played with John Dean.

Saturday, July 20, 1940—Cleaned house all day. Then went to Pauline's party. I had a good time.

Sunday, July 21, 1940—Helen, Virgil, and all of us went to Center Point to the quarterly conference. Had a real good time. Stayed home tonight.

Monday, July 22, 1940—I finished ironing and some work on my pillow slip. Then I tried to sleep some.

Tuesday, July 23, 1940—Back to town again. Wanted to get my hair cut but didn't have time.

Wednesday, July 24, 1940—Bought some peaches for Helen and helped her pickle them, too, while I waited for the mail.

Thursday, July 25, 1940—Cleaned up the house really good and went over for the quilting at the schoolhouse.

Friday, July 26, 1940—Back to town again. I was sure tired of this job. No letter from John. I was really disappointed.

Saturday, July 27, 1940—Cleaned the house and ironed. Went to the mailbox, and boy, I really got a letter from John. Kinda surprised.

Sunday, July 28, 1940—Went to SS and came home and slept some in the afternoon. Went back to church that night. Boy was I tired.

Monday, July 29, 1940—Sat around and ironed some and read some. Then went to bed early, and boy, did I sleep.

Tuesday, July 30, 1940—Back to town again and delivered our stuff. Had my hair cut too and left my dress at the tailor shop. It was late when I got home.

Wednesday, July 31, 1940—Did some of my ironing. Worked on my pillow slips some too. Then read some on a story I had.

Thursday, August 1, 1940—Sybil and I went to the quilting and had a good time. Not very many there.

Friday, August 2, 1940—We delivered our stuff and came home early too. Stopped at Ellen's for a while, and I read some after. I came home. Received a letter from John.

Saturday, August 3, 1940—John came home, and we went to the Langfords's for ice cream. We sure had a good time.

Sunday, August 4, 1940—Went to SS and came home and slept all afternoon. Went to the singing at Jimmy and Opal's. It was good.

Monday, August 5, 1940—I ironed some today. I finished my ironing and did some handwork.

Tuesday, August 6, 1940—Back to town again. Came home real early and helped with the milking. Went to bed early.

Wednesday, August 7, 1940—Cleaned up the house good. Went to the mailbox. Went to Helen's for a while. I slept some and worked on my pillow slips.

Thursday, August 8, 1940—I ironed some more today. And worked on my pillow slips again. Went to the schoolhouse to take the butter.

Friday, August 9, 1940—Back to town again. Stopped at the Edens' for a while. Went to Bethel for a meeting. I was really late.

Saturday, August 10, 1940—I tried to sleep some today. Received a letter from John, and was I glad. But he wasn't coming home.

Sunday, August 11, 1940—Went to church as usual. No one came home with me for dinner. I slept some for the afternoon.

Monday, August 12, 1940—I ironed some more today, and I finished it or rather caught up.

Tuesday, August 13, 1940—Back to town again and came home early and went to church meeting by myself.

Wednesday, August 14, 1940—Stayed at home and did come handwork. I wasn't very sleepy.

Thursday, August 15, 1940—Carried butter to the Smiths' and stayed a while and played with John Dean. Went to services at Bethel.

Friday, August 16, 1940—Back to town to deliver our stuff. Went to church at Bethel.

Saturday, August 17, 1940—Cleaned up the house and did the milking as Dady was in town.

Sunday, August 18, 1940—Went to church. Talked to John Couch for a long while. He tried to get me to go to La Mesa with all of them.

Monday, August 19, 1940—Cleaned up the house and ironed some, too. Then tried to sleep some and work on my pillow slips and helped milk.

Tuesday, August 20, 1940—Dady went to town after the money, and I stayed here and cleaned up the house and got things ready to go to Aunt May's.

Wednesday, August 21, 1940—Left about five thirty and got there about ten. Saw all the kinfolks.

Thursday, August 22, 1940—Really had a great time visiting. Started home about 4:00 p.m. Got here about nine. Then milked.

Friday, August 23, 1940—Did the churning or rather part of it. Slept some and carried the butter to the Smiths'.

Saturday, August 24, 1940—Did our delivery and came home by noon. Sure tired and went to bed early.

Sunday, August 25, 1940—Went to church at Center Point. Came home and slept until bedtime.

Monday, August 26, 1940—I ironed some and helped around the house. Went to the mailbox as usual. Then I slept some till dinner.

Tuesday, August 27, 1940—Carried the butter and stayed awhile at the quilting. Came home. Helped milk.

Wednesday, August 28, 1940—I did all the ironing that I had to do and then went to the mailbox. Tried to sleep.

Thursday, August 29, 1940—Carried the butter and stayed awhile at the quilting. Came home and milked.

Friday, August 30, 1940—Went to town and helped deliver our stuff. Came home real early.

Saturday, August 31, 1940—Cleaned up the house real good and then worked on my print dress. I received a letter from John Couch.

Sunday, September 1, 1940—We went to church at Center Point. Came home. Rested in the evening. Hamlins came. John came for me to go to the singing.

Monday, September 2, 1940—Helped do the work around. Did some needlework on my pillow. Helped with the milking and read some after supper.

Tuesday, September 3, 1940—Back to town to deliver our stuff. Came home early. I was sure tired, and I rested before I went to bed.

Wednesday, September 4, 1940—Cleaned up the house and did some work on my pillowcases. I ironed some and then milked. Went to Richland.

Thursday, September 5, 1940—Carried the butter to town and stayed awhile and really enjoyed it. Helped with the milking and other chores.

Friday, September 6, 1940—After trip to town to deliver our stuff, it was late when we got home.

Saturday, September 7, 1940—Cleaned house. Baked pies. Then Juanita came over to visit. We went to Richland.

Sunday, September 8, 1940—We went to SS, came home early, and ate dinner. Then went to the baptizing. Snooks got my keys, so I had to chase after them.

Monday, September 9, 1940—Cleaned up the house real good. A letter arrived from John. Went to the singing at Richland. Went home and went to sleep.

Tuesday, September 10, 1940—We delivered our stuff to town. Came home and went to the singing at the school. I was real tired.

Wednesday, September 11, 1940—Worked on my box to carry to the box supper. Also went to the singing. Then had to sleep.

Thursday, September 12, 1940—Laid around all day and later helped with the milking.

Friday, September 13, 1940—We went to town to deliver. I was sure tired, but I worked on my box supper. It sold for fifty cents.

Saturday, September 14, 1940—Cleaned up the house and made some pies. I did most all the milking. Stayed at home tonight.

Sunday, September 15, 1940—Went to SS. Wore my new suit. I was sure proud of it. Went to singing at Richland. It was real good.

Monday, September 16, 1940—Cleaned the house and ironed some but not all that was to do. Went over to Helen's and stayed awhile.

Tuesday, September 17, 1940—Mother and I went to town to deliver our stuff. It was late when we got home, and I was tired, too.

Wednesday, September 18, 1940—Just did the work around the house and washed my hair and cleaned the house real good.

Thursday, September 19, 1940—Cleaned up the house and then went to the Smiths' to carry the butter. Talked to Mrs. Smith awhile and saw Juanita and played awhile with John.

Friday, September 20, 1940—Back to town to deliver out stuff. It was late when we got home.

Saturday, September 21, 1940—Cleaned up the house. Went with Dady to Knott to see about feed. Went to town. John came, but we stayed at home and cut up.

Sunday, September 22, 1940—We went to SS and came home. Lora Lee, Aubrey, and John came, and we made some pictures. I got stung by a wasp. It sure hurt.

Monday, September 23, 1940—I got to sleep some in the afternoon. It was lazy and quiet. I ironed some.

Tuesday, September 24, 1940—Back to town again. I was real tired by this job too. Stopped at the Edens' for a while.

Wednesday, September 25, 1940—Cleaned up the house. Went to the mailbox. Then I had to milk because Dady went to town after materials to fix our floor.

Thursday, September 26, 1940—I ironed some and went to the quilting for a while and helped Dady milk. I also did some handwork.

Friday, September 27, 1940—Back to town. Delivered our stuff. It was late when I got home. I was tired and went to bed early.

Saturday, September 28, 1940—Juanita spent the day with me, and I went home with her that night. We sure had fun. She read to me a lot.

Sunday, September 29, 1940—Up early and helped Juanita clean up the house and cook dinner. Then sat around all evening. Dady came for me, but I was late.

Monday, September 30, 1940—Cleaned up and we went to wash. We carried the car to have it worked on. It was late when we got home, but I hung out the clothes.

Tuesday, October 1, 1940—Back to town again and helped with the stuff. I came home early and went to Ackerly with the Edens to a steward meeting. I was tired.

Wednesday, October 2, 1940—Dady and I went to town to have a tooth pulled. Boy, it really hurt, and boy, did I bleed.

Thursday, October 3, 1940—Cleaned up the house and went to the Smiths' after dinner to take the milk and butter. Stayed awhile.

Friday, October 4, 1940—Back to town to deliver the stuff. I received a letter from John. He was coming home too. Boy was I glad.

Saturday, October 5, 1940—John came over real early, and we sat around. Then we went over to the Couches's to sing awhile.

Sunday, October 6, 1940—Went to SS. Then came home and ate dinner. We drove around for a while, and I wanted to go to the singing, but I didn't.

Monday, October 7, 1940—Stayed around the house and ironed some too, but I didn't get through. Wrote a letter to John.

Tuesday, October 8, 1940—Back to town again, but I sure was tired of the job. It was late when I got home. I wanted to go to the steward meeting, but I didn't.

Wednesday, October 9, 1940—Dady and I went north of Colorado and over to Snyder to look for maize but couldn't find any. Came back home.

Thursday, October 10, 1940—Helped around and felt kinda bad but not so much that I couldn't do the work.

Friday, October 11, 1940—Back to town. Had my teeth worked on. It hurt but not as bad as the other one.

Saturday, October 12, 1940—Pulled cotton for a while. Then came home and cleaned up real good. Washed my hair. Read awhile and then went to bed.

Sunday, October 13, 1940—Was supposed to go to Ackerly, but a friend came over. Went to church.

Monday, October 14, 1940—Washed a lot in the morning. Went to the mailbox as usual. Did some handwork and milked.

Tuesday, October 15, 1940—Back to town to deliver as usual. It was late when we got home, and I sure was tired.

Wednesday, October 16, 1940—Pulled bales all day. Carried my dinner to the field. I pulled 256. Couldn't work too hard for the first day.

Thursday, October 17, 1940—I had a bad cold so I didn't feel like doing nothing. Stayed around the house.

Friday, October 18, 1940—Went to town again. Dady went too. We got home late.

Saturday, October 19, 1940—I pulled bales most of the day. I stopped a little before night. I was sure tired when night came.

Sunday, October 20, 1940—Mother and I went to Center Point to church. It was late when we came home, and I was tired. I slept in the afternoon.

Monday, October 21, 1940—Helen and I went to wash in town. Came home about 2:30 p.m. and I hung up the clothes. Went to bed.

Tuesday, October 22, 1940—Back to town again. I sure was tired. Went to bed early.

Wednesday, October 23, 1940—Pulled bales all day. Pulled 256. I helped with the milking. My back was really hurting.

Thursday, October 24, 1940—I didn't pulled bales in the afternoon because it was raining, and it was too wet to pull. I sure was glad.

Friday, October 25, 1940—Back to town again to deliver our stuff. It was late when we got home, and I helped Dady milk.

Saturday, October 26, 1940—Cleaned up the house real good and planned to go to town after post. Home real late.

Sunday, October 27, 1940—Dady carried me to Juanita's so I could go to the singing at La Mesa. Came back through the oil fields. [First mention of oil wells.] Had a good time.

Monday, October 28, 1940—Cleaned up the house in the afternoon. Helped with the work too. My, I was sure tired.

Tuesday, October 29, 1940—Back to town again. Did our work in a hurry and got home in the afternoon. Helped with the work too. My, I was sure tired.

Wednesday, October 30, 1940—Pulled bales all day. I was really tired too. I helped Dady with the maize stalks.

Thursday, October 31, 1940—I did not pull because I wanted to go to the sack supper at Gay Hill. I sure had fun.

Friday, November 1, 1940—Back to town again. It was late when we got home, but I helped Dady with the milking. Did some needlework.

Saturday, November 2, 1940—Cleaned up the house real good and then did some ironing. John came, and we went over to Juanita's. She came home to spend the night with me.

Sunday, November 3, 1940—SS. Dinner at home. Took a nap. Handwork.

Monday, November 4, 1940—Helen, Virgil, Juanita, and I all went to Stanton to see the Hambys. Really enjoyed the day. Juanita and I attended the singing at Richland Sunday night.

Tuesday, November 5, 1940—It was sure cold this morning, but we went and washed anyway. Got home early enough to dry our clothes. I was sure tired.

Wednesday, November 6, 1940—We delivered our stuff in town, and we didn't get home too early, but I really liked our delivery day.

Thursday, November 7, 1940—It rained some today. Dady and Mother went to town to see about his eye, and I pulled some cotton before it rained.

Friday, November 8, 1940—I cleaned up the house and carried the butter as soon as I could because it was raining. I felt bad but not enough to hurt.

Saturday, November 9, 1940—We finally made it to town, but it was raining. We finally got home. Practiced the play.

Sunday, November 10, 1940—Cleaned up the house and changed up all the things in my room. John and Asa came, and we went to Davis and Allie's and made candy and ate peanuts.

Monday, November 11, 1940—Went to SS and Pauline came home with me. Then we went to the singing and then went back to the church. John rode home with me.

Tuesday, November 12, 1940—Stayed around the house. I ironed some and also did needlework after supper.

Wednesday, November 13, 1940—Mother and I went back to town and delivered. It was late when we got home. I was sure tired when I got home. Went to bed early.

Thursday, November 14, 1940—Dady and I went to the sale and tried to buy a calf. We couldn't find one. It sure was cold. I like to have froze. Bought our doors.

Friday, November 15, 1940—Cleaned up the house and did needlework on my vanity set. Went to the Smiths'. Carried the milk and butter. It sure was cold. I like to have froze. Bought our doors.

Saturday, November 16, 1940—Back to town as usual and came home early.

Sunday, November 17, 1940—SS. Cleaned up the house. John came, but we stayed at home and talked. John stayed until 11:00 p.m.

Monday, November 18, 1940—We went to wash and finished quickly and on to home.

Tuesday, November 19, 1940—Back to the city to deliver milk and butter. Came back real early and I helped milk. I sure was tired.

Wednesday, November 20, 1940—I really did a big ironing. I did it all so I could get through it.

Thursday, November 21, 1940—Carried the milk and butter as quick as I could before the roads got slick.

Friday, November 22, 1940—Back to town with our goods to deliver. Weather was still bad.

Saturday, November 23, 1940—Back to town again. Delivery complete and we came home.

Sunday, November 24, 1940—Stayed at home all day. Still bad weather.

Monday, November 25, 1940—Helped with the milking. It was still cold.

Tuesday, November 26, 1940—I sat around and helped with the churning and helped with the work.

Wednesday, November 27, 1940—Back to the city to help on the route. Mailed John a letter.

Thursday, November 28, 1940—I cooked dinner while Mother and Dady went to Vealmoor to check on some cans.

Friday, November 29, 1940—Carried the butter early because they wanted it real early for dinner.

Saturday, November 30, 1940—Back to town again. Came home real early so I could go to the play at Gay Hill.

Sunday, December 1, 1940—Just did the work. Went to SS. I hoped John would come, but he didn't. Went to bed early.

Monday, December 2, 1940—I ironed some. John came after dinner.

Tuesday, December 3, 1940—Helped with the work. Took laundry to town and came home to get our clothes dry.

Wednesday, December 4, 1940—Back to the city to deliver our stuff. It was late when we got home. Mailed John a letter when I was in town.

Thursday, December 5, 1940—Cleaned up the house real good and did the ironing by myself, but I was finally finished before night.

Friday, December 6, 1940—Cleaned up the house real good and finished the ironing. Did all the milking by myself.

Saturday, December 7, 1940—To the city again. Delivered the stuff. It was late when we got home, and I was tired.

Sunday, December 8, 1940—SS. Same routine for the day.

Monday, December 9, 1940—Milked by myself. Stuff around the house. To bed early.

Tuesday, December 10, 1940—Cleaned up the house real good and did not go anywhere.

Wednesday, December 11, 1940—Mother and I went to town again. It was real late when we got home. I worked on my scarf.

Thursday, December 12, 1940—I tried to iron some, but I didn't quite finish. I helped Dady with the milking and did some other things around the house.

Friday, December 13, 1940—Cleaned up the house and finished the ironing and went to the Smiths' with butter and stayed awhile.

Saturday, December 14, 1940—Cleaned up the house as usual and I ironed some too. Worked on my scarf some too. John Couch came over.

Sunday, December 15, 1940—SS. Made a pie. Did some needlework.

Monday, December 16, 1940—Didn't go nowhere. Weather was bad. Cooked up real good.

Tuesday, December 17, 1940—Helen and I went to town to wash. Boy, we really had a big wash. Came home early so we could dry our clothes.

Wednesday, December 18, 1940—Back to the city again. Helped Dady with the deliveries. Home.

Thursday, December 19, 1940—I helped Dady with the feed. I was sure tired too, but I helped do the work.

Friday, December 20, 1940—Just worked around the house and went to the Smiths' to deliver the milk and butter. Worked on my scarf.

Saturday, December 21, 1940—Back to the city to take the milk and butter. It was late when we got home.

Sunday, December 22, 1940—SS. Laid around some in the afternoon. I looked for John, but he never came by.

Monday, December 23, 1940—John came real soon after dinner for a visit. We went to the singing. Got my Christmas present.

Tuesday, December 24, 1940—Cooked cakes for Christmas and helped around the house. Worked on my scarf.

Wednesday, December 25, 1940—Back to the city again. There was a crowd of people. Was not sure that I was going to get home.

Thursday, December 26, 1940—Cooked up some pies. Had a great dinner. No one here but us. John came over for supper. John and Lora Lee came also.

Friday, December 27, 1940—Went to Luther to mail some letters. Then went to the Smiths'. It snowed some and was really messy.

Saturday, December 28, 1940—Mother and I went back to town. I wanted to go to Mrs. Dietz's but could not.

Sunday, December 29, 1940—Dady and Jimmy finished hauling the feed. I was sure glad too.

Monday, December 30, 1940—Sat around and finally decided to go to Juanita's. She came home with me.

Tuesday, December 31, 1940—I did the churning so Dady could haul the feed from town. I sure felt bad. My whole body hurt.

January 1, 1941–December 31, 1941

Wednesday, January 1, 1941—Cleaned up the house and thought maybe John would write, but he didn't.

Thursday, January 2, 1941—Cleaned up the house and ironed some too. Received a letter from John.

Friday, January 3, 1941—Mother and I went to town again. It was late when we got home.

Saturday, January 4, 1941—Cleaned up the house and stayed at home. John didn't come home, and how sad I was.

Sunday, January 5, 1941—Went to SS as usual and came home and laid around and read some too.

Monday, January 6, 1941—Helped with the work. Then we went to town and washed.

Tuesday, January 7, 1941—Back to town again as usual. I was sure tired when night came. Came home real early.

Wednesday, January 8, 1941—I ironed today and did a little bit of everything. Did some stitching.

Thursday, January 9, 1941—Carried the butter and milk over to the Smiths'. Stayed awhile and played with John Dean.

Friday, January 10, 1941—Back to town as usual. Then came home real early. Sure was tired.

Saturday, January 11, 1941—Cleaned up the house. Then John came and stayed for a while. We sure had fun too.

Sunday, January 12, 1941—Stayed at home all morning and went to the singing at the church in the evening.

Monday, January 13, 1941—Cleaned up the house and worked on my scarf some. I did some of the ironing before it got too late.

Tuesday, January 14, 1941—Mother and I went to town as usual. I was sure tired too.

Wednesday, January 15, 1941—I finished ironing and worked on my scarf toward night. I was sure tired too.

Thursday January 16, 1941—Went to the Smiths' to carry the butter and milk. Stayed awhile and talked some. Went to Ackerly.

Friday, January 17, 1941—Back to town again as usual. Bought a lot and came home. I helped Dady milk when I got home.

Saturday, January 18, 1941—Cleaned up the house and finished my scarf and cooked some for Sunday.

Sunday, January 19, 1941—Went to Center Point to church and came home and laid around all afternoon and slept some too.

Monday, January 20, 1941—Helen and I went to town and washed. Then came home and tried to dry the clothes being as the wind was so high.

Tuesday, January 21, 1941—Mother and I went back to town to peddle. It was late when we got home, and I was sure tired.

Wednesday, January 22, 1941—I really ironed today. I sure had a big one too, and I was tired.

Thursday, January 23, 1941—Helped with the work. Then I went over to Jeanette's and stayed and played with John Dean awhile.

Friday, January 24, 1941—Back to town again and helped peddle. I was sure tired. We sure had the mud to pull home.

Saturday, January 25, 1941—Cleaned up the house real good and cooked some pies for Sunday. Went to Juanita's.

Sunday, January 26, 1941—Stopped around Hamlins' and we all went to La Mesa. We went to the singing and had fun, and I was proud too.

Monday, January 27, 1941—Helen and I went to wash. Got home and dried them too. Worked on a pair of pillow slips.

Tuesday, January 28, 1941—Went back to town. Had good luck and got through before night and came home.

Wednesday, January 29, 1941—I ironed some today or rather did it on and off. I was proud to get through.

Thursday, January 30, 1941—Went to Jeanette's in the afternoon and then just helped around the house.

Friday, January 31, 1941—Mother and I went back to town again. We got there early and came home and helped Dady.

Saturday, February 1, 1941—Cleaned up the house and finished my ironing, then cleaned myself up.

Sunday, February 2, 1941—Cleaned up the house and fixed dinner. Then John came out, and we sure had fun too. He stayed until late.

Monday, February 3, 1941—Helen and I went to town again to wash. I was sure tired too. We finally got our clothes dried.

Tuesday, February 4, 1941—Mother and I went to town to peddle. It was sure a long job of it, but we finally got through.

Wednesday, February 5, 1941—Cleaned up the house as usual. Then went to the mailbox and then to Smiths' to carry the milk and butter.

Thursday, February 6, 1941—Cleaned up the house as usual. Then went to the mailbox and then to Smiths' to carry milk and butter.

Friday, February 7, 1941—Mother and I went to town as usual, and we got done early, but it was late when we got home.

Saturday, February 8, 1941—I ironed today until I finished it, but it didn't like much so I did some handwork on a pair of pillow slips.

Sunday, February 9, 1941—We went to church at Bethel. Then we went to Web Nix, and I went over to Juanita's to stay awhile.

Monday, February 10, 1941—Cleaned up the house as usual. Then we went and washed in town and came home and dried all the clothes.

Tuesday, February 11, 1941—Mother and I went back to deliver. Had good luck so we got home early, and I had to help with the milking.

Wednesday, February 12, 1941—I did the ironing, and I finished my pillow slips after I finished my ironing. Helped with the night work.

Thursday, February 13, 1941—Cleaned up the house. Then went to the Smiths' to carry the milk and butter and played with John Dean.

Friday, February 14, 1941—Mother and I went to town. I received two valentines, one from Jeanette and the other from John.

Saturday, February 15, 1941—Cleaned up the house as usual and read some before I went to bed. Also did some needlework.

Sunday, February 16, 1941—I intended to go to church at Center Point, but I was tired and didn't go to the night service either.

Monday, February 17, 1941—Cleaned up the house. We went to wash and came home early and hemmed too.

Tuesday, February 18, 1941—Back on the same old job. It was always a gob seam to me. We got home early.

Wednesday, February 19, 1941—I did all the ironing and then worked on my pillow slips, but I didn't quite finish them.

Thursday, February 20, 1941—I cleaned up the house and then went to the mailbox. Then I finished my pillow slips and went to the Smiths'.

Friday, February 21, 1941—Mother and I went back to town as usual. It was late when we got home. I helped with the milking.

Saturday, February 22, 1941—Cleaned up the house real good and then cleaned up and ate supper. Then read some before I went to bed. Juanita came.

Sunday, February 23, 1941—Cleaned up the house and then Juanita and I cooked dinner. We sure had fun.

Monday, February 24, 1941—It was bad, and we didn't get to go to wash. I helped with the work and also did needlework.

Tuesday, February 25, 1941—Back at the same old job. It was very late when we got home, but I helped with the milking.

Wednesday, February 26, 1941—It was still bad, and we just did the work. Then I helped Mother wash some. I ironed some too.

Thursday, February 27, 1941—It was fair so we went and washed. There was sure a lot of people there too.

Friday, February 28, 1941—Mother and I went and peddled. It was better and not so cold and bad.

Saturday, March 1, 1941—Cleaned up the house real good and went to bed real early as I was really tired. Also washed my hair.

Sunday, March 2, 1941—Went to SS as usual. Then John came, and we just sat around as usual. Went to singing at Richland.

Monday, March 3, 1941—Helen and I went to town and washed and came home early, and we got our clothes dried before night.

Tuesday, March 4, 1941—Mother and I did our delivering. I am always so tired when our peddling day is over.

Wednesday, March 5, 1941—Cleaned up the house and then tried to do our ironing. And I finally finished it too.

Thursday, March 6, 1941—Helped with the work as usual. Then carried the milk and butter over to Smiths' and stayed for a while.

Friday, March 7, 1941—Mother and I went back to town as usual. It was late when we came home, and I was sure tired too.

Saturday, March 8, 1941—Cleaned up the house and did some of the ironing. Stayed at home the whole day.

Sunday, March 9, 1941—Went to SS at Bethel and came home and laid around all evening. I slept some too.

Monday, March 10, 1941—Helen and I went to town and did the washing. It was late when we got home, and I hung out all the clothes.

Tuesday, March 11, 1941—Mother and I went and did the peddling. I was tired too. I was supposed to go to the steward meeting.

Wednesday, March 12, 1941—Cleaned up the house and did all the ironing. I was sure tired. Then I worked on my rug for a while.

Thursday, March 13, 1941—Helped around with the work. Then went to the Smiths' with the milk and butter and stayed for a while.

Friday, March 14, 1941—Mother and I went back to the city and did the delivery. It was late when we got home.

Saturday, March 15, 1941—Cleaned up the house real good and washed my hair. I was sure tired after I finished baking my pies.

Sunday, March 16, 1941—Back on our route again. I was sure tired of this job. Came home early and helped Dady with the milking.

Monday, March 17, 1941—Helen and I went to town to wash and came home. We hung out all the clothes and got them dry before it was too late.

Tuesday, March 18, 1941—Helen and I went and washed in town and came home. We hung out and got all the clothes dry before it was too late.

Wednesday, March 19, 1941—Back on our route again. I was sure tired of this job. Came home early and helped Dady with the milking.

Thursday, March 20, 1941—Helped with the work and then went to the Smiths' with the butter. I played with John Dean.

Friday, March 21, 1941—Back to the city and did the delivering and bought our groceries and came home before night. I was tired.

Saturday, March 22, 1941—Worked around the house. Cleaned it up real good and then went to bed real early.

Sunday, March 23, 1941—Stayed at home all day. Boy, I was really lonesome. I wonder why.

Monday, March 24, 1941—Helen and I went to town and washed and got them dried before it was late.

Tuesday, March 25, 1941—Went to the route and helped Mother. It was late when we got home, but I helped Dady anyway.

Wednesday, March 26, 1941—Did the ironing and mopped and cleaned up the house real good.

Thursday, March 27, 1941—Helped with the churning. Then I went over to the Smiths' with the butter and milk.

Friday, March 28, 1941—Back on the route again and it was bad weather, and how. I sure dreaded the wind and sand.

Saturday, March 29, 1941—Cleaned up the house real good and washed my head. We did the work up good so we could go to the singing.

Sunday, March 30, 1941—Mother and I and Neil went to the singing at Valley View. It sure was good.

Monday, March 31, 1941—We went back to town again to wash and finally got them dried.

Tuesday, April 1, 1941—Mother and I went back to town again. Went by Mr. and Mrs. Edens' and stayed for a while. It was dark when we got home.

Wednesday, April 2, 1941—Cleaned up the house and did the mopping. I also finished my ironing, and was I glad.

Thursday, April 3, 1941—Helped around with the churning and then went over to the Smiths' with the milk and butter and played with John Dean.

Friday, April 4, 1941—Back on our route again and we went to see Mr. Dickson about working on our care the next day.

Saturday, April 5, 1941—Cleaned up the house and washed my hair and went to Helen's to see about my dress. Jeanette came over. I helped with the election.

Sunday, April 6, 1941—Went to SS as usual. Came home. Jeanette was with me. John came, and we all went over to the Simpsons', but they weren't at home. The calf was birthed.

Monday, April 7, 1941—Helen and I went and washed as usual. Got home early and dried our clothes. Was sure tired too.

Tuesday, April 8, 1941—Went to town as usual. Jack Darren died at eight o'clock. I sure felt sorry for the rest of the family.

Wednesday, April 9, 1941—Cleaned up the house and went to Jack's funeral. I sure felt sorry for them.

Thursday, April 10, 1941—Just helped around with the work as usual. Then churned some and traveled to the Smiths' with the milk and butter.

Friday, April 11, 1941—Mother and I went back to town again. It was late when we got home. I was sure tired.

Saturday, April 12, 1941—Cleaned the house all day and finished the ironing. Washed my head and did some needlework too.

Sunday, April 13, 1941—Juanita and I went to church in town. Came home, ate dinner, and laid around all afternoon.

Monday, April 14, 1941—Helped with the churning and some other work. Ironed too. I was sure tired when night came.

Tuesday, April 15, 1941—Back to the city on our route. We also had some rain, but it was pretty on this day.

Wednesday, April 16, 1941—We went and washed and came back. Got all of our clothes dried before it was too late, and I was so tired too.

Thursday, April 17, 1941—Helped with the work and then went over to Jeanette's to carry the milk and butter. I stayed awhile and played with John Dean.

Friday, April 18, 1941—Mother and I went back to town again. We had the milk to pull, and it was really muddy too.

Saturday, April 19, 1941—Cleaned up the house real good. Then worked on Mother's pillow slips too. Cleaned and took a bath.

Sunday, April 20, 1941—I felt bad all day, so I stayed in bed nearly all day. But I felt better so I went to church at Center Point.

Monday, April 21, 1941—Cleaned up the house real good and finished the ironing some to help churning some and help Dady out.

Tuesday, April 22, 1941—Back on the route again. I sure felt bad, but I helped anyway. Came home early and I went to bed early too.

Wednesday, April 23, 1941—Helen and I went on our usual trip to town early to deliver our eggs and butter. We also washed our clothes. I helped with the milking when we got home.

Thursday, April 24, 1941—Helped with the churning as usual and then went over to the Smiths' to carry the milk and butter.

Friday, April 25, 1941—Mother and I went to town as usual. Then came by and stopped at Edens' for a while.

Saturday, April 26, 1941—Cleaned up the house and finished my ironing. Washed my hair and did some handwork.

Sunday, April 27, 1941—Stayed at home and helped with the work. Cooked a real good dinner. Helen was over here.

Monday, April 28, 1941—Helped with the churning and worked on my pillow slips for a while, or rather what spare time I had.

Tuesday, April 29, 1941—Back to town as usual. Delivered the milk and butter and came home early to help with the work.

Wednesday, April 30, 1941—Helen and I went to wash. It was late when we got off, but we managed to finish.

Thursday, May 1, 1941—Helped with the work and did some ironing. Then went to Smiths' to take the milk and butter.

Friday, May 2, 1941—Back on our route again. It looked like it would rain, so we hurried up and finished so we could come home.

Saturday, May 3, 1941—Cleaned up the house real good and went to the mailbox to get the mail. Went over to Helen's.

Sunday, May 4, 1941—Went to SS. Then John came for a while. He brought me a locket for my birthday [her actual birthday was April 28]. I was sure proud of it.

Monday, May 5, 1941—Helped with the work. Then went over to Helen's and stayed for a while. I helped Dady churn. The little horse birthday.

Tuesday, May 6, 1941—Back on our route again. It came a rain and was we scared. It didn't rain more than I wanted it to.

Wednesday, May 7, 1941—Helen and I went and washed again. We got home pretty early, and I dried our clothes and then helped milk.

Thursday, May 8, 1941—Back on the same old job and helped around with the work. Also went to Smiths' with the milk and butter.

Friday, May 9, 1941—Mother and I went back on the route. She had a sore toe, so I had to do all the deliveries.

Saturday, May 10, 1941—Cleaned up the house and finished ironing. I was sure tired but also did some handwork too.

Sunday, May 11, 1941—Went to SS as usual. Then came home and tried to sleep some.

Monday, May 12, 1941—Helped around with the work as usual and worked on my pillow slips until late. Then helped with the milking.

Tuesday, May 13, 1941—Helen went on the route with me, and I was unusually tired when I got home. Mother had a bad temperature.

Wednesday, May 14, 1941—Helen and I went and washed. Came home early and hung out our clothes.

Thursday, May 15, 1941—Helped with the churning as usual, and carried Smiths' the butter and played with John Dean.

Friday, May 16, 1941—Mother and I went back on the route again. It rained some, so we had the mud to pull.

Saturday, May 17, 1941—Cleaned up the house and finished my ironing. Washed my hair and helped cook supper and read some before I went to bed early.

Sunday, May 18, 1941—Stayed at home all day and read some in the afternoon. Wanted to go to church but didn't want to go by myself.

Monday, May 19, 1941—Helped with the work and helped churn some too.

Tuesday, May 20, 1941—Mother and I went back on the route again. I was always tired too. Saw John. He was still at home.

Wednesday, May 21, 1941—Helen and I went to wash. Got home early and got all of our clothes dried. Helped wash the bucket and milked.

Thursday, May 22, 1941—Helped with the work and then went to Smiths' to take the milk and butter. Played with John Dean.

Friday, May 23, 1941—Back on our route again. Saw John. He was leaving on the nine o'clock train for El Paso to the army. It came up a rain.

Saturday, May 24, 1941—Cleaned up the house and rested some before I baked some pies. Went to bed early.

Sunday, May 25, 1941—Went to SS as usual. We sure had a lot of fun out her sometime.

Monday, May 26, 1941—Helped around with the work some and ironed me a clean dress to wear to town.

Tuesday, May 27, 1941—Mother and I went to town as usual and then came home early and helped with the work.

Wednesday, May 28, 1941—Helen and I went to town to wash. Did some trading and then came home early to get our clothes dried.

Thursday, May 29, 1941—Helped with the work and stopped at Ruby's for a while.

Friday, May 30, 1941—Mother and I went to town to deliver the stuff. It came up a rain, and we were scared too.

Saturday, May 31, 1941—Cleaned up the house. Then worked on my pillow slips for a while.

Sunday, June 1, 1941—Cleaned up the house and went to Sunday school. Came home and slept some in the afternoon.

Monday, June 2, 1941—Helped around with the work as usual. Went to Helen's and stayed awhile.

Tuesday, June 3, 1941—Mother and I went on the route as usual. I received a letter from John, and was I glad.

Wednesday, June 4, 1941—Helen I went and washed as usual. Came home and got our clothes dried.

Thursday, June 5, 1941—Helped with the work and I ironed some so we would have some clean clothes to wear.

Friday, June 6, 1941—Went to SS as usual. Then came home early and worked on a puzzle. Also read some.

Saturday, June 7, 1941—Cleaned up the house real good and ironed some, or rather finished it.

Sunday, June 8, 1941—Went to SS as usual. Then came home early and worked on a puzzle. Also read some.

Monday, June 9, 1941—Worked around the house as usual and helped with the churning. Also went to the mailbox.

Tuesday, June 10, 1941—Worked around. Then Mother and I got off to town as early as we could. Came home early and helped with the work.

Wednesday, June 11, 1941—Helen and I went and washed as usual. Did our trading and got home in time to dry our clothes.

Thursday, June 12, 1941—Helped with the work as usual. Then finished some ironing as usual. Also worked on my scarf for a while.

Friday, June 13, 1941—Mother and I went back to town as usual. It was sure hot, but we made it OK. It was sundown when we got home.

Saturday, June 14, 1941—Cleaned up the house and washed my hair as usual, and then took a bath and helped milk.

Sunday, June 15, 1941—Cleaned up the house and went to SS. Came home and rested some in the afternoon and read some too.

Monday, June 16, 1941—I helped with the work and worked on my rug some too. I had to iron a few pieces, but I finally got through.

Tuesday, June 17, 1941—Mother and I went on the route again. It rained some, but the roads didn't get so bad.

Wednesday, June 18, 1941—Helen and I went and washed. Got home about noon and got our clothes dried. I mopped and helped with the other work.

Thursday, June 19, 1941—I cleaned up the house and worked on my rug for a while. I was really slow on it, but I got it done.

Friday, June 20, 1941—Back on the route again and I sure get tired of it too, but nothing I could do about it.

Saturday, June 21, 1941—Cleaned up the house and went to the mailbox. Came back by the Spencers' and stayed for a while.

Sunday, June 22, 1941—Went to SS as usual and came home. I slept for a while. And boy, did I enjoy it.

Monday, June 23, 1941—Helen and I went to town to wash as usual. Came home pretty early and got our clothes dried.

Tuesday, June 24, 1941—Mother and I went to town and finally got through and came by Edens' for a while. Came home and helped milk some too.

Wednesday, June 25, 1941—I did some of the ironing and some work on my rug. I started the milking as Dady had gone to town.

Thursday, June 26, 1941—I helped with the work and did some of the churning as Dady wanted to work on the fence.

Friday, June 27, 1941—Went back on the route. Had a nice day, and it wasn't so hot.

Saturday, June 28, 1941—Cleaned up the house real good and finished my ironing. Washed my hair and set it.

Sunday, June 29, 1941—I went to church at Center Point by myself. I really enjoyed it.

Monday, June 30, 1941—Cleaned up the house and Helen and I went to wash. Finally got home and got our clothes dried.

Tuesday, July 1, 1941—Mother and I went to town as usual. It was late when we got home, and I was sure tired.

Wednesday, July 2, 1941—Helen and I went and washed. Got home a little after dinner and got our clothes dried. Received a letter from John.

Thursday, July 3, 1941—I helped around with the work and helped churn. I had to iron a few pieces so we would have some clean clothes to wear to town.

Friday, July 4, 1941—Back to town. We ate our July 4th dinner with Mrs. Wilson. She sure had a good one, too.

Saturday, July 5, 1941—Cleaned up the house and worked on my rug for a while. Then I slept some after dinner. I sure enjoyed it too.

Sunday, July 6, 1941—Went to SS as usual. Came home and went to bed and slept some too. I was sure tired.

Monday, July 7, 1941—Helen and I went and washed and did some shopping. I bought some thread for my rug.

Tuesday, July 8, 1941—Mother and I went to town as usual. Met the mailman and got a letter from John.

Wednesday, July 9, 1941—Up real early and did all the ironing that was supposed to be done. Worked on my rug some.

Thursday, July 10, 1941—I helped with the churning and worked on my rug some too. I also washed my hair.

Friday, July 11, 1941—Up early to get to town. I really felt bad, but I went anyway. It was late when we got home. We had the car worked on.

Saturday, July 12, 1941—Cleaned up the house real good and went to the store to mail some letters.

Sunday, July 13, 1941—I went to Bethel church. I went by after Helen, but she had already gone.

Monday, July 14, 1941—Helen and I went to wash in town. Did some shopping as usual. Bought some thread for my rug.

Tuesday, July 15, 1941—Back on our route again. I was sure tired when I did get home. It was late too.

Wednesday, July 16, 1941—[She started writing in ink!] I did all the ironing before dinner and then worked on my rug some too.

Thursday, July 17, 1941—Did up the work. Then Uncle Charley and Aunt Annie came over to see us. Felt bad also.

Friday, July 18, 1941—Back to town again. I was really tired and my job too. I received a letter from John. I went home with Aunt Annie. Saw Peanut.

Saturday, July 19, 1941—Went to see Oma Lee. Went to town in the car. Then went to church and to the midnight show. I saw *I Wanted Wings*. It was late when we got home. Saw Woodrow.

> *I Wanted Wings* follows the training and personal lives of three recruits in the Army Air Corps—a wealthy playboy, a college jock, and an auto mechanic. The love interests are played by Constance Moore and Veronica Lake. Directed by Mitchell Leisen. (Source: IMDb.com).

Sunday, July 20, 1941—Went to Crews to church, up to Aunt Dora's for dinner, and home with Uncle Pat for supper. They carried me over to Aunt Annie, and I went to church.

Monday, June 21, 1941—Aunt Annie carried me to the bus. Ate dinner with Elerene. Got to Big Spring at 4:45 p.m.

Tuesday, July 22, 1941—Mother and I went back to town again. I was really tired too because I had lost so much sleep while I was gone.

Wednesday, July 23, 1941—Cleaned up the house real good. Was supposed to go and wash, but Helen went to Mildred's to can corn.

Thursday, July 24, 1941—Up early and fixed to go wash. Got back about eight o'clock and got our clothes dried. Was I glad too.

Friday, July 25, 1941—Mother and I went back to town. It was sure hot, and I kinda felt bad too. I sure was sleepy too.

Saturday, July 26, 1941—Cleaned up the house real good and did all of the ironing. I slept some in the afternoon and also worked on my rug.

Sunday, July 27, 1941—Cleaned up the house and went to Sunday school and church. I also slept some in the afternoon.

Monday, July 28, 1941—Helen and I didn't go and wash, but I really did iron. I worked on my rug too. I will sure be glad when I get it finished.

Tuesday, July 29, 1941—Mother and I went back to town again on our route. I was sure tired of the job.

Wednesday, July 30, 1941—I worked on Ruby's pillow slips. I finished one and started on the other. I had to do all of the milking by myself.

Thursday, July 31, 1941—I worked again on Ruby's pillow slip. I like just a little having the other one finished.

Friday, August 1, 1941—Mother and I went back to town as usual. It was late when we came home. I helped Dady milk.

Saturday, August 2, 1941—Cleaned up the house real good and finished Ruby's pillow slips. I finally got them done.

Sunday, August 3, 1941—Sharlot and I went to SS. I tried to sleep some in the afternoon. I also read some too. Juanita came over.

Monday, August 4, 1941 – We all went and washed, and Juanita went too. We carried Sharlot back to town. It was four o'clock when we came home.

Tuesday, August 5, 1941—Mother and I went to town again. It was late when we got home because we had so much to do.

Wednesday, August 6, 1941—I did the ironing, and boy was I tired. I also had to do all of the milking because Dady went to town.

Thursday, August 7, 1941—Helped do part of the churning and then worked on my rug some. I got a letter from John.

Friday, August 8, 1941—Mother and I went to town again. It tried to rain some, and boy was I tired. I helped Dady milk too.

Saturday, August 9, 1941—Cleaned up the house real good and worked on my rug some too. I washed my hair.

Sunday, August 10, 1941—Cleaned up the house real good and went to SS at Bethel. Came home and slept some in the afternoon.

Monday, August 11, 1941—Helen and I went and washed. It was three o'clock when we came home, but we got our clothes dried.

Tuesday, August 12, 1941—Mother and I went back to town again on our route. It was sundown when we got home, and was I tired.

Wednesday, August 13, 1941—I did some of the ironing and worked on my rug some. I didn't like so much, but I was sure slow about it.

Thursday, August 14, 1941—I helped with the churning and worked on my rug in between times. Received a letter from John. Was I glad.

Friday, August 15, 1941—Back on the same old job. To town again. I was sure tired when I came home. We came home about sundown.

Saturday, August 16, 1941—Cleaned house real good and worked on my rug again. I tried to sleep some in the afternoon.

Sunday, August 17, 1941—Stayed at home all day and helped with the work. I wanted to go to Sunday school but didn't go.

Monday, August 18, 1941—Helen and I went and washed. It was late when we got home, but we finally got our clothes dried, and I was glad.

Tuesday, August 19, 1941—Mother and I went back to town again. I was sure glad to get home because I was tired too.

Wednesday, August 20, 1941—I did all of the ironing and was I glad to get through. I also worked on my rug some.

Thursday, August 21, 1941—Helped with the work and I did some of the churning so Dady could rest.

Friday, August 22, 1941—Mother and I went back to town again. I bought some thread for my rug too. It was late when we got home.

Saturday, August 23, 1941—Cleaned up the house and went to Juanita's to spend the weekend. Went to town with Gertrude Hamlin. Worked on my rug.

Sunday, August 24, 1941—Cleaned up the house and cooked dinner. Laid around and read some, and we talked a lot. Dady came after me about six o'clock.

Monday, August 25, 1941—Helen and I went and washed. Got home in time to dry our clothes. I help with the milking. Worked on my rug some.

Tuesday, August 26, 1941—Mother and I went back on the route again. It was a pretty day, and we got home before night. I was sure tired.

Wednesday, August 27, 1941—I had to do most of the milking because Mr. Clayton came to work, and Dady had to help him. They were supposed to stack feed, but it rained.

Thursday, August 28, 1941—I did some of the ironing and also helped churn. Worked on a pair of pillow slips that I had started for a time. Rained again.

Friday, August 29, 1941—Mother and I went back to town again. I felt really bad, but I managed to help with the work.

Saturday, August 30, 1941—Dady went to town, and I had a lot to do. All the milking to do in the evening.

Sunday, August 31, 1941—Cleaned up the house. Mother and I went to Coahoma to a singing convention. Sure enjoyed it too.

Monday, September 1, 1941—Helen and I went to town and washed. Irene was here, and she went with us. Sure had some fun.

Tuesday, September 2, 1941—Mother and I went back to town as usual. I was sure tired of this job. I was sure looking for a letter from John but none.

Wednesday, September 3, 1941—I cleaned up the house as usual, and I also ironed some or nearly all of it. I worked on a pair of pillow slips.

Thursday, September 4, 1941—I helped around with the churning and worked on a scarf some. Still no letter from John, and was I sad and how.

Friday, September 5, 1941—Mother and I went back to town. John came in, but he had to stay at La Mesa because it was late when he got there.

Saturday, September 6, 1941—Cleaned up the house real good and washed my hair. I really had a letter from John. He came out about 8:30 and had to be back at town at 10:00. So he didn't stay long.

Sunday, September 7, 1941—Stayed at home all morning and made some ice cream. John came, and we went to the lake and made some pictures. Ate supper with John and went to hear the preacher. Sure had some fun. Went to the lake and made some pictures.

Monday, September 8, 1941—Irene, Helen, and I all went to town to wash. Saw John and Mrs. Couch. Talked to John a long time. It rained some toward night.

Tuesday, September 9, 1941—Back on our route again. Had a date with John. He came, and we went to Juanita's and went to the show. Saw the movie *Moon Over Miami.*

> In *Moon Over Miami*, sisters Kay and Barbara arrive in Miami from Texas looking for rich husbands. It stars Don Ameche, Betty Grable, and Robert Cummings. Director was Walter Lang. (Source: IMDb.com)

Wednesday, September 10, 1941—Cleaned up the house and ironed some too. Also worked on a pair of pillow slips, the ones Jeanette gave me for my birthday.

Thursday, September 11, 1941—Worked around the house and helped with the churning. I was sure tired when night came and how.

Friday, September 12, 1941—Mother and I went back to town as usual. John had gone back, and I was sure sad and how. We sure had a good time while he was here.

Saturday, September 13, 1941—Cleaned up the house and mopped, and I changed my bed and cleaned my room real good. Boy, I was sure tired.

Sunday, September 14, 1941—I really went to Sunday school. First time I had been in a long time. I slept all afternoon. I really slept too.

Monday, September 15, 1941—Helen and I went and washed. Got off real early. We got home about twelve, and I hung out our clothes and got them all dried.

Tuesday, September 16, 1941—Back on our route again. I was sure tired of this job, but I had to keep it up. Got home about dark.

Wednesday, September 17, 1941—I cleaned up the house real good, and I ironed some too. Also worked on my pillow slips.

Thursday, September 18, 1941—Cleaned up the house and went to the mailbox. Helped cook dinner and finished a pair of pillow slips that I had started.

Friday, September 19, 1941—Back to town again. It was late when we got home, but I went and helped Dady milk the rest of the cows.

Saturday, September 20, 1941—Cleaned up the house real good and helped around the place the rest of the day. I also worked on another pair of pillow slips.

Sunday, September 21, 1941—Dady went to church at Center Point. Reverend Hollowell and family came up here for dinner. We sure had a good time. Dady and I went back to church.

Monday, September 22, 1941—Helen and I went back to wash again. Got off real early. We got home about eleven and put out our clothes and got our clothes dried.

Tuesday, September 23, 1941—Mother and I went back to town again to do our delivering. I was sure tired when we got home too.

Wednesday, September 24, 1941—I did some ironing today and worked on a pair of pillow slips, the ones Jeanette gave me.

Thursday, September 25, 1941—Cleaned up the house and helped Dady do some of the churning. Went to milk real early and I came back before night.

Friday, September 26, 1941—Mother and I went back to town again. I received a letter from John, and boy was I glad and how.

Saturday, September 27, 1941—I cleaned up the house, and in the afternoon I went and picked some cotton. I picked 130 pounds. That was really good for me.

Sunday, September 28, 1941—Cleaned up the house real good and helped others with the work and cooked dinner. We had a real good dinner. We had a chicken.

Monday, September 29, 1941—Helen and I went and washed and got our clothes dried before night. Was I glad, and how, because we had a lot to do about night.

Tuesday, September 30, 1941—Went to town as usual. It started raining about night. We had the mud to pull home, and it rained on us a lot.

Wednesday, October 1, 1941—It rained some more today, and we were about out of cow feed. Boy, all the mud to pull.

Thursday, October 2, 1941—Helped with the churning and also ironed some. Helped milk and worked on my pillow slips after supper.

Friday, October 3, 1941—Mother and I went back to town again. Had a real nice day for delivering, and was I glad. Got a letter from John.

Saturday, October 4, 1941—Cleaned up the house real good, finished my ironing, and worked on my pillow slips again. I had them done.

Sunday, October 5, 1941—I went to Sunday school and came home and ate dinner. Then I slept some after dinner, and I really caught up with it too.

Monday, October 6, 1941—Helen and I went and washed again today. Got home about noon and we got our clothes dried. I helped with the churning and then milked.

Tuesday, October 7, 1941—Mother and I went to town again to do our delivering. We got home about dark and went about work and helped with milking.

Wednesday, October 8, 1941—Cleaned up the house real good and helped wash the buckets. Then milked and worked on my new scarf.

Thursday, October 9, 1941—Helped work around the place and helped do some of the churning. Worked on a scarf in between times.

Friday, October 10, 1941—Mother and I went back to town again. Boy, I was sure tired of this job, but I had to go anyway, regardless.

Saturday, October 11, 1941—Cleaned up the house, washed my hair really good, and cleaned my scarf. Worked on my scarf again.

Sunday, October 12, 1941—Stayed at home all day and helped Mother cook dinner. Mr. and Mrs. Hamby were supposed to come for dinner but came in the afternoon.

Monday, October 13, 1941—Helen and I went back to wash again. Came home about noon and got our clothes dried before night. Was I tired.

Tuesday, October 14, 1941—Mother and I went back to town as usual, but we had so much to do that we didn't get home very early.

Wednesday, October 15, 1941—Cleaned up the house and tried to iron some, but I never got very much done because I was so tired.

Thursday, October 16, 1941—Cleaned up the house and went and washed and got our clothes dried and Helen's, too.

Friday, October 17, 1941—Mother and I went to town to peddle. It was late when we got off and late when we got home. I was sure tired.

Saturday, October 18, 1941—Cleaned up the house and headed some maize. We were gone nearly all day. I was sure tired when I got through.

Sunday, October 19, 1941—Dady and I went to Center Point to church. Stayed at home in the morning. Mrs. Eden came up here for dinner, and I went home with her and stayed after church.

Monday, October 20, 1941—Cleaned up the house and helped around the house. Then went and headed some maize. I was really tired too.

Tuesday, October 21, 1941—Mother and I went back to town again. It was nearly dark when we left town. Helped Dady milk.

Wednesday, October 22, 1941—I helped head some maize. We headed about six acres and rows. I was sure tired.

Thursday, October 23, 1941—Helped with the work and headed maize by myself. Dady came and unloaded it for me.

Friday, October 24, 1941—Mother and I went back and peddled again. Had some work done on our car so it was late when we got home.

Saturday, October 25, 1941—Cleaned up the house real good, and went back and helped Dady head some more maize.

Sunday, October 26, 1941—Cleaned up the house. Then Helen, Mother, and I went to the singing in town. It was sure good.

Monday, October 27, 1941—Helped with the work and headed some more maize. I did most all of the heading by myself.

Tuesday, October 28, 1941—Mother and I went back to town on our route again. Did some trading before we came home.

Wednesday, October 29, 1941—I went to town and did the washing. Came home and dried our clothes.

Thursday, October 30, 1941—Cleaned up the house and headed up some more maize. I sure worked hard.

Friday, October 31, 1941—Mother and I went back to town again. I was sure tired too. I had a letter from John.

Saturday, November 1, 1941—I cleaned up the house. I still helped with heading up some maize. I worked hard all day.

Sunday, November 2, 1941—Helped with the work and went to SS. Came home after church and we stayed around all evening.

Monday, November 3, 1941—I headed some more maize, and I churned some while Dady was loading the maize. I was sure tired.

Tuesday, November 4, 1941—Back on our route again. I was sure tired, and I also received a letter from John. He was just fine.

Wednesday, November 5, 1941—Back to town and did our washing, and came home and dried our clothes. I headed some maize.

Thursday, November 6, 1941—I headed some maize. Then there was the churning to do and other things around here.

Friday, November 7, 1941—Back on our route and it was a pretty day. I received a letter from John, and I was glad.

Saturday, November 8, 1941—Cleaned up the house real good and helped Dady head some maize. I was tired.

Sunday, November 9, 1941—Helped around and finally got off to SS. Came home and slept some in the afternoon. Helped do up the work.

Monday, November 10, 1941—Back on my maize-heading job. I did not like it so much, but I did the best I could with working all the time.

Tuesday, November 11, 1941—Back to town again. We got through pretty early, but it was dark when we got home.

Wednesday, November 12, 1941—Back to town to wash. I got home early and got our clothes dried before too late.

Thursday, November 13, 1941—Cleaned up the house and headed some maize after dinner. I was sure tired when I quit before night.

Friday, November 14, 1941—Mother and I went back to town to do our delivering. It was late when we got home as usual.

Saturday, November 15, 1941—I went back to town to wash again, and I got home in time to dry our clothes. All dried and I worked with the maize.

Sunday, November 16, 1941—Helped around with the work and went to SS. Came home and we went to Mrs. Deats's to stay for a while.

Monday, November 17, 1941—I worked around all morning, and I headed some maize in the afternoon. I was sure tired too.

Tuesday, November 18, 1941—Back to town again with our stuff, and we had good luck. I received a letter from my dear John.

Wednesday, November 19, 1941—Back to town again to do our washing, and I got them all done before it was late.

Thursday, November 20, 1941—Helped with the work and headed some maize in the afternoon when I was through with the work.

Friday, November 21, 1941—Mother and I went back to town again. I really was tired when I got home. It was late when we got home.

Saturday, November 22, 1941—Cleaned the house real good and cooked some pies. Went to the mailbox and received a letter from John.

Sunday, November 23, 1941—Went to SS as usual abd came home. After dinner I laid around some and read too.

Monday, November 24, 1941—Helped with the work as usual. I also did some of the ironing and worked on Mother's scarf.

Tuesday, November 25, 1941—Back on our route again. Boy, I was sure tired of this job, too, but I couldn't do any better.

Wednesday, November 26, 1941—I went to town and did the washing. Got home about two o'clock and got our clothes dried before it was too late.

Thursday, November 27, 1941—I helped with the work around and worked on Mother's scarf some. I really felt bad.

Friday, November 28, 1941—Mother and I went back to town as usual, and we had some work done on our car. Received a letter from John.

Saturday, November 29, 1941—Cleaned up the house. Dady let me go to town, and I bought my watch. I sure was proud of it.

Sunday, November 30, 1941—I went to SS. Came home as usual and stayed at home by my lonesome. No one came.

Monday, December 1, 1941—Cleaned up the house as usual and ironed some. Went to the mailbox and got a letter from John.

Tuesday, December 2, 1941—Mother and I went to town as usual with our butter and stuff. It was pretty cold, and I was glad when we got done.

Wednesday, December 3, 1941—Helen went and done our washing, and I cleaned up our house real good and dried our clothes when she got home.

Thursday, December 4, 1941—I ironed some more and worked on Mother's scarf some, but I didn't have time to work much.

Friday, December 5, 1941—Mother and I went back to town again. It was late when we got home, as we had the car worked on.

Saturday, December 6, 1941—Cleaned up the house and washed my hair and set it. I helped do the milking too in the evening.

Sunday, December 7, 1941—Went to SS as usual. Jeanette was over here for dinner. Helen came also.

Monday, December 8, 1941—I helped with the work as usual and went to the mailbox. I got a letter from John, and was I glad.

Tuesday, December 9, 1941—Back to town again on our route. We had a real pretty day for it, and I was glad too.

Wednesday, December 10, 1941—I went and done the washing, and I got back about one o'clock and got our clothes dried before night.

Thursday, December 11, 1941—I helped with the work as usual. I helped Dady with the churning and did some other things around the house.

Friday, December 12, 1941—Mother and I went back to town again. I was really tired when I got home, as I am always tired.

Saturday, December 13, 1941—I cleaned up the house as usual, and I ironed some. Worked on my scarf some too during my spare time.

Sunday, December 14, 1941—Went to SS as usual. Came home as usual. I laid around for a while.

Monday, December 15, 1941—Cleaned up the house and ironed some. Did some handwork and worked on Mother's scarf. I received a letter from John, and I sure was glad.

Tuesday, December 16, 1941—Mother and I went back to town again. It was a real nice day. It was late when we got home, and I was tired.

Wednesday, December 17, 1941—Helen and I went and did our washing, and I helped Mother around the house and dried our clothes after she got back from town.

Thursday, December 18, 1941—Helped with the work as usual and ironed some too. I finished Mother's scarf in my spare minutes.

Friday, December 19, 1941—I went back to town again, and my cold was better. I went to the Christmas tree when I got back from town.

Saturday, December 20, 1941—I received a letter from John, and was I glad. He came home, but I didn't know it. He got here about ten o'clock. My cold was better.

Sunday, December 21, 1941—John came out about ten o'clock, and I went home with him for dinner. We sure had a good dinner, and I came home about seven. I hated to see John go back.

Monday, December 22, 1941—I went and helped Dady with the work and helped churning. I did some handwork too when I wasn't churning.

Tuesday, December 23, 1941—Mother and I went and did our delivering and got back about 7:30 p.m. I was sure tired.

Wednesday, December 24, 1941—I went and did the washing and got back real early and dried our clothes. No letter from John. I was sure worried.

Thursday, December 25, 1941—We went to Helen and Virgil's for dinner. I sure felt bad, and I was afraid to eat very much because I was afraid I would vomit.

Friday, December 26, 1941—We churned today. I received a letter from John, and was I glad he got home safe and sound.

Saturday, December 27, 1941—Mother and I went to town again, but we had to deliver on Saturday because of Christmas day. It was late when we got home.

Sunday, December 28, 1941—Went to SS and I went home with the Andersons. We went to town after Neil. Sure had lots of fun. I came home before the sun went down.

Monday, December 29, 1941—Cleaned up the house as usual and went to the mailbox. I helped do the churning, and I was tired too.

Tuesday, December 30, 1941—Mother and I went back to town again. We sure had trouble too. Mother dropped my watch. Had some work on the car and had a flat.

Wednesday, December 31, 1941—I went again and washed and got back in time to get our clothes dried. Was I glad to be home.

CPSIA information can be obtained
at www.ICGtesting.com
Printed in the USA
LVHW052259030220
645691LV00001B/125